HONEY AND ASHES

OTHER BOOKS
BY JANICE KULYK KEEFER

The Paris–Napoli Express

White of the Lesser Angels

Transfigurations

*Under Eastern Eyes: A Critical Reading
of Canadian Maritime Fiction*

Constellations

Reading Mavis Gallant

Travelling Ladies

Rest Harrow

The Green Library

Marrying the Sea

Janice Kulyk Keefer

HONEY AND ASHES

A Story of Family

Harper*Flamingo*Canada

First edition

Excerpt from *Black Sea Blue* by Natalka Husar. Pamphlet produced by Rosemount Art Gallery.
Reprinted by permission of Natalka Husar. Excerpt from *Bloodlines: A Journey into Eastern Europe*
by Myrna Kostash. Copyright © 1993, published by Douglas & MacIntyre. Reprinted with
permission. Excerpt from *The Heart of Europe: A Short History of Poland* by Norman Davies.
Published by Oxford University Press, 1986. Reprinted by permission of Oxford University
Press. Excerpt from *Housekeeping* by Marilynne Robinson. Reprinted by permission of Farrar,
Straus & Giroux. Excerpt from *An Imaginary Life* copyright © David Malouf 1978. Reproduced
by permission of the author c/o Rogers, Coleridge & White Ltd., 20 Powis Mews, London,
W11 1JN. Excerpt from *Land to Light On* by Dionne Brand. Used by permission, McClelland &
Stewart, Inc. *The Canadian Publishers*. Excerpts from *Russia, Ukraine and Belarus: Lonely Planet
Survival Guide* Edition 1, 1996. Copyright © Lonely Planet Publications. Reprinted by permis-
sion of Lonely Planet Publications. Excerpts from *Shtetl* by Eva Hoffman. Copyright © 1997 by
Eva Hoffman. Reprinted by permission of Houghton Mifflin Company. All rights reserved.
Excerpts from *The Songlines* by Bruce Chatwin. Copyright © 1987 by Bruce Chatwin. Used by
permission of Viking Penguin, a division of Penguin Putnam Inc. Excerpt from essays by John-
Paul Himka and Frank Sysyn in *Ukrainian–Jewish Relations in Historical Perspective* Second
Edition. Published by the Canadian Institute of Ukrainian Studies, University of Alberta, 1990.
Reprinted by permission. Excerpts from Isaac Babel, "Crossing the Zubrich," in *Lyubka the
Cossack and Other Stories*, translated by Andrew R. MacAndrew, New York, New American
Library, 1963, pp. 108 and 109. Used by permission.

Canadian Cataloguing in Publication Data

Keefer, Janice Kulyk, 1952–
Honey and ashes : a story of family

Includes bibliographical references
ISBN 0-00-255443-7

1. Keefer, Janice Kulyk, 1952– — Biography.   2. Keefer, Janice Kulyk, 1952– — Family.
3. Staromischyna (Ukraine) — Social life and customs.   4. Toronto (Ont.) — Social life and
customs.   5. Authors, Canadian (English) — 20th century — Biography.*   I. Title.

PS8571.E435Z53 1998   C813'.54   C98-931387-5
PR9199.3.K4115Z468 1998

98 99 00 01 02 03 04 HC 10 9 8 7 6 5 4 3 2 1

Printed and bound in the United States

Tomasz Solowski (1900–1964)

Olena Levkovych Solowska (1902–1979)

vichnaia pam"iat'

There is so little to remind us of anyone—an anecdote, a conversation at table. But every memory is turned over and over again, every word, however chance, written in the heart in the hope that memory will fulfill itself, and become flesh, and that the wanderers will find a way home, and the perished, those whose lack we always feel, will step through the door finally and stroke our hair with dreaming, habitual fondness, not having meant to keep us waiting long.

Marilynne Robinson, *Housekeeping*

Contents

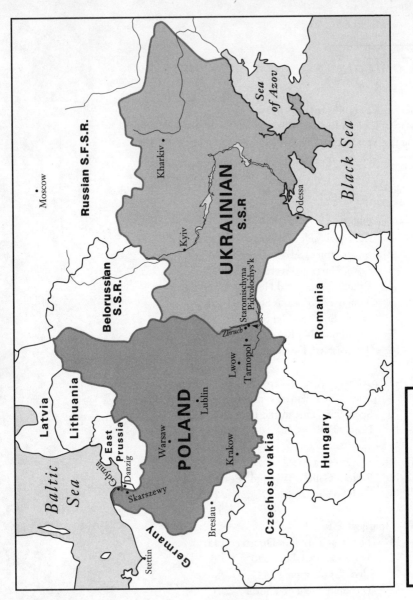

EASTERN EUROPE 1936

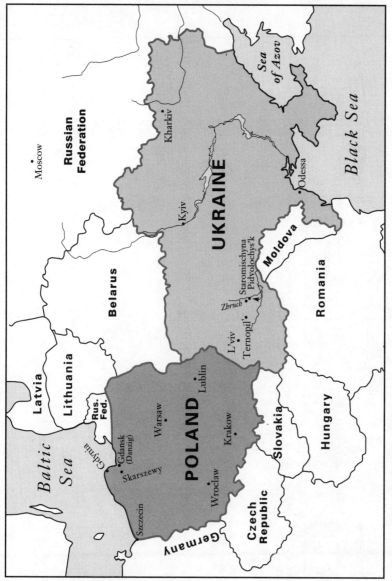

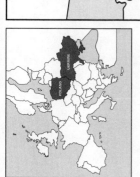

On Polish maps pre-WWII, Pidvolochys'k would have appeared as Podwoloczysk, Staromischyna as Staromiejszczyzna, Zbruch as Zbrucz, and Ternopil' as Tarnopol. When the borders between Poland and Germany, and Ukraine and Poland shifted after the war, place names also altered, so that Breslau became Wroclaw, Stettin, Szczecin, and Lwow, L'viv. Kiev, the Russian spelling of Kyiv, would have been used in most atlases.

EASTERN EUROPE 1997

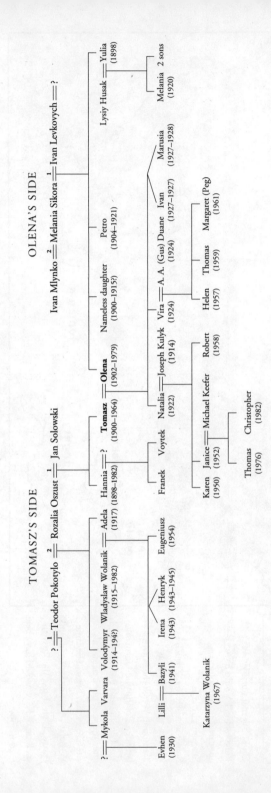

For the sake of simplicity, not all marriages and children have been included in this family tree.
Some birth and death dates are approximate.

Author's Note

Staromischyna (pronounced Star-o-*mees*-chin-a) is a rendering from Cyrillic into English letters of the Ukrainian name for the village where my mother was born. The name appears on prewar Polish documents in my family's possession as Staromiejszczyzna.

In referring to place names during the interwar period in Poland (1918–1939) I have used the Ukrainian forms for those places frequently referred to in my family's stories: thus, Ternopil' instead of Tarnopol, and Zbruch instead of Zbrucz, but Lwow instead of L'viv. I have also omitted the accents from Polish names.

In the transliteration of Ukrainian to English, I have used the standard system whereby *y* is pronounced like a short *i* and *i* like a long *e*. Thus *spy* (the imperative of *spaty*, to sleep) is pronounced like the English word *spit* without the *t*; *pich* sounds like *peach*.

Olena is pronounced with a short *e*, and accented on the second syllable; *Tomasz* as To-*mash*, with the *a* sounded like the *a* in *father*. The *a* in *pan* is pronounced likewise. *Skarszewy* is accented on the second syllable: *szewy* is pronounced like the name of the car, Chevy. Volodko is pronounced as it looks, with the accent on the middle syllable. The *rz* in *Katarzyna* is pronounced *zh*, like the French *j* in *joie*.

I have used Ukrainian instead of Russian names and spellings where appropriate: thus Kyiv instead of Kiev; Chornobyl instead of

Chernobyl; *borshch* instead of *borscht*. The politics of naming make an already fraught and shifting territory even more complicated.

Sources for all quotations will be found in the endnotes, ordered according to the pages on which they appear.

HONEY AND ASHES

prologue

a bridge of words

I stand by a river, looking over the water to a distant shore. When I was a child, I crossed this river as though water were as natural an element to me as the air I breathed, the earth under my feet. But now I know the strength of the river's current. Were I to step into these waters, they would tug me upstream or down, anywhere but across; anywhere but where I long to be.

Forty years divide me from the child I was then; seventy years divide me from that child I can still glimpse across the water: the child my mother once was. I see the vanished world where she grew up as if I were looking through the wrong end of a telescope: a world brilliant, precise, impossibly small. Yet when I was a child, I stood with my mother on that distant shore, or walked with her up the road, past orchards of plums and pears, past fields narrow as piano keys. To the village where she was born, and her mother before her; all other mothers, all the befores that ever were.

The village is called Staromischyna, a name that means, roughly, "the Old Place." When my grandmother was born there in 1902, Staromischyna belonged to the Austro-Hungarian Empire; twenty years and a world war later, my mother was born in this same village as a citizen of a newly created Polish Republic. Twenty-three years on, after yet another world war, Staromischyna became part of the Soviet Union. My mother and her family had the immense good luck to leave their village just before that war began. Yet despite these shiftings of armies and borders, the Old Place as it was told to me seemed a timeless, self-sustaining world, one I never dreamed of looking for in any atlas or history book.

A story, it's been said, "is a wish, or a truth, or a wish modified by a truth." Children listening to a story will ask if it is true, but they will also ask of it "what they ask of a dream: that it satisfy their wishes." My childhood was filled with astounding stories of the Old Place, stories that fed my experience of, my desire for, difference. If, with a name like Kulyk, I didn't belong in a world of Smiths and Browns, then I longed for that place where I did belong to be something richer and finer. When I left my parents' home, married, had children of my own, my dreams and wishes altered: the Old Place vanished from my consciousness the way a river travels underground. I was making a new life, a new self as distant as possible from what my childhood life and self had been. But over the last few years I've come to hear the river of the past, my family's and my own, more insistently than ever. I knew that it was time to write down the stories that had so obsessed me—write them down for my children, who are strangers to the Old Place, and for the dead, whose lives would otherwise become invisible as air.

Yet in trying to write what had only been spoken, in greeting as an adult the faces I had first met as a child, I found myself consumed by curiosity as well as wonder. What came home to me then was not just the delight, but also the tyranny, of wishes: that when we most need to see beyond ourselves, they may offer us nothing but mirrors. Remembering the stories I was told of the Old Place, I began to ask myself about the larger world surrounding them—what were its politics, its history? Who else besides my family lived within its borders, whose stories hadn't I heard? There were people who seemed to be signalling to me, although

I'd barely noticed them before. People like the Jewish couple who ran the store where my grandmother exchanged cream for the cloth that she sewed into dresses for her daughters; sewing and singing to a husband lost in a string of desolately foreign syllables: Saskatchewan, Ontario. This curiosity meant following what had been private images, family myths, into the vortex of context—a public world full of other people and events that the storytellers of my childhood had never known, or had forgotten or suppressed.

And as I wrote down the stories my family had told me of their lost home, as I pored over maps and encyclopedia entries and history books, I realized that I would have to make another kind of journey to the Old Place. In July 1997 I travelled for the first time to western Ukraine, to a small village an hour's drive from the city of Ternopil'. I was looking for whatever traces might remain of my grandparents' lives: for the place where their house had stood; the orchard in which they'd fallen in love. I wanted to walk through that very orchard, down to an actual, and not imagined, river. What happened to Staromischyna between the time my family left and the time I found it, what must always happen to the imagined under the pressure of the actual, is part of the story this book has to tell.

✳◈✳

Honey and Ashes is, more than anything, a story of family. I do not claim to know or tell The Truth about my family; what I am doing is sieving memory and retelling the stories that make memory material, and public. The difference between what I was told and what I heard; what memory hides and what imagination discloses—all this is part of the book I have written. The stories I grew up with, or have since discovered, deal only with my mother's family: to my great regret, my father's parents never talked to me of their life in their own Old Place, which they fled in 1914. And while my father finds it difficult to recall the texture and particulars of his early life, my mother finds that as she grows older, she sees the intricate world of her childhood more and more clearly, as if time were quiet water, or unblemished glass.

To write of family can be an act of homage and of trespass. *Honey and Ashes* is my own version of what I've salvaged of the enormously complex lives of four people whom I've called Tomasz, Olena, Natalia, Vira. I have slightly altered the spelling or sound of the names by which my mother and aunt were called on coming to Canada; I have also restored to my grandparents, whom I always knew by pet names, their given names. This has been partly to gain enough distance to write of my immediate family, and partly to show the slippage between my family's actual lives and how I've represented them. Though I've tried to be as accurate as possible, I know I must have introduced errors into the stories I've retold. I also know that these stories, in being translated from one language to another, have had some of their most important resonances altered or extinguished. And as for the secret stories I have come across, they are no more or less The Truth than any of the others. For we never give ourselves entirely away, least of all to ourselves. We keep something back, even in the most urgent confession.

Some of the stories I was given had their threads cut short by their tellers: some of them I have salvaged from years of silence. All of them bear the impress of my own desires. The duty we claim to owe the dead, to let them rest in peace, their secrets undiscovered—what does this give us but holes in a scrap of cloth? It's the holes I need to examine as much as the weave, holes that will take me deeper into the lives of the dead. Imagining patterns, fleshing out scenes, trying to stay true to what I've been told and the manner of the telling. The way that photographs, those compounds of time and light, of fact and artifice, are true.

Writing of the Old Place and of Staromischyna as it exists today, of the tortuous history of Poland and Ukraine and my experience of these two newly independent countries, I speak for no one but myself. I grew up a Ukrainian-Canadian with a thread of Polishness in her, someone who found French and German easier to learn than the language my Saturday-morning Ukrainian school tried to pound into my tongue. For me, ethnicity has been no voluntary affair of food and dress but a mesh of old place and new, of personal and public history—a mesh that cuts deep into the skin. In writing as briefly as I do of the history of my family's homeland, of the tragic relations between Poles, Ukrainians, Jews, I am not trying to take sides but to explore a common space that is both blank and scored through.

I hope to tell a story that will speak across any number of borders, to anyone who lives in two countries of the heart and mind at once. We live in a time when to be a migrant or refugee is one of the commonest human conditions; we also live in a time when many immigrants are flagrantly attacked or covertly despised. And though there are tremendous differences among immigrants—differences of culture and history, language and looks, that compound the difficulty of making new lives in strange countries—I believe there's a continuum of experience and, most of all, imagination that can bring us all, however momentarily, together.

Imagination, Toni Morrison reminds us, is bound up with memory. Writing of how the Mississippi was straightened out "to make room for houses and liveable acreage," and of how the river on occasion floods these places, Morrison argues that the river is not flooding but remembering:

> All water has a perfect memory and is forever trying to
> get back to where it was. Writers are like that: remem-
> bering where we were, what valley we ran through,
> what the banks were like, the light that was there and

the route back to our original place. It is emotional memory—what the nerves and skin remember as well as how it appeared. And a rush of imagination is our "flooding."

I stand by my river, gazing at the shore so far across from me, the figures gesturing there, or walking up the road and out of my range of vision. I stand by this river with my heart in my mouth, remembering, imagining—trying to build a bridge out of words.

I

The Old Place

1

an equal spill of beauty and blood

On a surface no larger than the circle you can make with thumb and finger, an old man is drawing home, the home my mother left behind some sixty years ago. Against a sky so dark it looks like blood stirred into earth, he puts the whitewashed house: in the thick gold of its thatch, storks are nesting. They bring good luck, the very best luck. No other kind will do in this place where the land is so rich and the people so poor that, for as long as anyone can remember, they have been making the long, rough journey to the mines and factories and cheap acres of the Americas. Sometimes the men take their families with them to make a new life; sometimes they go alone, sending money home to buy more land. To feed the children to whom they've become strangers; to feed the children waiting to be born.

A brash angel, this stork on the roof of my mother's house. His legs, strict as yardsticks, lock into the shape of a backwards 4; his head is cocked towards the marsh where his mate is hiding in the reeds. One of her feet is plunged into cool and oozing muck, the other prints its shadow on a lily leaf. She waits with the patience of the reeds themselves, then jabs her long red beak through the belly of a frog. Nearby, goslings snap at a broth of weeds; they eat and eat till they're as round as they are yellow. A dozen small downy suns and a long peeled stick, a poplar wand that a child begins to wave around them, driving them out of the water into the dust of the road.

A horse and cart are paddling through the same soft dust; before the child can intervene, the horse crushes one of the goslings under its hoof. The child, who is my mother, does not grieve or dig a hand-sized grave. She drives her goslings down the road, till she comes to a farmyard thick with the jabber of geese and ducks. Taking her poplar wand, she prods at one of the neighbour's goslings, weaving it into her own diminished flock, then rushes home to the whitewashed house with its golden thatch. But just as she starts to unlatch the gate, the neighbour's gosling breaks free and darts down the road, too fast for her to catch it. When her mother counts the goslings, as she's sure to do, there will be a beating. In this lush, hungry place there are always beatings, the back of love's hand.

It takes a long time for the old man to fill in the shapes he has drawn with beeswax melted over candle flame. He lowers them into jars of dye—gold, orange, green, a brown so deep it's almost black—sealing each colour with beads of wax. His hands work as surely as if there were no nerves beneath the skin, just bones tied up with blood. When the pattern is complete, he paints it with varnish and leaves it to dry. A whole world on the curve of an egg, a world so delicate a fingertip could smash it.

※◇※

I grew up in two worlds at once, and my passion for one could make the other as unreal as the images on the screen of that sacred toy, the television, home of Howdy Doody, Roy Rogers, the Three Stooges. For their adventures paled beside the stories my mother told of her childhood in a village named Staromischyna, or "the Old Place," a world as rich and strange as embroidery, and as different from the world where I was born as long-legged storks are different from television aerials.

My parents had lived as immigrants in the dark, narrow houses, the noise and rush, of downtown Toronto until, in the early 1950s, they were able to build a house of their own on the city's western edge. Most of the streets in their suburb bow to minor members of the House of Windsor, or harp on royalty and riches: the Kingsway, Royal York, Richview, Prince Edward Drive. On the immense, empty lawns that had once been farmland, the city staked birch and maple saplings. Forty years on they've grown luxuriant, and the birdsong is as fine as you'd find in any English hedgerow. It's even harder now to think back to the longhouses and fields of maize and beans, the tracts of dense and unmolested green this suburb would have been when only Native people lived here. Now the small streams have almost all dried up or run forlornly under asphalt; everywhere are blue-blue swimming pools, their filters humming through the summer days and nights. Garden stores sell newly hybrid species of this or that subtropical plant, specially designed to withstand Canadian winters. How can you see what used to be here, how can you imagine it back into being?

My parents' house is built of yellow brick; no wolf could ever blow it down. The street they live on is a cul-de-sac; on it I skipped rope, played tag and rode my bicycle in perfect safety. Yet the bright open-plan house where I grew up with my older sister and younger brother, the weedless lawns I walked past on my way to school were haunted by another house, another landscape, where everything was stingingly real. *Real*, however much it hurt, was always better than the custard skin that formed over everything in the brick house on the cul-de-sac. And *real* kept jumping over the border between there and here, then and now, so that many times when I was a child, and my mother spoke in her own language that was never mine, shouted or laughed at something I'd done just as her own mother had shouted or, far more rarely, laughed, I hardly knew where or when or even who I was. Except that I was split and doubled: wanting nothing else than to be haunted.

✕◈✕

In 1927 my grandfather Tomasz Solowski left the village of Staromischyna and boarded *The Empress of France* in the Free City of Danzig. He was as old as the century itself; he was leaving his wife Olena and their four children, two of them newborn, to find work in Canada, work that would buy more strips of black Polish earth for his family. He returned to them in 1932, only to leave again after ten months, finding it impossible to live under Poland's repressive martial regime. Before he left, he pleaded with his wife to bring their surviving children—my mother Natalia, my aunt Vira—to Canada. It took my grandmother four years to make up her mind, and even then, though she sold her house, she could not part with the land she'd bought so dearly. She had contracts drawn up between herself and the neighbours who'd agreed to rent her fields till she returned one day. And though she lost those fields in 1941, when the invading Soviets collectivized the land round Staromischyna, she kept the contracts, with their seals and stamps and purple ink, till the day she died, thirty-eight years later.

My grandmother never returned to the Old Place, nor did her daughters, who were fourteen and twelve when they abandoned their village and the narrow future it had dug for them. But in many ways they brought the Old Place with them when they crossed the ocean, hiding the past in embroidered shirts, the folds of woven rugs. I was born in Canada, which for my family meant a place as blank, as free, as the future itself. But I was born out of their lives as well, out of all they were and all they came from. They've given me the gift and burden of a past that often seems to me an equal spill of beauty and blood. It's not metaphorical, this blood, and it's not exhausted by genealogy: it oozes into a black necklace for a would-be bride; it spurts from a man's legs, severed at the knees.

Why do we become obsessed with where and whom we come from? With that country mapped by genetic repetitions that gives me, for example, my grandmother Olena's near-sighted eyes, my grandfather Tomasz's height and temperament? Repetitions, variations, borne by my children and whatever children they may have. Family, it's been written, "is all we know of infinity, the insolence of fate." We may try to flee this fate, but as we run, we carry it inside our very cells. Yet families are more than gene pools: their stories travel through and map us, too. When they talk of the manure heaps and blossoming orchards of the Old Place, or of the school where, for punishment, they had to kneel on mounds of dried peas, my aunt Vira, my mother Natalia become the most fascinating of strangers to me: the children they once were. Or perhaps I take on through them the eyes and ears of childhood, so that the world becomes once more a startling place, all its dead skin peeled away. Sometimes, as a story's being told, a chance word lights up years and years of forgetting, and I see my grandparents once more, if only the shape of their shadows.

They were the two people I loved most as a child, loved with my whole heart. After they died, I had dreams in which they came back and spoke to me. My grandfather Tomasz, whom I lost when I was twelve, materialized at the dinner table, first as a skeleton made out of wire, then slowly putting on his flesh as if it were something cumbersome, an overcoat worn to please someone he loved. And my grandmother Olena, who died while I was living in England, appeared to me on the cellar steps of her emptied house in Toronto. She was holding out a basket of provisions: bread, cheese, a jar of the strawberries she'd preserve each June. As we faced each other—unexpectedly, yet with the calm of those who have loved each other forever—I knew that I was both taking leave of and greeting her forever.

I do not mean anything so fantastical as that my grandparents appeared to me in dreams, demanding that I write down the stories of their lives. What I mean to say is that love is one of the debts we can never repay, something that leaves us all the needier the more we receive of it. That to make good our debts, we speak love out, write it down, an act of exorcism that desire itself sabotages every time, turning it into one more form of haunting. I think of Virginia Woolf's *To the Lighthouse*, the phrase that must wring the heart of all those who have the cherished dead in their keeping: "to want, and not to have—to want and want." Perhaps all we do in writing of the dead is realize our perpetual indebtedness to them, the way our lives will always feed on what they've given us.

Rolnik, or labourer, is written into Tomasz's and Olena's Polish passports and, for good measure, *agriculteur*. Writing of their lives, I became a different kind of labourer, coaxing details and sometimes whole new stories from my family. The few documents I've inherited are among my most precious possessions: passports embossed with faded eagles, birth and death certificates filled out in Latin, a few photographs of family who were left behind. But what of those whose names or faces only the dead remember? The ones whose lives are leaves fallen on a pond, leaves slowly filling with clear, cold water until they are nothing but dark shapes, submerged.

To write of the dead, to conjure them through love into even momentary being, is an enormous task. What Orpheus attempted: to bring back the dead from an underworld of silence and forgetting. Or Odysseus, spilling blood for the ghosts to drink, so they might speak of their lives to him and thus disclose his own true shape, his very future. What can I offer my dead, the ones I loved so dearly, and the ones I never knew? Is the blood we pour out for the ghosts only our endless longing for them? Or is it also curiosity in its most intense and dangerous form? The desire "to walk with the dead and yet see them with our own eyes, from our vantage point." To disenchant them, or diminish the mythic shapes they once held for us, but also to reveal their difficult, remarkable, profoundly human lives.

Courage, then, and love—these are what I need to take along with me as well as passports, visas, scraps of foreign languages. As I make this journey, first into a world of stories and then to the very place where those stories start, a place that belongs not only to my family but to those who hover ghostlike at the edges of storytelling, who materialize in the differences between Staromischyna as it is now and the Old Place as memory fashions it. Between the shaded, complex lives of the people who lived there, and their images as handed down to me—bright, clear as the pictures on an Easter egg.

---

sweet home, sweet home

For as long as I've known that there's an Old Place, I've known that it lies on a river. The river is called Zbruch: the land on either side of it rises gently, like the sides of a shallow cradle. But the Zbruch is deep enough that when a horse and rider plunge from the bridge at Staromischyna, they vanish beyond all hope of rescue. For the current of the Zbruch is as treacherous as it is strong; it can drag you under and away, all the way into another country.

In the world of my family's stories, the wide, inky waters of the river Zbruch form the border between Poland and the Soviet Union. In one of his *Red Cavalry* stories, Isaac Babel describes how he and a host of other cossacks cross this river—he calls it the Zubrich—on their way to conquer Warsaw. It is 1920, the year my grandparents marry:

> The smell of yesterday's blood and of killed horses drips into the coolness of evening. The blackened Zubrich growls, tying its rapids in foamy knots. . . . The horses' backs are awash and the sonorous stream gurgles among the hundreds of horses' legs. Someone is drowning, loudly abusing the Mother of God. The

river is strewn with the black squares of wagons; it is
full of booming, whistling, and singing, floating above
snakes of moonlight and gleaming pits.

By the time my grandparents' first child is born, two years after
Marshal Jozef Pilsudski crushes the Red Army on the very
outskirts of Warsaw, the Zbruch is empty of horses and wagons.
But soldiers are stationed on either side of the river: the Russian
ones shoot at workers trying to escape the drudgery of collective
farms, the Polish ones aim at students striking out for the Workers' Paradise. As for the villagers, they keep their distance from
fugitives, soldiers, bullets. It's not to the Zbruch but to a smaller
shallow river that the women take a summer's worth of hemp and
flax each year. They place the plants under the water, weighing
them down with stones and mud; softened by the current, the
stalks can then be dried and flailed and woven into thread. All
winter long the women's looms hum and clatter; come spring,
when the sunlight's strong enough, the woven cloth will be spread
across the grass to bleach. Children will be set to shoo the geese
and ducks away from all these brilliant squares of summer snow.

Snow out of season: the hovering pink snow that fills the
orchards every spring, orchards running right down to the river.
Petals of what will be plums, cherries, apples, turning the air so
sweet that ten-year-old Natalia runs between the trees with her
mouth open and her arms outstretched. Falling straight into the pit
where an outhouse used to stand. Her cousins find her, screaming,
up to her neck in slime; they give her a stick to grab onto; they haul
her out and dump her in the shallows of the river Zbruch. Speech-
less, staring up at cold, white clouds, she feels the current tugging
her and starts to thrash about. Her cousins, thinking she's trying to
wash herself, return to their work, while she nearly succeeds in
drowning. Somehow she gets to her hands and knees, crawling back
to the place where water stops and something like ground begins.

Years later she will claw the face of a Toronto boy who tries to throw her into Sunnyside Pool. Blood will pour down his cheeks— her only way to speak her terror at the sight of even shallow water.

※◈※

Staromischyna is one of a host of villages strewn through the valley, joined by roads that are crusts or soups of mud, depending on the season. Each village has a church, a school, a reading room or *chytalnia* where people go to read the newspapers from town, or hear them read aloud. Sometimes there's a co-operative store, selling salt and sugar, tobacco and flour. Always there's a fine house belonging to the priest and his family, for the churches here are Greek Catholic, owing allegiance to the Pope-in-Rome, but following the Byzantine rite and permitting their priests to marry.

Tomasz's cousin Myhailo Petrylo is a priest: he serves a neighbouring parish but often comes to Staromischyna to help out at the church of St. Nikolai. When Tomasz leaves for Canada, Myhailo is kind to his cousin's children, taking them for Sunday afternoon outings in his wagon. While the hired man drives, the priest gestures to the vast yellow fields on the Soviet side of the river. "Pay attention," he tells my mother and my aunt. "That's the future over there." They stare at the flood of ripened wheat and then look back at their own fields behind them, small slashes of gold and green and ochre. Myhailo Petrylo knows which way the wind is blowing: straight from godless Russia. His sons will grow up to be engineers instead of priests; his daughters, dentists.

When Vira and Natalia go to church to confess their sins— stealing fruit from a neighbour's orchard, cream from the larder— Myhailo interrupts them with questions. "Has your father written lately? When is he going to take you away from here? Say your prayers three times over and tell your mother I'm expecting chicken for dinner." This during Lent, when it's sinful to taste even a lick of butter. But he's a better man, Myhailo Petrylo, than the regular priest of Staromischyna. Izydor Swystun, a big, sloppy bear of a man, wears enormous unbuckled overshoes; they flap so hard wherever he goes that his nickname is "Thunder." He believes in printing the fear of God into even the youngest of his flock. Passing him on the road while you're talking with your friends, or just daydreaming in the delicate shade of the ash trees, you have to call out *Slavuizuskhrysta*—"GlorytoJesusChrist!" If you're not quick enough, he'll tug at your earlobes till they feel like hot, bruised plums.

Being the nieces of a priest, Natalia and Vira are expected to behave not well, but perfectly. Natalia never can. Standing (for the church has no pews) through the endless liturgy on Sunday mornings, her thoughts are not on God but on the monstrance the priest raises during mass, an egg-shaped glass holding the Host in a frame of golden fire. If she can only get close enough to that glass, she'll be able to see everything that's going on in the village of heaven. But the priest always locks the glass away, leaving her nothing to look at but the icon screen, with its rows of frozen saints. She's tired of having to set an example, of having to stand in the front row, where the priest can keep an eye on how many times and how fervently she crosses herself. One Sunday, when Olena is home with a headache and the girls have come to church alone, Natalia grabs Vira's hand and wheels round, turning her back on the saints and Thunder. She hears him falter in his chanting; she is all defiance and all eyes. What is everyone wearing, which of their friends are missing, who's that snoring by the door? The priest steps forward, grabs her shoulders and tugs first her, then Vira, round to face him. Once the service is over he rushes to their house, galoshes charging like twin bulls. For half an hour he lectures Olena, who must promise to deliver the lesson—with the back of her hand—when her daughters dare to creep home.

And yet there's great beauty in the church, in the festivals and processions that break up the plod of the year. In autumn the whole village marches round the fields with shining banners, thanking God for a good harvest. On the feast of St. Nikolai, Natalia's greatest joy is watching her grandmother's sisters drive up to the house in a sleigh pulled by four white horses: the women are wrapped in furs; the little bells on the horses' necks make quicksilver music. In spring the priest puts on his most gorgeous brocades to lead his congregation over mucky roads to the cemetery, for the blessing of graves. And always there are funerals where hired mourners, black-shawled women, keen behind the coffins trundled over every twisting lane in Staromischyna.

The cemetery lies at the bottom of a hill; it's Natalia's refuge when she knows she's earned a beating. When, for example, she gives a wailing baby a soother made of green poppy seeds, and the baby doesn't wake for two days; or when she beats a tree full of ripe pears and knocks her sister out cold with the end of her stick. On spring afternoons, Vira brings the cows to graze in the field at the cemetery's edge, and falls asleep between the graves, where she's been picking violets. She sleeps for hours, violets like bits of blue paper in her fists, till she hears her mother or her sister shouting out her name. It's as though they're calling her from the dead, or from the death that always threatens her through diphtheria or scarlatina or any of the nameless fevers that are just as lethal. And that always bow, at the last moment, to her thin, stubborn body, as if there were something too tough in it for even death to swallow.

It's Vira who senses the presence of the dead. Just outside the cemetery gate lies a clump of graves the priest has never blessed. The boy who hanged himself is buried here, the seventeen-year-old boy who used to tease her by tossing a ball too high for her to catch. She can never go up to his grave, and yet she stands at the edge of this burying ground, waiting for something she can't explain. Fearing the boy will stretch out his arms and pull her down beside him; longing for the bright ball to sail higher, farther, than she will ever reach.

When she is all of eleven, old enough to attend the school in town, Vira stops on her way to pull up flowers, leaves, even grasses from the ditches. She takes them to the building that's been turned into the local morgue. Slipping through the heavy doors and past the guard sleeping at his desk, holding her breath in the chilly air, she leaves her crushed bouquets by the bodies of beautiful young men in dark blue capes with silver buttons. University students shot trying to cross the river into paradise, led by commissars instead of cherubim.

※◇※

The house where my mother was born, and her mother and grandmother before her, is not a house but a world. Acres of orchards, a yard and garden closed off by wooden palings and a high gate so narrow that the children always scrape their ankles when they ride their cousin's horse inside.

Through this gate you step into a crowd of sounds: hens squawk, geese cackle and, from the rooftop, storks clack their bills or fly off to the marsh, their wings beating like long soft sticks. Sitting on the *pryspa*, the low clay ledge that runs the whole way round the house, a woman sings, shelling peas that drop like green bullets into the basin on her lap. The garden's a tangle of lilac and peonies, daisies, sunflowers, poppies. Feeding this bloom and all the rows of corn and beans, onions and garlic; fed by the animals and all the people in the house: the manure pile. A drunken buzz of flies rises up from it in summer; in winter, heady plumes of steam. Close by the manure pile are the chicken coop, and the barn where the cow nurses her calves and the pigs are penned. In the loft, sweet-smelling hay is piled: the children love to lie here, just to listen to the rain.

The house itself is simple, with the beauty of essential things. Its whitewashed walls are built of mud and straw; its floors are made from yellow clay renewed each spring with a fresh wet paste left to dry as hard as marble. You enter the house by the *siny*, a closed-off hallway with only one small window to let in the light; on your way to the kitchen you pass the *komora* with its sacks of grain and flour. When six-year-old Natalia tries to help her mother by emptying a pot of boiling water, it's to the *komora* Olena carries the screaming child, rolling her over and over in cool, soft clouds of flour.

Apart from the attic where salt pork is stored and apple rings are hung to dry, there are only two rooms of any size in this house. The *mala khata* or "little house" is where everyone lives from November till the end of April. At the heart of this room are the two stoves, an iron one for cooking and a tall clay *pich*, heated with sizzling stones, for baking bread. On its warm, wide ledge grain is spread to dry; when they were very small, the children would sleep here on winter nights. But now that they're older, Vira shares her mother's wooden bed, pushed against a sheepskin-covered wall; Natalia takes the *bambatel*, a wooden bench with a hinged seat in which goose-down quilts are stored. The finest bed of all belongs to the second room, the *svitlytsia*, with its grand wooden floor. This bed is covered with thickly embroidered pillows: your wealth, your standing in the village are measured by the pillows piled on this bed, kept only for your guests, or your dead. Reaching up to the highest pillow one winter morning; finding a small, cold hand—this is how Natalia learns that her youngest sister has died in the night.

For as long as I can remember, my mother has told this story without tears, without a catch in her voice. Until now, talking of a project she's involved with in the Ukrainian museum on Spadina—pillows embroidered with a Tree of Life design, needing to be displayed in some eye-catching fashion. She was showing the women she works with how her mother had arranged a pyramid of cushions on the guest bed in the spotless, chilly *svitlytsia*. "That's when it came home to me," she says. "My memory snapped." Snapped like a switch that floods a room with light. A woman of seventy-four becomes a five-year-old child again, knowing everything's wrong, though no one will explain what has happened. So she has to discover for herself, arched on the tips of her toes, the hand that feels like a small stone in her own.

※◇※

The one fairy tale my mother remembers from her childhood has to do with a brave soldier who rescues a king's daughter from a gang of thieves. To show his gratitude, the king bestows upon the soldier not the princess he's rescued, or half his kingdom, but furniture—a walnut dining table and a set of finely carved chairs. Sitting on their kitchen stools, listening to their mother's story, Natalia and Vira would look down at the rough-hewn table, its clumsy scars of knives and burns. They are unable to imagine *dining, finely carved*. What kind of happy-ever-after can this be?

Most houses in Staromischyna have very little furniture: there are few closets or wardrobes, only chests to store things in and high wooden bars over which to hang linen or Sunday clothes. The walls are bare under their rows of holy pictures: fat-cheeked saints, maidenly Christs pulling open their tunics to reveal hearts like hot-water bottles. Only the few wealthy families have a *svitlytsia* where you might find a cabinet, even a writing table, as well as the guest bed. Yet though Olena and Tomasz have no money between them and barely enough land to feed themselves, they, too, possess a *svitlytsia*. In it Olena's father's books are shelved; on one of the walls hangs an oil painting of some sacred scene; on the other a foxed portrait of Emperor Franz Josef, whose huge moustaches Vira secretly kisses. The other glory of the *svitlytsia* is a cupboard topped with a tilting mirror.

One of the few objects my grandmother was able to bring with her on her long journey across the Baltic and North Seas and over the Atlantic was a miniature cupboard with a swing-top mirror framed by scalloped wood. Far too big for any doll's house, much too small for holding anything but pocket-sized secrets, it stood on a shelf in the furnace room of my parents' house. The cupboard was made of red mahogany; it had a small black metal latch and the glass of its mirror was flawed—you could never find your true reflection in it. I never asked why this odd piece of furniture was hidden away, or whether I could have it in my room to use in place of the shoe box that held my treasures. I must have realized how out of place it would have felt among the plain pine furniture in my room, all blond Scandinavian modern.

I can't remember how I came to learn that the miniature cupboard with the swivel glass had been made by my grandfather's half-brother Volodko. He was a cabinetmaker, and so handsome that the village schoolteacher, who considered herself many cuts above the men of Staromischyna, had fallen desperately in love with him. He made Vira a set of skis out of seasoned wood; he would often come to Olena's house the year before she and her daughters left for Canada. This is all I learned of Volodko when I was growing up. The albums held not a single photograph to prove he ever existed; no one knew what had happened to him after 1936. Of all the family left behind in the Old Place, he was the most mysterious, the most seductive. He was an artist of sorts, making this miniature of the one fine piece of furniture Olena owned, the seed for the dining room suite that furnished the happy ending of her fairy tale. A replica, holding the memory of everything she'd had to leave behind. Holding, too, the touch of the hands that had fashioned it.

⁂

For the child I was, listening to my mother's stories of the house where she was born, the place of most magic was never the *svit-lytsia* with its wooden floor and spotless furniture. It was something that at first glance might seem as humble as a chicken coop: the *lyokh* or root cellar, its door like an upside-down U, its sloping walls made of earth and plunging down so far that neither frost nor soldiers' bayonets could reach the wealth it held.

The root cellar lies apart from the house, and yet the life of the house depends on it, storing as it does the piles of beets and potatoes, apples and cabbages that feed the family all through winter. Its walls are plastered with yellow clay, and you must count the fourteen steps down, because apart from two small windows at the top of the stairs, there's nothing to light your way. Once you touch bottom, you stretch out your hands, taking short, slow steps past piles of puckered vegetables and the frogs that make their home among them. You push into the black lying before you until your foot bumps a crate pushed against the wall; only then do you fish for the matches and candle stub buried in your pocket. You make a scratch of light, enough to see the treasures piled up before you: gilded cherubs, porcelain translucent as communion wafers, tablecloths like starched spiderwebs. Locked in the deepest, darkest corner of the root cellar, this treasure you must never speak of or bring outside into the light. It doesn't belong to you; it's a mystery you visit each time you're sent into the dark to fetch a basket of onions, a garlic wreath.

When I was old enough to ask my mother for an explanation—to want explanations instead of mysteries—she told me that the lace and silver and china had been left behind by wealthy families from the town, Poles or Jews or Ukrainians fleeing the region when war broke out between Russia and Austria in 1914. Late at night people would knock at Olena's father's door; they would be holding tightly wrapped bundles too fragile to take with them, too precious to be left in their hastily abandoned houses. My great-grandfather, who was the reeve of the village, was esteemed for his honesty and good sense. Certainly he honoured his promise to look after his neighbours' possessions till the war was over. He hid them in the depths of the root cellar, and while foreign armies rushed through the region, smashing or grabbing whatever they could lay their hands on, the treasures stayed safe in their hiding place. I want to think of them as being there still, waiting for the dead to come back and claim them.

XOX

Like nested boxes, the different parts of this vanished world. The innermost box is the house surrounded by its orchard, its flowers and wooden gate: around it the village of Staromischyna, my grand-parents' narrow fields scattered at its edges. Then Pidvolochys'k, the market town a kilometre to the south, where Olena takes cream and butter and eggs to Helka and Blumen, the Jewish couple who sell sandals and socks and underwear; printed fabric for dressmaking. Far beyond the market town lies the city of Ternopil', where trains run and telegrams fly like birds singing in a foreign tongue. Poland surrounding Ternopil', and then the ocean, and finally the emptiness where Tomasz has gone. Twice every month, like a threaded needle working its way over a vastness of linen, comes a letter from a place so unimaginable that it becomes another word for nowhere.

Nine years after my grandfather left Poland for Canada, that nowhere into which he'd disappeared became home for his wife and daughters. Living in rooming houses, working in factories, Tomasz and Olena managed, over the next six years, to save two-thirds of the sum they needed to buy a house of their own. Every bank in the city turned Tomasz down when he asked for a loan;

even fellow immigrants, people from their own village, had nothing but discouragement to offer him. But when Tomasz had all but given up, Olena spoke to a Lemko man, Theodore Yawyliak, who made a living selling fruit to corner stores on Queen and Dundas, fruit he'd buy each morning fresh from the St. Lawrence market. He knew my grandparents because his daughter Anna and their Natalia had become best friends; he agreed to loan my family the two thousand dollars they needed to buy outright a house on Dovercourt Road in downtown Toronto.

It was Olena who persuaded Tomasz they could take on the loan and pay it back; who drove her husband and daughters and the many friends who pitched in to help through the swabbing and shovelling out, the painting of walls and stripping of varnish that restored the house's splendour. Chaste Ionic columns gleamed once more from the small brick porch; stained glass turned the sun or streetlights pouring through the transom amber, emerald, crimson. For my grandmother, who'd had to sell the house she was born in and who'd lost the land she'd tried so hard to keep in Staromischyna, the Dovercourt house became the whole world; whenever she was called away to the homes of her daughters or taken on outings in the country, she would always sing out as the car pulled down her street. *Sweet home, sweet home*, she'd cry, getting it slightly out of synch, this one English phrase she knew by heart.

❀

Squeezed into a long backyard, serenaded by car horns and radios advertising bread or plumbers in half a dozen languages, my grandparents' garden in Toronto must have seemed a mirror of their narrow strips of land in Staromischyna. Here, as there, runner beans, strawberries, cucumbers thrived, feeding the family through summer and winter. Zinnias, dahlias, morning glories: these were Canadian translations of the poppies and hollyhocks growing by the *pryspa* in Olena's yard. Working the earth of her garden, back stooped and hands blackened, my grandmother had no time to mourn for the Old Place, or lament the new. The rich gravity of earth: this was her one true home.

Inside the house on Dovercourt Road, oak and brass were made to gleam; crystal shone from chandeliers or hung like unshed tears from the satin shades of table lamps. But the rooms I remember best, and which must hold, even now, some echo of my grandparents' lives, are the small kitchen and dining room that overlook the garden. The least elegant but most important furniture was here: the *shafa* or glass-fronted cupboard that stored plates and bowls and the small gold-rimmed glasses from which the men in the family drank what I grew up calling *viski*. The *shafa* and the long wooden table seating all twelve of us with room to spare. And in the kitchen, adjoining the dining room, the small enamel-topped table on which gargantuan meals were prepared for us each Saturday, to be served and lingered over every Sunday afternoon.

At the very end of the dining room lay a relic encased in a large wooden box and crowned with flowering plants—coleus or chrysanthemum or poinsettia, depending on the season. Inside the box was a treadle sewing machine, serviceable enough but lacking the beauty of the one my grandmother had left behind in Poland. Black that shone so you could find your face in it, garlands of golden leaves and flowers—the only sewing machine in all of Staromis-chyna. At which Olena sat, singing love songs to the man she wouldn't see again for years and years. What else should she be singing? For it's love that has given her the children whose clothes she's sewing, children whose very existence has forced her husband to live so far away. To earn the bread she puts into their mouths, to earn such consolations as this glistening machine. It's love she married for, not bread: what I'm about to tell you is a love story from a world where bread is hard and sour, honey rare as amber.

3

---

love, marriage, secrets

She's not my grandmother, or anyone's mother yet, but a girl of eighteen: Olena. Not beautiful, but fair, that word from fairy tales: as a child, she'd been so blonde that her brother had called her *bilenka*, little white one. Olena's grey eyes are both sharp and nearsighted; her mouth wears the smile of someone who has learned early on to disguise the limitless meaning of that small word, pain. She stands in a knot of girls her own age, in a corner of the barn where a harvest dance is taking place. Unlike the other girls she wears a kerchief on her head; her head is bald except for an ash-blonde sheen. A month ago she caught typhus from her father, Ivan Levkovych: he died, but she pulled through. Typhus is spread by lice or fleas caught from infected rats: no one is more fastidious than Olena's mother, Melania, yet at the age of eighteen the girl contracts typhus. The fever that comes with this disease runs dangerously high and can last for as long as two weeks; it's the fever, not the typhus, that makes the patient's hair fall out, as if burned from the root.

It prickles her scalp, the new-grown hair on Olena's head, just as stubble in newly scythed fields pricks her bare feet. But whatever she feels at the loss of her hair, her face gives nothing away.

Nothing but that pride marking her out as different from the other girls, the simpering or grievously shy ones who'd rather be hiding with the cows than exposed to view like this at a village dance, on a brilliant autumn night.

Musicians have come in from town, fiddlers in tight suits with whisky-watery eyes. The barn fills up with farm boys, who tramp on toes as if they were clods of earth. Local boys, and a stranger from a neighbouring village, someone who has gone away to war and managed to come back again, alive and whole. He's only a little older than the others; he can't be more than twenty. Whatever uniform he once owned has rotted long ago; he's wearing the same rough trousers and hemp shirt as the others, but the straight way he stands makes him look distinguished, like someone from a city. And when he starts to dance, there's suddenly no other man in the room, for he glides across the floor as if he were an angel off an icon, shod in clouds, not leather.

He dances again and again with the proud-eyed girl wearing a tightly fastened kerchief. Another girl stands by the wall, refusing every boy who asks her, wanting only to dance with the stranger. At last, with the night wearing on and her spine feeling like a row of little knives, the girl runs to where the stranger is standing with Olena, waiting for the musicians to chase the dust from their throats. She grabs Olena's kerchief, whisking it away so everyone can see the nakedness beneath. Olena runs out into the night. And Tomasz rushes after her, finding her at last in an orchard by the river.

In one of the tenderest of Ukrainian songs, a lover calls to his sweetheart to join him in the orchard—the moon is so bright, he says, that she could find a needle on the ground. If she is tired, he will hold her; if she is afraid of getting her feet soaked with dew, he'll wrap them up in his cap. More than anything else, it must be Tomasz's tenderness that wins Olena in those hours spent together among pear and apple trees; the way he takes her head in his hands and, bending it towards him, kisses again and again the plush of her scalp.

❊❖❊

In the gallery of Ukrainian art in Kyiv, a sad, severe building with weather-eaten lions guarding its cracked steps, there are many paintings of village weddings, the Ukrainian variant of Dutch tavern scenes. And in painting after painting an elderly drunken lout is parading with some horrified girl, wreathed and ribboned for the sacrifice. All the songs sung by mothers of Ukrainian brides-to-be are in a minor key, and nothing can disguise the fact that they are lamentations. In peasant cultures marriage is often a time of sacrifice, the bitter culmination of a long process of surrender. From the moment a daughter is born, her dowry's begun: feather quilts and pillows, hand-woven rugs or kilims, the same necessary treasures Olena carried with her over the Atlantic to Canada. Quilts that remained shut in cedar closets when her daughters married, kilims that found their way into their children's playrooms, scarred by tricycle wheels till holes wore through the patterned roses.

Three of my mother's grandparents married more than once. Rozalia, Tomasz's mother, had two other children with her second husband, a man named Pokotylo. Ivan Levkovych was a widower with one daughter when he married Melania, the young teacher who became Olena's mother. After Ivan died of typhus, Melania married yet another widower who'd worked a long time in the United States and come home with enough money to buy land and a new wife. Ivan Mlynko was his name. What Vira and Natalia remember best about him is his trousers, sewn out of a marvellous cloth called corduroy. They'd listen for the swish he made coming into the house; stare at the ridges left in their skin after he'd sat them on his knees. He had three grown sons at home that

Melania had to cook and clean for, but it wasn't the labour she complained of. Her sorrow was that he was *prostiy*: uncultured, coarse, however kind. "Just look how he eats," she'd complain. "Instead of breaking his bread, he takes bites big as horseshoes. How can I hold my head up, married to a man like that?"

In the Old Place people marry not for love, but land: scattered ribbons of soil from which everything comes, not only wheat and rye and flax, but your entire past, your only future. In the Old Place you are born and die a peasant; to be a landless peasant is like being born with a stomach and no mouth. Land is your one defence against poverty and hunger: in overpopulated places like Staromischyna, land is desperately hard to come by. Olena's parents have as good as engaged her to a much older man with land adjoining the Levkovych fields; Tomasz is supposed to marry his stepsister Varvara and join her lands to his. He has no love, no ability for farming—he was supposed to have become a priest but ran past the seminary door and off to be a soldier. Now that he's left the army, he wants to marry. He wants to marry Olena, and he does.

No one has ever told me—could tell me—whether Varvara was sullen and plain, three years older, with a squint or faint moustache. Perhaps she was lovely, gentle, wise—but she wasn't Olena. Who, for her part, would have no one but Tomasz. *Let them marry then.* Is this what their parents agreed at last? *Let them lie down in the dust together—what little dust they can scrape up between them.* For this is all they'd inherit from their families by way of land. Perhaps Tomasz, like many others, did hired work for the man who owned the largest fields in Staromischyna, a rich man living in the far-off city of Lwow. But even so, he'd have earned no more than a few sacks of wheat. Without fields of their own, he and Olena would have barely been able to feed themselves. How did they manage to survive?

As Ivan Levkovych lay dying of typhus, the story goes, he called for a lawyer and made out his will. Out of belated love or a panic of guilt, he left his house and orchard to the Cinderella of his daughters, Olena. As soon as Olena married Tomasz, Melania, who had fought the match as fiercely as she could, went off to live with Yulia, her favoured daughter. It must have irked Melania to see Olena and Tomasz get by, somehow, with the house that used to be her own and the acres of orchards lying behind it, the vegetables from the garden in the yard. Irked her so much that when Olena was in labour with her first child, Melania came back to the Levkovych house once more. She sat in a chair outside her daughter's room, her arms folded high and tight. Between Olena's screams Melania called out, "You wanted Tomasz, you've got Tomasz."

This was one of the stories I heard again and again when I was a child. The rancour of that woman who folded her arms outside her daughter's door, her daughter's pain: this was passed down to me as the very truth of life. All joy, all desire, all freedom come to this: a gaunt, black-kerchiefed hag crowing at the threshold of your heart. Not that anyone ever called my great-grandmother names like hag or witch—even though it was her own daughter she cursed, folding into her malice the only person who'd ever shown that daughter anything like gentleness. *You wanted Tomasz, you've got Tomasz.*

When she first left the house her husband had willed to Olena, Melania looted everything she could lay her hands on, including the damper from the chimney. To Yulia and Yulia's husband, a man named Husak, she signed over, bit by bit, every one of her possessions and all the strips of land she owned in Staromischyna. When the last field was in his grasp, Husak threw Melania out of his house. Where did she go for shelter and to salvage her pride? To Olena, with whose help Melania arranged her only way out: marriage to a widower in a neighbouring village.

In telling me this story, no one says anything of Olena's goodness, her largeness of heart in taking in the mother who so mistreated her. To me, it's as astounding as if Snow White had taken in the wicked queen who'd fed her poisoned apples. In my mother's mind Melania simply wasn't to be judged, any more than were the customs of the Old Place. Judgement was a luxury you couldn't afford. And here's the other phrase that haunts my childhood: "That's the way it was, and that is that." Each *that* a hammer driving home a nail.

I know only one story of Olena's childhood. When she was four or five, her mother sent her, alone, to fetch water from a distant spring. The child's eyes were infected, the lids so crusted over she could barely open them when she woke each morning. Years later Vira will diagnose the same disease that afflicted the five-year-old Olena, advising her patients' mothers to dip a clean, soft cloth in a salty solution, then gently press it against their children's eyes until the crusts soften. The children will be frightened, she'll warn: they'll need to be consoled, persuaded that their eyes will once again let in the world.

Olena may have been sent, Vira suggests, to a healing spring, *but even so.* There's a silence after that last phrase, in which my aunt and I, ninety years on, see the child feeling her way to that spring, splashing icy water on her eyes so that she can finally see more than needles of light. We watch her fill a metal pail with that same ice-cold water and struggle home with it, the pail rubbing against her bare shins, making a bright, raw mark. Only a few feet from home the child stumbles, spilling the water and earning another of the beatings that make up the rhythm of her life: running from a beating; being caught and beaten; running away again and into the same arms that beat her.

She was not supposed to have been born; they wanted a boy, not another girl. Even when the longed-for son was born at last, the one killed by lightning when he was just seventeen, Melania would not relent, as if selective cruelty were some habit she couldn't break, or else the right and proper privilege of mothers. This power to blight or ease her children's lives—what was it, after all, but the one power she possessed after marriage? For she had no control over how many children she would bear, how many would die of typhus or diphtheria or war or weather. The day she first married, pulling a wreath of wildflowers from her hair, pulling on a drab kerchief, she would have known all this, as her own mother had known it, and her mother's mother. *And that is that.*

※◇※

Defying the massed weight of family, Tomasz and Olena marry, only weeks after their first meeting. What takes my breath away is not the romance of this wedding so much as the stubbornness it shows. Or is stubbornness the very heart of romance? How, then, do I read this other story, one I've known as long as I've known about the country dance, the moonlit orchard?

In this other story, lovers are forbidden to marry for the same simple reason: like Olena and Tomasz, they have no land between them. But for these lovers, there must have been no house and orchard, and certainly no Canada, no place vast or distant enough to translate poverty into possibility. Instead of crossing an ocean, they walk out together one summer evening, dressed in their finest clothes, spending the night in the fields by the river. When it comes time to go to sleep, they steal to one of their fathers' barns, slip stout hemp cords around their necks and walk together off the beams to which they've tied these cords.

The whole village comes to their burial in the unblessed field at the edge of the cemetery. Olena brings her daughters to stand a moment at the open coffins. What's to be seen in the faces of the dead? A stubbornness that prefers death to division—the kind of division Olena's come to know by heart, now that Tomasz has gone to Canada to earn the price of Polish fields? Or is it submission that she finds on the lovers' faces? Has Olena brought her children here to inoculate them against the terrible beauty of hopelessness? Against surrendering to instead of making your fate, as she and Tomasz have tried to make theirs? Young as she is, Natalia knows that the girl's black braids are wrapped so thickly round her neck to hide the bruises left by the rope. That the scarf binding the boy's throat, propping up his chin, keeps his swollen, purple tongue from sticking out.

And Vira? She stares and stares into the face of that tall, beautiful boy who used to tease her, throwing a ball so high it seemed to disappear, caught by one of the stern angels looking down from paradise.

※◇※

Falling in love and marrying as they did, what do they make of their daughters' romances, Tomasz and Olena?

Natalia's first love affairs are theatrical: she's inherited her father's passion for the stage, and soon after her thirteenth birthday makes her first appearance in one of the plays performed at the *chytalnia*. The plots are starkly generic: lovely maiden, brave soldier, fallen soldier, maiden dead of grief. The last part Natalia ever plays in Staromischyna is that of a girl bidding farewell to her sweetheart, who is going off to war. The play is based on a patriotic Ukrainian poem, and two Polish soldiers come to the house after opening night, warning Olena that her daughter's far too young for such a role. The play closes after the first performance.

In my youthful fantasies Natalia wept for her lost lines, keeping all her life a hatred for censorship and the silencing of poets. I could never accept my mother's verdict: that the soldiers had been right to close the play. Later I learned that Ivan, the twenty-four-year-old who'd played the lead, had asked Natalia, eleven years his junior, to marry him offstage as well as on. He'd proposed in a long and desperate poem he slipped to her during rehearsals: her first years in Canada, Natalia received letters from him, equally poetic and intense. Could she help him get out of Poland? Things were very bad there now. Would she promise never to forget him? And then the war started, and the letters stopped.

In the Old Place childhood was a time of work, not play; children grew up quickly. My thirteen-year-old mother, acting the role of a soldier's sweetheart, had been close to marriageable age; that same year, visiting an aunt in a neighbouring village, she'd been astonished to look up at the window and find it filled with the faces of young men. "Smile at them," her aunt had urged. "They want to marry you. Thanks to your father, you've got land. If you were a goat and had land, they would want to marry you." Things are very different in Toronto, where my mother's parents are faced with a phenomenon unknown in Staromischyna: adolescence. This means Natalia showing up one day with crimson fingernails, and Tomasz, innocent of the chemistry of nail polish, bringing her a dish of soap and hot water.

But far worse is what Natalia does with her hair—the long, thick braid or *kosa* that, in the Old Place, would have been a sign of virginity as well as beauty. All it signifies on Queen Street is that she's a bohunk straight off the boat. More than anything, Natalia wants to look like the girls at school or, better still, like Paulette Goddard in *Modern Times*, the first film she's ever seen. And so one afternoon she goes with a girlfriend to a beauty salon to ask for a perm. The hairdresser is Ukrainian; she charges nothing for her work, which is just as well. For the girl who emerges from her hands is shorn, her hair more fuzz than curls. Natalia runs home from the shop, exhilarated at the breeze fanning her neck, terrified at how light her head feels.

She runs straight into her father. He's too shocked to say a word: perhaps he has a vision of the girl he met sixteen years ago, the nakedness of her scalp beneath a tightly tied kerchief. He marches his daughter back to the beauty salon to ask the hairdresser for the *kosa*. "I swept it up long ago—I threw it out with the rubbish," she insists. Of course she's hidden it away to sell to a wig-maker, this lustrous braid of red-brown hair. They walk slowly home, father and daughter; nothing more is said about the *kosa*. But the loss of it lasts far longer than the ghost of Natalia's permanent wave. It has taught her a curious, complex lesson to do with the body and its adornments; how much, yet how little, is ours to keep or change or give away.

When Olena has to speak to her daughters on the subject of their bodies, she says only two things: "Men are like that," followed, when her daughters ask, "Like what?" by a stern "You'll find out." The house rules? "If you ever get into trouble, you can walk straight into Lake Ontario." This is what that immense body of water at the edge of this huge, strange city comes to mean for Olena: not a waterway leading to the centre of a continent, not a source of simple pleasures—ferry boats, beaches and carnival rides—but the ultimate offstage for girls who bring shame upon their families.

What made Olena speak of Lake Ontario to her daughters, who knew even less about swimming than they did about the facts of life? What else but the village code of pride, trailing after it the inevitable weight of shame. Natalia and Vira weren't to know what went on between men and women in the dark, but they were to know exactly what to do should that dark catch up with them. Shameless women, after all, would go ahead and have their babies or seek out women with knitting needles in back alleys; good girls walked into Lake Ontario, just as they must have walked into the strong, fast current of the river Zbruch.

※◈※

When my mother was old enough to bring boyfriends home, my grandfather would sit with them in the parlour of the Dovercourt house, talking politics or history or even the weather if the young man proved dull. When the couple sat out on the porch on balmy summer nights, Tomasz would appear at eleven o'clock, look conspicuously at his watch and announce to the linden tree that it was well past the hour when his daughter should be safe in bed. They were always Ukrainian boys, sons of people my grandparents knew in Toronto or Poland or both. It was unthinkable, in the way television or space travel must have been unthinkable, that Natalia or Vira would go out with, let alone marry, someone who wasn't *nashi* or "our own." How could you know anything about the people of a Macedonian or a Scotsman? How could you protect your daughters, how could you make sure they were entrusting themselves and their future children to men who were solid enough to work hard without drinking up their wages, decent enough not to run around or lift their hands in rage?

I've been told that my grandfather glimpsed one of his future sons-in-law in 1928. On a snowy afternoon, shortly after he first arrived in Toronto, Tomasz saw a young boy carrying a large violin at Yonge and College. He watched as the boy vanished down the street, struggling to keep his violin case out of the slush. Twenty-one years later Tomasz would give Natalia away to the man this boy became. At this point he was no longer toting violins but drilling teeth: when he'd left high school, he'd had to decide whether to go to New York to study music or to try for a profession in Toronto. It was the Depression; he was the only son of immigrant parents; toothaches, unlike concert stages, are never in short supply.

To her great regret, my mother never heard my father play his violin. She was still in Poland when he performed Paganini's *Perpetual Motion* at Massey Hall; she was on a boat crossing the Atlantic when he loosened the strings of his bow, laid it alongside his violin in its case with the blue-velvet lining, wrapped the lump of rosin in its scrap of silk, snapped the whole case shut and buried it in the silence of a cupboard forever. But while she never heard my father play violin, she did fall in love with him years before they actually met. On her way to work one day—it was wartime, 1942 or '43—she stopped short in front of the window of a photographer's shop on Queen Street West. Staring at the portrait of a man in captain's uniform, staring into the brilliant whites and blacks of his eyes, she vowed she'd marry him when he came home. As it turned out, it was her sister who played Cupid. Having come down with toothache, Vira made an appointment with a Dr. Joseph Kulyk, newly back from the war. She happened to be the last patient of his long day; he offered her a drive home; her sister was sitting out on the verandah of the Dovercourt house when the car pulled up. And that, as my mother says, was that.

But when Vira first brought home a young man—the only young man in the world for her—the whole Ukrainian community rose up, including her parents. When Tomasz had seen the boy who was to become my father, when Natalia had stared at the portrait in Stasiuk's Studio window, they had known without needing to be told that he was *nashi*. Vira's suitor, on the other hand, was straight from County Galway. Those who had telephones called, those who didn't came to the house to express their astonishment that the Solowskis could give their daughter away to an *Anglik*—no one made distinctions then between different kinds of native English speakers. There were so many fine Ukrainian boys for Vira to choose from; there were even some going into business or the professions. Who was this "Gus"—what kind of a name was that? What were Tomasz and Olena thinking—had they no shame? And so, just as her own mother had forbidden her marriage to Tomasz Solowski, Olena fought Vira's romance with Andrew Augustine Duane, who'd joined the Royal Air Force at age eighteen and had come out to Canada when the war was done. Who'd met a wonderful girl, a medical student, at the hospital bed of a mutual friend, a fine Ukrainian boy sidelined by hepatitis.

I was four years old when Gus and Vira finally married, after a nine years' courtship. Along with my sister, then six, I was a flower girl at the wedding. Without understanding it, I must have perceived the distress Vira felt in marrying against the wishes of her parents, the advice of her sister and the judgement of all the people who'd helped her family through the terrible early days in Toronto. And it must have been the high-wire tension surrounding this wedding, combined with its taking place on and overshadowing my birthday, that led me to my mother's sewing room on the morning of June 2, 1956, and put into my hands a large pair of Swedish-steel sewing scissors. My mother tried to disguise the damage with a flower headband, but the evidence is there in the photographs. Beside my delighted uncle and my aunt, who looks both dazed and radiant without her glasses, a scowling child, whips of white-blonde hair sticking up against the flowers round her face.

There is, of course, more than a little irony about this marriage of a Ukrainian to an Irishman. For though Vira is marrying a man from another culture, country, language, she is immediately at home in the family of the Duanes: her mother-in-law is a country woman, like Olena: she raised twelve children as well as working the land. Gus's brothers and sisters, some of them in Canada by the time of this wedding, welcome Vira with kindness and cheer, whereas Natalia's new family is forbidding. For all that she is a good Ukrainian girl, no woman can ever be good enough for their Joseph, who might have married any number of Nadias or Olhas or Lidas: girls whose families owned businesses or apartment blocks. Even when Natalia has produced the necessary children, including the all-important son; even when she invites her husband's family to lavish birthday and Christmas and Easter dinners, they remain suspicious, grudging. "Did you really make this yourself?" they ask, pointing at the heaped platters of *holubtsi* or *varenyky*, stirring the *borshch*, the wild-mushroom gravy. Following her into the kitchen, looking for dirty pots and pans. As if what this intruder might be getting away with is no simple case of takeout food, but murder.

XOX

We are obsessed with our parents' and grandparents' courtships, with the unions out of which we slide into the light. For without this coming together of two people who might have been anyone else and yet had to be exactly who they were, without this urgency between a woman and man who once were perfect strangers, we would not exist.

We are fascinated, too, with missed possibilities, alternatives only shadowed, never seized. The figures in photograph albums no one will identify—"Him? Her? Just someone I used to know, nobody important." We are born with, or quickly acquire, a nose for secrets and a wisdom that helps protect the clues we chance upon. If we ask too many times about that unnamed young man who holds our mother so closely round the waist, we'll open the album one day to find a blank inside the mitred corners that once held his image. But if we hold our tongues, if we open our eyes and ears, we may discover just enough of what we need. Enough to help us make up other stories than the ones we're told.

All families have secrets: secrets are different from gaps, those empty spaces made by whatever we haven't desire or experience enough to imagine. Secrets are material; they speak to us through palpable absence—the missing document, the figure scissored out of the photograph, names that must never be spoken. And secrets can be double-dyed, pride and shame shot one through the other, as in a certain kind of taffeta that changes colour moving through the light.

XOX

In the kitchen of the house in Staromischyna there were wooden troughs for kneading dough, a long-handled paddle for taking loaves of bread out of the *pich* on baking days, enamel pots, earthenware bowls and a few glasses kept precariously clean. There was, as well, a carved chest whose hidden contents mystified and tantalized Olena's oldest daughter. "None of your business," her mother warns her when she begs to know what's kept inside. It's up to her, then, to imagine all the chest might hold.

Not knowing is more than this child of eight or nine can bear. Her curiosity has a practical turn: the end of wonder is to find things out, but in order to do this you have to keep things to yourself, find ways of making sure no one guesses what you're up to. Once, when she was younger and had hatched some terrible crime to be carried out in the kitchen—stealing sugar or eating her sister's share of the white bread baked for some festival—Natalia had climbed up on a chair to each of the holy paintings hung along the walls. With a small knife, she'd dug out the pupils of the saints' sad eyes. For her mother had told her that the saints were always watching; would tell of any mischief she got into when Olena wasn't there.

The saints are blind now, they cannot see Natalia prising up the lid of the *skrynia*, the old carved chest. No thief can have been more promptly punished: in place of gold, jewels, embroidery, are rags. Stiff red rags, giving off a meaty smell of blood. And now the child cries her own eyes out. Her mother has murdered someone and is hiding her guilt here, in this chest in the kitchen. The floor below must be soaked in blood; if the chest is moved, everyone will find out, her mother will be taken away, be killed in turn—and what will become of her children with no one to look after them? Who is the murdered person, where is the body hidden? Nowhere is safe anymore, not the chicken coop or cowshed, not even the manure pile. In a nightmare Natalia sees the dead man's legs sticking out of the muck, eaten by giant flies that lurch and stumble.

For days, my mother says, she lived in misery and terror. And then she discovered the truth of what was hiding in the chest, though she never explains how this came about. I tell myself she must have seen her mother, early one morning when everyone else was supposed to be asleep; watched as Olena removed from under her nightdress the blood-soaked rag, throwing it into the chest. To be emptied when the children were asleep at night; to be washed and dried in secret.

I am told this story not when I'm fourteen, but forty-five. Only now does my mother confide how, when she first began bleeding every month, it was her Canadian girlfriends and not her mother who enlightened her. They took her to Kresge's; showed her how, for a dime, you could buy a box of Kotex pads and the stiff elastic belts that could never protect you from your fear that, walking down the street or a school corridor, blood from deep inside might gush out and betray you. When my sister and I began to bleed each month, our mother gave us the same boxes of Kotex pads, the same belts and metal fasteners, warning us never to use tampons, which would ruin our wedding nights. Refusing such opaque advice, reading the ads in teen magazines urging us not to let "that time of the month" spoil the fun of swimming or skating—neither of which we did with any passion—Karen and I would head for the drugstore at the plaza, spending our allowances on small blue boxes of Tampax.

Perhaps it's just as well I never knew till now that story of the chest in the kitchen. How its true secret wasn't a pile of blood-soaked rags, but the sense of shame enveloping the body, mysteries you couldn't control and could never hide. How our mother, though only a child and only for the space of a few days, could have believed her mother capable of murder. The mother she feared and loved equally, who would never find out that her daughter knew her to be not just her mother, but someone far more powerful—the keeper of secrets her daughter would never let on that she knew. For not all secrets are small and silent enough to be hidden in an old carved chest. Some have voices that make themselves heard across corridors, across oceans. Voices of strangers, voices you recognize, at last, as ones you've always known.

4

families: ashes and honey

I know the faces in my mother's family. I know them from old albums, and I have them in my bones, for I take after the Solowskis, just as my sister favours the Kulyk side. "Take after"— how often did we hear this phrase as children, I with my mother's blue-grey eyes and hair as white-blonde as her mother's once had been; Karen dark-eyed, dark-haired like our father? What is it that we take, and what is taken from us, what other chances do we lose or fail to make when we're assigned this ancestor's height or walk, this forebear's heart or lungs or character?

In photographs of my grandmother when she was twenty, thirty, forty, I've found not just my eyes and lips, but at times my very expression. Sometimes, wrapping myself up in a *khustyna* or head scarf, I think I am more than Olena's granddaughter. I take the scarf, centre it on my head, making sure it covers my hair completely. I pull the cloth low on my forehead, as if the ghost of the *chador* hung in its folds, a memory of the time when whole villages were captured during Turkish raids, their people sold as slaves in the markets of Constantinople. I take the ends of the scarf and wrap them round and round my neck, then tie them at the back. Looking in the mirror, I see any woman from the Old Place, sixty or six hundred years ago. A twist of cloth, a slant of cheek-bone erasing the world that's made me, a world of computers and television and men on the moon.

Seductive, disturbing, this abracadabra with a length of patterned cloth. A shell, a noose, a shelter, a halter.

※◇※

In the ornate, cursive script of the parish priest of Staromischyna, Izidorus Swystun, the genealogies are laid out in Latin. Documents should act to tether our stray selves, but these forms and legal papers fail to do so, perhaps because they're written in three different languages, sometimes on the same page. On my grand-parents' marriage certificate, or *Testimonium Copulationis*, the name of the *sponsus*, or bridegroom, is Tomasz Solowski, born in Czerniszowka. He is the son of a Ukrainian woman, Rozalia, born Oszust, and Joannis or Jan Solowski, a Pole who died in an indus-trial accident in Pittsburgh—none of his family have ever seen his grave. As for Tomasz's wife Olena Levkovych, she also is the child of a Joannis—Ivan in Ukrainian—but her mother is Melania, née Sikora, a schoolteacher who, bored or exhausted by her charges, married a respected, reasonably weathy widower who, with only one young daughter, would have been in search of sons.

Melania stares at me from the album: a starved nun with beaked and hooded face. No photo exists of Rozalia, but I picture her as perpetually anxious, a woman forced to cut and contrive. For her second husband, Teodor Pokotylo, was an ogre according to the stories I have heard. He was so tight-fisted, Olena used to say, that Rozalia was forced to steal her own grain and sell it secretly, in order to give money to the church. Pokotylo was a man who never met your gaze, Vira remembers: he always kept his eyes on your feet, as if the rest of you didn't exist. Whenever Tomasz and Olena's children came to visit, Pokotylo flew into a rage: he had his own grandchildren to look out for, why should these brats come begging to his door? If Rozalia dared to give anything to Tomasz's wife—a jar of cherries, a twist of sugar—she had to cover her traces as cleverly as any master thief.

It's one of the stories my mother loves to tell, though like so many of these stories, she tells it against herself. Once Rozalia had been brave enough to kill two chickens for Olena, who'd just given birth to twins. As soon as she saw Pokotylo coming through the door, Rozalia started wringing her hands. "Would you believe it?" she cried. "The fox crept right into the hen coop and stole two birds!" The next day, when Natalia came to visit and Pokotylo asked her in his grunting way how her mother was, the five-year-old replied, "Our mother's so sick she can barely stand up, and yesterday Baba Rozalia sent her two chickens to pluck and boil into soup."

※◇※

In my mother's and my aunt's memories of the Old Place, food is the face of desire. Once Vira's schoolmates, deciding she's the smallest and skinniest of the bunch, push her through a gap in the fence round the schoolteacher's orchard. An older man, a bachelor, the teacher prides himself on the big, beautiful plums hanging from his low-branched trees. Vira wriggles through the fence, pelts towards the plums, begins to fill her skirt with fruit when she hears a growl behind her and something she learns much later to be Latin: *bestia carnalia!* It's the teacher, his stick lifted high over her head, his withered arms far more powerful than they'd ever looked in class. Half a dozen plums roll from the child's skirt into the grass: she races back through the gap in the fence, along the road and into the hayloft of her mother's barn. Sixty-five years on she remembers how fast and hard her heart beat; how her only plunder was words, forbiddingly delicious as the plums themselves: *bestia carnalia.*

Stolen fruit, and longed-for sweetness. Just after she tells me the story of the schoolteacher's orchard, Vira goes on to speak of Olena's older sister, Yulia, the favoured one. How she had trees in her orchard that bore small purple plums, the kind used for that marvel of Eastern European baking, plum and poppyseed cake. Some of the branches of those plum trees hung over the wall dividing Yulia's and Olena's gardens: "If I or your mother so much as looked at them, Yulia would swat us."

Yulia's husband, whom my aunt and mother nicknamed *Lysiy* or Baldy, was capable of setting fire to Olena's wheat if it looked as though her crop would be larger than his. He was hateful in other, subtler ways. In his orchard was an apiary: from pear and plum blossoms his bees made a slow, dark honey whose very fragrance was delicious. Olena's children would stand at the fence dividing Lysiy's property from their own, watching him take the combs out of the hives. Their cousins would be holding out huge chunks of bread for their father to dribble honey over: Vira and Natalia would be hanging over the fence, sucking on their fingers. "I'd have given anything for just a taste of it—even the wax," Vira tells me. The wanting is still there in her voice, after all these years of living in a world of doughnut shops and Danish pastries. I hear something else as she speaks to me, an awareness of something that shouldn't have been, the awareness children have but so often lose when they become adults. "The cruelty of it," she says. "To refuse a child so small a thing."

Cruelty—what others might call necessity, the way things were or had to be—is part of the landscape of the Old Place. It would be so in any comparable culture, but the fate of these children—grudgingly acknowledged by their grandmothers, resented or ignored by most of their aunts and uncles, fatherless for much of their growing up, fearing and loving their mother in equal measure—makes the cruelty far worse. Cruelty, it's been said, is only fear disguised. In the Old Place, in Olena's dealings with her children, it seems to me that cruelty, or harshness, is love in hiding. But how do we name the cruelty shown by a grown woman to her small nieces, denying them a handful of plums, a bread crust scribbled with honey? The kind of cruelty that fills the mouth with ashes.

✖◈✖

In fairy tales enchanted godmothers appear at the graves where ill-treated stepchildren mourn their mothers. Heroes meet ancient men at crossroads, gladly sharing their black bread and jugs of water, earning magical powers, unanticipated gifts. It's these gifts of sympathy and power that let the helpless and put-upon secure not just their fortune, but their very survival.

Olena's blessing was bestowed by her dying father. It wasn't just the property he left her, but something that speaks a different language from wills and testaments: the door he made for his house. It was an unusually strong and heavy door; beautiful, too, for he carved it with stars and birds and sunflowers. I heard its story only a few months ago, watching my mother sketch the house where she was born. In the door of that house she made a deep, thick mark, high up, where you'd expect a grown person's head to reach. When I asked her to explain the mark, she seemed surprised, as if it were nothing out of the ordinary for a door to be scarred in this way. And as she told me the story, I understood that my grandmother's life had in it the stuff of fairy tales, the violent evil that makes ordinary demons—illness, loneliness, worry—seem benign.

This evil wells from envy. It pushes Yulia's husband, Lysiy, to open the gate of Olena's yard one day, not long after he's rid himself of Melania. Olena has stepped out into the garden, leaving her mother to hide her shame and bitterness inside; leaving the door to her house wide open. Perhaps Olena has come outside to collect a pot drying on one of the pointed staves of the fence;

perhaps, though this is barely possible, she simply wants to feel the sun on her face. But as she stands there in the yard, a shadow cuts across the light that washes over her; she whirls round to find Lysiy, brandishing an axe. Olena doesn't scream or plead. She races to her house and throws herself inside, slamming the door behind her. The axe lodges in the mouth of a carved sunflower.

✕◇✕

Stories speak one language: documents another. With the help of a friend who was born and grew up in Poland, I go through my treasure hoard of official papers. The sheets are waxy or grained, sometimes coarse as cornmeal; they are pasted with stamps bearing the Polish eagle and various denominations of zlotys. 1926, 1928, 1930: these are the dates of the papers, all of which have to do with land—the renting or buying of earth parcelled out in morgs and valued according to measures of grain, namely "rye, clean and dry." What these papers tell me is that my great-grandfather Ivan Levkovych, who carved the sunflowers into the door that saved Olena's life, was a man of substantial property, and that he died on February 2, 1920, without having drawn up any will at all. Thus the deathbed bequest I've been told of was not made in the presence of a lawyer; it appears to have launched a battle that was only resolved six years later, in a notary's office in Pidvolochys'k. A typed, sealed Statement of Bequest declares that, according to the established laws of property and a sworn statement regarding his father's intentions, given by one Petro Levkovych, who died a year after his father, the following disposition of Ivan Levkovych's estate must be respected: his house and garden, along with thirty-five square metres of land bordering the road to the river, are the lawful property of his daughter Olena. The land, but not the house and garden, is to be shared with Yulia.

Other bequests of property are made to Ivan Levkovych's two surviving children and his widow Melania. Much of the land is tied up, so that a daughter may have the use of a certain number of parcels until her death but acquires no ownership and thus cannot pass this land down to her children. Some of the other "contracts of sale and rental" in my possession show that Tomasz, for example, was given a gift of land by his mother Rozalia after his marriage, but that, again, the property is tied up in such a way that his children cannot inherit the land. The need to possess as many strips of earth as possible is countered by the fear that these strips will end up divided into nothing.

As I puzzle through this intricate scheme of provisions and restrictions, I begin to see that my grandparents' dilemma was more poignant than I'd thought: between them, they had enough land to guarantee their own present but nothing that would give their children any future. And so, the year after the legal resolution of this dispute regarding Ivan Levkovych's estate—the year Olena's twins are born—Tomasz sets out for Canada. Three years later, his name appears on a document stating that he's paid the considerable sum of one hundred and fifty American dollars for a narrow strip of land in the township of Staromischyna.

The documents tell me one thing more, something to add to this story of the thatched house with its storks on the roof, its axe mark in the carved front door. When Ivan Levkovych lay dying of typhus, he confided his wishes regarding Olena not to a lawyer but to his sixteen-year-old son, Petro, who might have expected that he, not Olena, would inherit the family home. Petro honoured his father's request; it is Petro's sworn statement that shapes the legal document I hold in my hand, a document that validates Olena's very existence. And Petro suddenly comes alive for me: Petro, who was struck dead in a freak electrical storm one February day in 1921, when he was only seventeen.

※◇※

When it came time for Olena to leave Staromischyna, perhaps only for a few years, perhaps forever, she remained outside the gate of her sister's house, sending her daughters in to say farewell. Yulia nodded at the girls; Lysiy lay in bed with his hand over his eyes, saying nothing. And the cousins, what did they do? The boys with whom Natalia and Vira barely got along; the daughter, who'd been given her grandmother's name, Melania. Of all Yulia's family, she is the only one on whom I've set eyes. Thirty years after Olena and her daughters left their village, years of war and explosive peace as the Old Place was absorbed into the Soviet empire, Melania finally made contact with her newly Canadian cousins and aunt. Letters flew to the house on Dovercourt Road, harsh-textured envelopes with ugly stamps. And each one made the same demand: Olena must buy a ticket for her niece to come to Canada.

What must have gone through Olena's head, reading these letters? She could have left them unanswered, she could have written to say it would be impossible to secure a visa. She could have forgone excuses altogether and reminded her niece, if not of the axe thrown at her head, then of the bread and honey denied her children. There's a part of me that longs for even small injustices to be acknowledged: this was cruel and this unfair, and until you recognize this—recognize, let alone apologize—there can be nothing between us but bitterness. Yet Olena held out her hands to her niece, and kept the peace she'd finally made with the sister who'd refused to bid her goodbye. For years Olena had been sending Yulia parcels of all the perfectly ordinary things her sister needed but could never find in the People's Republic of Shortages and Shoddy Goods. She may have done this mainly out of pride—would she have wanted it said that she'd turned her back on her own family, however vicious Yulia had been? "Let my sister's daughter come to Canada," Olena may have said. "Let her see what my daughters have made of their lives. Let her sit at my table, eating ashes with honey."

My parents, who live near the airport, went to meet Melania's plane. My mother, dressed to kill, stood at the arrivals gate, looking out for a fortyish someone who, transformed by age and hardship, might be that snooty, swaggering girl she could never forget. And saw Melania, encased in the sweat-drenched cotton housedress she'd been wearing for the past thirty hours, diffusing the unmistakable Soviet smell of unshaved, unmusked armpits. Melania, waving imperiously, refusing to give up rank or power, even now.

There must have been some gesture of greeting, even in that family so wary of open affection. But what could it have been? A mere shaking of hands, a grabbing of suitcases, a combination of relief and panic on my mother's side, and on Melania's the arrogance of expectation shown by all invaders. For it soon became clear that Melania's visit was a pretext for plunder. Throughout the long weeks of her stay (which she'd gladly have extended forever), Melania kept assessing which of her cousins had done better and in what regard—from whom she could demand a car, and from whom a house, from whom a Touch'n'Sew machine, from whom a colour television set. Even my grandmother, who was renting out the top two floors of her house and living modestly in a small apartment on the ground floor, became a possible source of luxuries as Melania turned herself into a goods train to be loaded up at every stop.

She spent most of her time at Dovercourt Road, holding court among Olena's friends. They'd come by for a cup of *chai* and poppyseed cake and the chance to talk with someone from the Old Place, who might have news of family or friends. Sometimes Melania would deign to peel potatoes or string beans: always she'd make fun of her aunts' and nieces' anglicized Ukrainian. "*Na selaryu,*" she'd snort, "*na selaryu!* There's no such word in Ukrainian as 'cellar.' How can you tell me to go *na selaryu* to fetch the onions?" To give her mother a rest, Vira took Melania up to her cottage on Georgian Bay. On her return Vira phoned her sister. "You know how wonderful the view is from the bluff, looking out over the water? And the birds in the morning, and the trees tunnelling over the road? She had all that to enjoy, and all she could do was say, 'How much does that cost? Buy me one. You're rich, you have three bathrooms in your house.'"

I don't know how Melania imagined she would take all the possessions she coveted back to Ukraine. Perhaps she reasoned that if only she could accumulate enough objects—toasters, vacuum cleaners, lawn mowers—their sheer accumulated weight would guarantee her immobility, if not asylum. But when it finally came time for her to leave, and she'd failed to squeeze out of her relations anything more than room and board, plus trips to cottage country and Niagara Falls, Melania resigned herself. Though she did ransack my mother's closets and sewing room, demanding at least as much as she could wear or carry home. The woman who boarded the Aeroflot jet back to Ukraine looked substantially different from the woman who'd arrived six weeks before. "They didn't let her starve," the steward must have thought as Melania staggered up the ramp. For not only was she wearing, this hot August day, a wool dress over a jersey pantsuit and a full-length merino coat, but under the coat she'd cocooned herself in yards of brightly patterned crimplene to be sold on the black market towards the purchase of a Lada, if not the Cadillac she'd coveted in Canada.

Perhaps some people have spite in their genes. Shortly after Melania's return, someone from the village wrote to my grandmother asking if it were true, what Melania had said. Had Olena really grown so fat she couldn't walk and had to be carried everywhere in a litter? For answer my grandmother put on her best dress, called up her Irish son-in-law and had him bring his camera to the Dovercourt house. He took picture after picture of Olena in her garden, standing between her red and white rosebushes. Standing unaided, a woman who was—what did they say back then?—full-figured but certainly not fat. She sent all but one of these pictures to the person who had written her. The last one she had framed, displaying it on the top of her *shafa* along with the school photos of her grandchildren.

I was fourteen the summer Melania visited. My memories of the woman I saw—large, loud, with fizzy reddish hair and stain-less-steel teeth that might as well have had CCCP stamped on each one of them—have merged with the stories I've heard my mother and my aunt exchange about her visit. But there would have been things unspoken or said beyond my hearing. There would have been shame, that of all their family the only one to have come here was this greedy, brazen woman. And there would have been pain, too, the sense of having been refused something as natural for them to want as plums and honey.

Speaking to me now, more than thirty years after Melania's visit and long after Olena's death, my mother can't keep the lone-liness out of her voice. "I wish I had more family," she says. "I wish the family I still have over there were closer. I can't help wishing my brother and my other sister had lived—Ivan and Marusia. I keep seeing my mother standing at the kitchen table with a cradle on either side of her. She's kneading dough and, at the same time, swaying her hips, rocking first one child and then the other."

※◇※

Although her mother had disinherited her and her sister had aban-doned her, Olena could look for some help from Tomasz's mother Rozalia and from Adela, Rozalia's daughter by the terrible

Pokotylo. Adela was only five years older than Natalia; it was Adela, my mother remembers, who helped to look after Ivan and Marusia when Olena was left alone, after Tomasz set out for Canada. Unlike Yulia or her children, Adela is remembered with affection by my mother and my aunt; they send her packages from time to time, and letters written in Polish cross back and forth between the city on Lake Ontario and the town near the Baltic coast where Adela and her family were resettled after the war.

In the few photographs brought from the Old Place, Adela gleams, dark-haired, dark-eyed. Looking at these images, I correct my vision of her father as fat and thick-necked. For his daughter is beautiful and his son Volodko, my mother says, looked just like Errol Flynn. I will meet Adela this summer; I will ask her about her father, her brother, and what she remembers of Tomasz. And I'll take her a photograph my mother has unearthed of Tomasz's sister Hannia, the daughter of Rozalia Oszust and Jan Solowski. Something terrible happened to Hannia and her family during the war. Letters came from Staromischyna, many years after the war's end; they told of how one of Hannia's sons was tortured: how she was forced to watch as his tongue was cut out, his ears torn off. By partisans, it seems, but as to which of the many groups operating in the area and why, no one knows for sure.

Shortly before I'm to leave for Poland, my mother will hand me a photograph. "When you meet Adela," she'll tell me, "ask her who these people are, and what happened to them." The photo is one I've never seen before: two women, one round-faced and in her late twenties, the other looking twice as old, though perhaps this is only the effect of her black dress, her thinness, the way her hair's scraped so tightly from her face. Either of them could be Hannia. Apart from the women, there are three children in the photograph: a black-haired, big-eared handsome boy as tall as the women, and a small, blond boy in short trousers, his hair unevenly cut—he may be seven or, at the most, nine.

And all in white, with a wreath in her hair and with a prayer book, rosary, white lilies in her hands, a girl of thirteen, the age for a first communion. She has the same deep-set, downward-slanting eyes as the older woman; the same delicate features and wide, narrow mouth. Her pearl-drop earrings make me think of the luminous girls Jan Vermeer once painted. A young, fair-haired girl standing here before me, in the black and white graveyard of a photograph.

✖◈✖

They tell us nothing but the truth: the truth someone—if only the photographer—has wanted us to see. Or else the truth that's somehow drawn by the flash of light hitting their skin, truth startled into showing. It's not their fault if we make up stories about the people in these photographs, invent lives, resemblances, futures for them they could not possibly have had, may never have wanted. We appropriate them for our purposes, making mysteries or moral fables out of the way they stand; the clothes, the very faces they wear. Sunday faces, for these are studio photographs in my mother's album, the only kind of photographs that could be taken in the Old Place.

Olena Levkovych dressed for her wedding, wearing a blouse with embroidery as heavy as the earth in her fields. Her long vest is woven with patterns of leaves and blossoms; she holds a wreath of field flowers and ribbons in her hands. On her face is an expression that turns the eighteen-year-old girl into someone utterly free of her role as daughter, sister, even wife. For one moment she stands alone, wearing the face of who she really is, a face lit up by possibility.

This portrait of Tomasz, taken somewhere in Toronto, in those plummy days before the Crash when work was plentiful and wages good. The young man in a good suit, with an indefinable air about him—not the air of a scholar or gentleman, for there's too much hard experience in his face, the set of his shoulders. Not the air of a labourer, unless that term embraces work done by the mind, the heart. He wears the same expression of expectancy I find in Olena's face. And what speaks most clearly to me now is only this: the right they claim to be expectant. To treat the future as something not yet written down, or off—as something they can make for themselves. This miracle of possibility: their happiness together.

5

Tomasz: a glorious stranger

For as long as I can remember, I have known the story of my grandfather's first departure for Canada. The very day his twin son and daughter were born, Tomasz had to take leave of them, of his wife and of his other children, who were only three and five years old. Just before he boarded ship, Tomasz sent a letter to Olena— he'd had bad dreams while travelling to Danzig; he was afraid for the children who'd just been born. On his arrival in Canada a letter was waiting for him, saying that his only son, Ivan, had died the night after his birth—the very night of Tomasz's dream.

I have a sheaf of documents before me now, documents in Latin and Ukrainian, Polish and English; together, they tell me a different story. When Tomasz boarded *The Empress of France* of the Canadian Pacific Line, the twins were four months old. Ivan would live for another three and a half months after his father was "legally and permanently admitted at the port of Quebec under the name of 'Tomasz Solowski'" on June 4, 1927.

The Latin inscribed on Ivan's death certificate seems a distillation of necessity and grief: *die 18 septembris mortuus est; 19 septembris sepultus est*—died on September 18; buried September 19. The documents also tell me that Ivan lived to the age of eight months, his sister to a year and a half. This agrees with my mother's memory of Olena kneading dough between a pair of cradles, swinging her hips to rock both babies at once. The *qualitas mortis* for Ivan looks like *debilita(n) de natu* or birth defects, but this explanation does not appear on his sister's certificate. For her there is one word, *scarlatina*, though according to other stories I've been told, Marusia as well as Ivan suffered from epileptic seizures.

Out of this mesh of fact and story I know—in the same way I know my own name—that long before any news from Staromischyna could reach him, my grandfather dreamed of his son's death, perhaps on the very night that the child stopped breathing. It seems that this dream occurred on a Saskatchewan farm, rather than on a Polish train, and yet I'm haunted by the pathos of the other version of departure: how Tomasz's taking leave of his family to explore that fairy story, Canada, is mirrored by his son's taking leave of a life too short to be made into any kind of story. Perhaps there's no such thing as a true story, just the echoes between different versions, and the desire to know, that keeps us speaking, and listening, at all.

※◇※

Like so many others from his corner of the world, Tomasz got off the boat into a world he knew only from tales of plentiful work and easy money. At Halifax he stopped the first passerby he saw on the street and spoke one word: "Toronto?" He ended up on a CPR train, heading west. To Saskatoon, says the card issued by the Ukrainian Colonization Board of Saskatchewan, 234 1st Avenue South. It was stamped on the day he'd been "passed by the surgeon" and certified fit to work. The card tells him that "it should be kept carefully. It should be shown to government officials whenever required." That the card still exists proves it was kept with great care—but I wonder to how many officials it was ever shown. For my grandfather was a man with the wits and courage to act for himself, and he was no great friend of authority. Sent to work for a farmer—whether of English or Ukrainian extraction no one knows—Tomasz found the conditions atrocious, the men treated far worse than cattle, forced to sleep in rough bunks built into the barn and given slops to eat. So he and a friend took off one night in the middle of winter. They walked for hours along section roads harder than iron under their worn boots, past snowfields thick with moonlight, till they came to a frozen river. Halfway across, Tomasz sank through the ice; somehow, his friend managed to fish him out, and Tomasz walked the rest of the way with his arms flapping like crazy birds, just to keep himself from freezing. Without map or compass, only the memory of the way they'd come, the two men reached a railway depot just in time to hop a freight car and ride the hundreds of hungry, thirsty miles to Toronto.

A year later Tomasz had found a job at a foundry attached to General Electric, where he learned to design and pour moulds. In the ever-to-be-cleaned-out basement of my parents' house, there's a memento of my grandfather's years at GE—a sturdy-legged, bronze-coloured dog, about eight inches high. When you pull on his tail, his jaws open to receive a walnut or almond; if you shove the tail down hard enough, the nut will crack. It used to fascinate me, the clumsy power of the dog's jaws, the hardness of the nut that proved no stronger than a wishbone. What that dog signifies of my grandfather's view of life I haven't decided. Some simple allegory about how even the strongest are crushed, their bravest hopes smashed by the powers that be? And yet he never seemed to me a broken man, my grandfather. In fact, he'd been famous for his powers of healing. Both in Staromischyna and Toronto, people with shoulders wrenched from their sockets would seek him out to be made right again. They valued him as much for the gentleness as for the strength and sureness of his hands.

But what did happen during those first lonely years that Tomasz lived in Canada? In 1927 hard work was still a ticket to independence, dignity, mobility. This is what I've been told: that once he came to Toronto he worked long shifts at the foundry, pouring molten metal into moulds made out of sand. That every month he sent a letter home, a letter enclosing a money order to buy boots for the children, oranges at Christmas, but most of all to buy more land. That he shared a room with three or four other men; that he often ate with Ukrainian families who always had a place for him at their tables. Perhaps he sang for them after supper in his rich baritone, performing an aria from *Taras Bulba*, the opera he was helping a group of fellow immigrants to stage. Perhaps he played counting or clapping games with the children, who may have reminded him of his own.

This, too, I've been told: he was such a handsome man, so strong and straight-shouldered, and yet so kindhearted, so well-mannered, there was no end to the mothers trying to marry him off to their daughters. Or to the women who'd signal to him, just by the set of their shoulders, the tilt of a hat, that he could walk beside them, if he pleased; buy them a cup of coffee, take them to Centre Island some Sunday afternoon. And to every such appeal, my mother says, Tomasz would reply in words or simply by the way he carried himself, walking down the street, coming into a room: "I have a wife and children at home." Saying "home" in such a way that it was clear he'd be going back to them, or they'd be coming out to join him.

Yet his papers tell me it is four years before Tomasz returns to Poland, in December 1931. And he heads back to Canada just before his birthday the next year, in early November. It's the thick of the Depression: his old job at the foundry has vanished, and he is one of thousands of men sleeping rough by night, scrounging for work by day, with no rights at the soup kitchens that have sprung up across the city—they are only for married men, with families. He gets a job picking cherries for twenty-five cents an hour—you could survive on that, if you didn't do anything but sit all day. But just walking to and from the farm exhausts you; you can barely hold onto the ladder as you pick the ripe and sticky fruit, and you spend everything you make on the little food you can afford to buy, food that never fills you. Walking to the farm with a friend early one morning, Tomasz is hit by a car and rolls into a ditch; with his friend's help he gets up, slowly, and hobbles back to the city. People from the Labour Temple on Dupont find him a room, visit him to make sure his back is healing, bring him whatever food they can. When he's better, he hears there's work shovelling coal in Guelph, a small town sixty miles west of Toronto. He walks there with the same friend who rescued him from the ditch. They arrive at nightfall on the second day, and as they wander the freezing backstreets, they catch a glimmer of fire, the smell of potatoes roasting. Calling out in their broken English, they hear a voice answering in Ukrainian. "Who was the *durak* who told you there was work in Guelph?" the voice asks. It belongs to a man who invites them to sit a moment by the fire; while they're warming their hands, he offers them each a potato to eat on the long walk home.

My source for these stories, and for the one I'm about to tell, is someone outside my family, though I meet him at my mother's house. A small, elderly Ukrainian man who came to Canada when he was just a boy, he lives in an old-age home, having lost his wife to Alzheimer's. He has no children. His name is John Matushak, and my mother describes him as "an engineer without a degree." He has a nose like a small potato and a high, domed forehead; what little hair he has left shines perfectly white. His immaculate grey suit looks as if it were made out of some space-age material, and his tie is grey, too, with a pattern of small red spots. He met my grandfather, he tells me, during the Depression. He was twenty; Tomasz thirteen years older. "He looked after me like a father," Mr. Matushak explains. "He made sure I didn't starve."

Before he met Tomasz, John Matushak had worked with French

Canadians in the bush north of Quebec City; later he went to Sudbury, to the mines, which he quit after an accident that left one of the men on his shift with his lower leg hanging from the knee, attached only by a strap of skin. John hopped freight trains to get to the West, jumping off the boxcars whenever a town came into view, knowing that policemen with dogs would be waiting for him at the station. Once, crossing a stretch of Saskatchewan wilderness late at night, he saw a lantern shining and felt such pure, sharp loneliness that he jumped from the train and made his way to what turned out to be a Doukhobor settlement. They fed him, he says, and put him up for the night, though he was sent on his way the next morning. The children, he tells me, were beautifully dressed—it was a paradise: a *kommuna*, not *kommunisma*.

My mother's guest tells me all this in English, sitting in a stiff, satiny chair in what's called the living room. I wish we were sitting in the kitchen, over cups of tea—what in the Dovercourt house was always called *chai* and bought in brightly painted tins with Russian lettering. I feel uncomfortable, I feel wrong, making this man speak to me in a language not his own; although my mother addresses him in Ukrainian, he insists on using English. But he also speaks another language that is foreign to me—because I've never travelled anywhere without purchasing a ticket; because I've never gone hungry or without shelter. I, the professor of English literature, from the university in that very town this man walked to with Tomasz, gaining nothing but a roast potato for his pains. I want to tell him how grateful I am to him for sharing these stories with me, telling me things about my grandfather's life that no one else could, but my words come out stiff as the clothes we wear in this formal, tidy room. My mother has wanted to honour him by seating us here; he has wanted to honour her by dressing up for this meeting. The honorary engineer and my mother—they share something I've lost or never had, the customs of the Old Place, its language of dress and occasion.

And then Mr. Matushak tells a story of the thirties that neither I nor my mother has ever heard before. Things got so bad in Toronto that they couldn't afford even the worst of the rooming houses: they had to sleep on park benches, making pillows out of abandoned newspapers, huddling in torn jackets with too-short sleeves. Then one night, when the police are busy raiding the parks to pick up what they call vagrants, Tomasz and John and half a dozen other men walk up and down a maze of streets until they discover a basement window they can jimmy open. The basement belongs to a church; they are eight men, huddling next to the furnace, sleeping as best they can while keeping their ears cocked for the sound of feet on the stairs. They return to this place night after night; one morning they wake to find a priest—is his name Smith?—staring at them with his arms crossed. He's a man of sixty, tall and big: a man you could respect. And he says something that floors them: "Don't fool with the window, you'll only draw attention to yourselves. I'll leave the basement door open; lock it after you come in at night and when you leave each morning."

And they do, for a whole six weeks, in the thick of winter, until one night the police, who are stepping up their beat, look in the windows to find a basement full of ragged sleepers. They force their way in, beat them up and haul them off to the station, all except for Tomasz, who manages to slip away. He makes his way back to the church that night, betting that the cops will be hunting elsewhere. He finds the priest waiting for him, insisting that something must be done. God, he says, never meant human beings to be treated worse than dogs, who sleep in warm kitchens, eating scraps from their masters' plates.

Mr. Matushak shifts in his chair, closes his eyes. I am trying to imagine my grandfather's face as he listens to these words from a priest who could have come straight out of some Hollywood seminary—*The Bells of St. Mary's*. Tomasz had no time for the priests of the Old Place; how they'd frighten people into paying tithes, attending mass: your children will pay for your sins, they'd say, pay with birth defects or early deaths from typhus or pneumonia. The same children the priests let go hungry while they collected loaf upon loaf of Easter bread, almost the only white bread you'd see all year, brought to them to be blessed and left as a tribute to heaven. Mountains of golden bread adorned with rosettes and crosses and doves, collected by priests and thrown in their barns to feed the pigs. Is this what Tomasz thinks of, heat from the furnace rocking his bones, as he listens to talk about action and justice? What can he do but trust this priest who's treating him like a man, not a tramp: a man with a mind as well as a belly. And what can I do but take Mr. Matushak's story as he tells it—*a wish or a truth, or a wish modified by the truth.*

Tomasz and the priest talk all night; the next night the other men come back to the church basement and the talking gets louder and stronger. The priest organizes a march to protest the denial of relief to single men. They set out, thirty thousand of them, Mr. Matushak declares—surely he means three thousand, three hundred? Ordinary working men without work of any kind, except the labour of keeping themselves alive. With the priest at their head, they make their way to city hall. By the time they arrive, the police are waiting for them on the front steps, their batons swinging. "If you come up these steps, we'll use them," the police chief shouts. The priest doesn't budge. "This is my country, my city. This is my city hall. And these"—he points to the men standing behind him—"these are my kids." Two of the policemen lunge at the priest, throw him into a snowdrift. He picks himself up, starts to climb the stairs towards the doors that lock the mayor safely inside. At this point the Mounted Police arrive. Tim Buck, leader of the Canadian Communist Party, looks at the police on their tall horses, the defenceless men—and according to Mr. Matushak, Tim Buck shakes his head and turns away. Policemen are barring the priest from entering the doors, and the priest turns as well. But not away.

"You see those bricks over there?" he calls out to the men. A building has been demolished nearby, and the rubble's heaped up all around them. "Each one of you grab a brick and walk up these steps where I'm standing. Just hold on and keep walking."

When the police realize what's happening, one of them slips inside to confer with the mayor. Suddenly the door opens and the priest is asked to come inside. He agrees on condition that he's recognized as the delegate of all these homeless, jobless men. And only when they finally agree to this demand does he let the men disperse. He asks them to trust him. They wait for a moment, fingering the bricks in their hands, and then, one by one, return them to the rubble piles and walk away.

Later, the relief laws will be changed: single, unemployed men will be given the right to the same small help as married ones—a bowl of soup, a roof for the night. Not all of them, but more than the law would allow before, Mr. Matushak tells me. He falls silent then, sitting cautiously in his beautifully upholstered chair as if afraid to touch its back with his own. I thank him for these stories he's given me, and then I, too, fall silent. I have so many questions I need to ask about my grandfather, his first years in Canada. What other friends did he have, how did he survive the loneliness he must have felt? I want to know about that man in his early thirties: not the grandfather I adore, or the adopted father who took a twenty-year-old under his wing, but the actual man, Tomasz. Mr. Matushak stays silent. To him I am, before anything else, my mother's daughter; even when she has left us to see to something in the kitchen, we both feel her presence. A presence marked by love of the father she barely knew before her fourteenth year, a love so intense it keeps him from being human, turns him into someone as rigid in his devotion to his wife and children as that bronze dog from the foundry: as rigid, and as true.

※◈※

My mother and my aunt have never said as much in talking of their father, but Tomasz was a political man. Perhaps this had to do with the early death of his father, a needless death in the new world to which Tomasz followed him. My grandfather's politics leap up at me as I write of his life in an Ontario that more and more resembles its condition in the Dirty Thirties. Toronto itself—no unreal city, no such luck to be only a metaphorical wasteland, but an "unjust city," in ways my grandfather would have immediately recognized.

Tomasz was political, not in the sense that he joined a party, stood for or worked for someone else's election, agitated according to the dictates of this organization or that. But he cared deeply about justice and the lives of ordinary, working people. In the late thirties, two years after his wife and daughters had arrived from Poland, he was hired back at General Electric, only to take part in a strike there some years later. It had been called to protest the company's refusal to allow a union, and the bulk of the workers went out on the picket line.

It was wartime: Tomasz was a skilled worker, expert at pouring the moulds needed for making ammunition. So the foreman came to the house one night, telling Tomasz that the others were done for but he could have his job back; they needed men like him, they could forget and forgive, provided he never joined a picket line again. Tomasz refused. The strike collapsed, and he went back to work. But he couldn't stomach the taunts of those who'd sided with the bosses: "We stayed in and kept our paycheques, and what did you get? Worse than nothing." So he left General Electric for good.

When postwar prosperity came round, he didn't forget what had happened to so many people like him in the thirties; what could so easily happen again. A photograph has just surfaced from some cupboard in Vira's home: it shows my grandfather marching in a

Labour Day parade on September 6, 1948, part of a large group of men wearing white caps of the kind I associate with train conductors. Unlike some of the marchers, Tomasz wears no tie. He is one of the tallest men and his face is in profile, for he's looking straight into the eyes of a dark-uniformed policeman. Seeing this photograph for the first time, I am struck by the calm intelligence of my grandfather's gaze. The assurance of his bearing, the strength conferred on him by marching in the company of all these other union men.

※◇※

Most immigrants belong to one ethnic organization or another, depending on their politics, their education, their religion or lack of it. Ukrainian immigrants arriving in North America before the Second World War had needs that their new countries could or would not meet: education for their children in the language and history of the homeland; social and cultural expression in their own tongue, to steady them after all their fumbling in English. Hence all the Ukrainian schools, the orchestras and ensembles, dance groups and theatrical troupes, the "national homes" that sprang up even in this worst of times. I've been told that some of Toronto's ultranationalist Ukrainians, seeing Nazi Germany as the natural enemy of the Soviets who'd so brutally occupied their homeland, hung swastikas from the windows of their headquarters and collected donations for a wristwatch to be sent to Adolf Hitler. Tomasz gave them a wide berth, joining the Labour Temple instead, a nationwide organization hoisting that unwieldy banner, *The Ukrainian Labour Farmer Temple Association*. Its concerns were social, educational, cultural and political: in the Dirty Thirties many of its members were not only socialist, but pro-Communist. Tomasz, as far as I can tell, was a lifelong socialist whose politics never constricted his affections. He'd often go for walks with the priest at the Ukrainian Orthodox cathedral, the one up the road from the Labour Temple at 300 Bathurst Street. They'd zigzag through the city, exchanging wildly opposing views in the most civil fashion. On Sundays, while his wife and daughters went to church, Tomasz would sing Gregorian chant as he shaved or worked at his carpenter's bench.

I know that Vira and Natalia went to the Labour Temple, too, learning mandolin and singing in the choir. Natalia may even have sung the *Internationale* and carried red flags down University Avenue after Russia finally joined the Allies in 1941. For the rest of the war Russian sailors could be seen walking the streets of Toronto, arm-in-arm with pretty Canadian girls. Many of the sailors were engineers who'd come from Odessa to build corvettes in Midland; others lived on Russian ships moored in Toronto harbour. The girls were from different Russo-Carpathian organizations and my mother's best friend was among them. The girls had been asked to act as translators and guides, and they couldn't help falling in love with the Russian sailors, despite the warnings of their aunts and mothers.

Did Tomasz ever meet with these men to ask them what conditions were like in their country, what they thought or feared they'd meet when they went home after the war? What did he learn of Stalin's self-made famine, the millions of Ukrainians who starved to death so that the Kremlin Mountaineer could play God with grain quotas? All I know is that throughout the fifties, my grandfather refused to become an armchair cold warrior. He never sang Stalin's praises, and he never swore, point-blank, that anything coming out of the USSR, whether Sputnik or the Red Army Chorus, had to be the devil's work. And he never forgot why he'd come to Canada in the first place, a year after the miltary coup that supplanted democratic rule in Poland. That he'd left his homeland not just to make money but to find a place where he could live and think and act as he chose, a place without curfews or censors.

※◈※

To me, they have an indissolubly romantic ring, the names of the ships on which my grandfather crossed the Atlantic. *The Empress of France*, sailing from Danzig via Cherbourg to Quebec in 1927; the steamship *Frederik VIII* of the Scandinavian American Line that took him back to Poland at the end of 1931; *The Montrose*, on which he returned to Canada the following year. Though he travelled in steerage, though he must have been miserable with missing his family, with knowing how hard Olena's life would be and how uncertain his own, I'm convinced he must have revelled in the strangeness of names and places, the sheer difference of everything around him, making him not only foreign but anonymous, the next best thing to free.

I'm obsessed by what the past leaves behind, mere bones of lives once full as our own. This scrap of yellowed paper is the ticket my grandfather used to cross the ocean from America to Poland. Tomasz once held it in his hands, showed it to officials, hid it in a breast pocket; he stored it away in a sheaf of old papers for me to find, sixty years later. The words this paper holds are, for me, incantatory:

DET FORENEDE DAMPSKIBS-SELSKAB

AKTIESELSKAB

SKANDINAVIEN-AMERIKA LINIEN

PASSAGER-AFDELING.

The logo of a small white cross in the centre of a black flag, its cloth already rippled by sea winds. The pointing hands, overlong index fingers extended, the others curled in, each hand lopped off at the wrist and cuff, to warn that **This order will not be honored unless stamped at the agency at the port of Debarkation**. The copperplate signature of A. Himursken, Purser, the address of the Danzig agent, L. Karlsberg, Spiro & Co., Langermarkt 41—an address I presume doesn't exist any longer, at least not in those very German words. The stamp, in large letters, NEW YORK, the port of embarkation. How had he travelled there—by train from Montreal, where he'd got his documents from the Polish consulate? How much time had he spent there, how much could he have spent, given how little money he could spare?

What of the photograph affixed to the Certificate of Identification, what does it show? A man in a suit and tie, a dignified man, his thick hair pushed straight back from his forehead, showing a widow's peak, a generous mouth that doesn't smile or frown but seems in possession of whatever words it will or will not speak. This photograph is furnished, the certificate says, "for the purpose of proving my identity." From the small black-and-white snap, cut off just below the shoulders, there's no way of proving that his height is tall, his hair chestnut, his eyes brown. But words and image must have carried authority, for there's a stamp in his passport, dated June 10, 1932, extending his stay in Poland from six months to a year, and the seal on his exit visa attests that the immigration inspector in Warsaw, a certain H. Taube, found in him nothing suspicious or wanting.

※◇※

To his children he's a glorious stranger bringing unheard-of gifts: a long, lily-shaped trumpet attached to a box crammed with hundreds of tiny people who start to sing at the crank of a handle. And something he calls "everlasting candy," which they'll find again in Canada under the less wondrous name of chewing gum.

To win back his daughters, who barely remember him, he talks about things he's learned in Canada: Darwin's or Marx's theories, or the magic called electricity—how you only have to push a button, just like the buttons on his shirt, and light brighter than daylight jumps into a room. While he tells them this, they look across at the naphtha lamp under which their mother sews each night, seeing for the first time what poor, pale light it throws, all the endless labour of cleaning and trimming, of filling the glass that, for all its heaviness, is so easily broken.

He tells them certain things about his time in the army. Of how, when he took off his shirt at night, it would get up and walk away from him, so terrible were the lice. Perhaps he describes the loneliness of the prairies and a farm woman he met there. Her husband had brought her to Canada forty years ago, and she still wept for the Carpathian mountains. In her first year of exile, looking out the window one spring morning, she'd given a clear shout of joy. She thought it was a lake in front of her, a lake on which she could sail home to her mountains, to spruce forests like fragrant ladders climbing the sky. Until her husband took her by the hand and walked her through waves of new wheat to convince her that she wasn't in the Carpathians but Saskatchewan, that there was only land before her and more land after that: flat, furrowed, dry.

When spring finally comes after an endless winter, Tomasz takes Vira with him for long walks into the countryside, but he hates the clogged roads, their glutinous mud a sign of everything that's wrong with the old forms, the old ways. And he hates the seven o'clock curfew, flouting it whenever he can, stopping to talk with people on the road and being stopped by militia who threaten to throw him in jail the next time they catch him out of doors after hours. He is no farmer, but he works all that summer with Olena in their fields; in the fall he helps to bring the harvest in. And then, after consoling his daughters with the last few sticks of everlasting candy in his knapsack, after pleading with his wife to come out to him in Canada, just once, just to see what it's like, he leaves.

What happens then? How does she feel, Olena, with her fields to work all day, and her sewing to be done at night, as she listens to the couples courting in the lane? Or when she writes letters to Tomasz by the light of the naphtha lamp, the children keeping strict silence, for she can never write if there's the slightest noise, and even then the letters of the words crowd so thick they look like the stitches in a sweater—if you pull one out, the whole thing will come undone. How can she keep from turning over in her mind what all the gossips are telling her: *How do you know he doesn't have a wife and children in Canada? Why else would he have gone back?*

How do you keep yourself from swallowing ashes? Of dying inside of thirst, of hunger?

✳◈✳

Tomasz survived three years of near-blindness in his youth; he came through typhus in 1919, and silicosis contracted in 1937 when he got a job in a fellow immigrant's foundry, one without protective gear for its workers. He survived a war and a fall through an ice-bound river; he weathered a bout of tuberculosis when he was fifty-three. But just as he began to find some measure of ease and happiness in his life, working in the garden with Olena, enjoying the company of his daughters, playing with his grand-children, a blood vessel in his brain exploded. He fell into a coma and died the next day, at the age of sixty-four.

I've heard different versions of my grandfather's death: that he tripped on a patch of ice, or simply lay down on his bed, saying he felt strange, and never got up again. But though the details vary, nothing changes the shock of it. My father's father had died when I was very young; I remember climbing a tall, narrow staircase to his room, holding out a fistful of daisies; how he grabbed my hand instead of the flowers, grabbed it so hard and so long that I screamed my terror. But it was only with Tomasz's death, when I was twelve, that I learned what the word *loss* meant, the unbreakable laws of subtraction. Someone I loved had gone away from me; I would never see him again. When I was told of my grandfather's death—it was a Sunday morning, my sister and I and our six-year-old brother were sitting at the kitchen table—I went up to my room and lay, face down, on my bed. I pressed my open mouth into the chenille spread, though my mother was still at the hospital and my father too busy making breakfast to listen for sounds of weeping. I made no sound at all. Not because I couldn't understand what had happened, but because I knew too well what I'd lost and could never have back. Not just my grandfather, but something of myself, my certainty that, like him, I would live forever and ever.

The year of Tomasz's death, Vira's youngest child was barely three. And though I had yet to learn about fixing things in memory, things I would otherwise lose without a trace, I've kept from that time a recollection of my grandfather playing with my youngest cousin. I remember not just the scene itself, but myself watching it, taking note as if it were happening in a book I was reading slowly, obsessively, wanting it to last forever. In this memory my grandfather sits at the dining room table in the Dovercourt house; my cousin is beside him, playing with a plastic comb. Tenderly, he bends his head towards her; with equal tenderness, she leans towards him, pulling the comb through his thinning hair. Her eyes are fascinated and uncertain: she is learning how the comb's teeth can both catch and, at the same moment, let go.

6

Olena: snow on her sleeves

She died when I was fully grown, living in England, an ocean away from her. I knew her always as Nana, she refused to be called *baba*, a word that means "old woman" as well as "grandmother." I loved her for the warm language of her body, language I could understand so much better than the Ukrainian she spoke with my mother and my aunt. I loved her quickness and strength in kitchens and gardens, and I loved her softness, too, especially when she came to look after us when our parents were away; when she'd lie down beside us at bedtime, telling us stories. Of her dearly bought piglets who ran across the bridge over the river Zbruch to become Soviet bacon; of a family of rabbits living in a garbage can, and how the mother had to leave her children all alone and hungry in the dark, while she searched the alleys for food to bring back to them.

In so many of the stories my grandmother told me, or that I've heard about her, she appears alone. Not just in her fields, with her husband gone to Canada, but in her house, the village, the town. Even though her children are always there to be fed and clothed and nursed through terrible illnesses. Even though the neighbours are forever offering her advice on how to take care of sickly Vira. And though her sister Yulia, who lives next door, keeps stopping by to parade her superior goods and good luck. Still, Olena is alone. Even Tomasz has become transient as memory, his image drawing her through dreams at night, dreams she's too exhausted to recall by day.

The only friend I've ever heard of in connection with my grandmother is Helka, the woman who ran the store in Pidvolochys'k. Whenever she is mentioned in the stories, this is what I'm told: that Helka is Jewish, and that she has long, red hair, like some great flame she wears on her head, the way country women wear kerchiefs. Of the friendship between Olena and Helka, I know only this: as a mark of affection and esteem, Olena named her most precious possession after Helka: the red cow she depended on for the cream that brought her ready cash to pay for Vira's doctors. When I was a child, I thought it an odd way to show friendship, but now, when I think of Helka and Olena, I see a kind of poetry in that act of naming.

I have no way of knowing whether Helka named anything she loved or needed after Olena; no way of knowing, either, what the two women talked of together, or whether they talked very much at all. But given the traditional hostility between Ukrainians and Jews, I find it remarkable that this friendship even existed. Twice a week Olena would take a sky-blue can of cream to Helka's house in Pidvolochys'k, cream for which she'd receive credit at Helka's store. I imagine the two women meeting and exchanging greetings; I imagine, too, the respect Helka would have shown for Olena's pride, the attention she would have paid to her loneliness—the kind of silent attention that a well pays to the water it holds within it. Or perhaps Helka had family in America or Canada, and she shared with her friend whatever news she'd gleaned of that foreign place across an equally foreign sea.

Perhaps Helka was the one person to whom Olena could speak of her longing for Tomasz; perhaps Helka was the only one who understood how hard it was for Olena to bear the spitefulness of gossip, the rumours that Tomasz had abandoned her and married some Canadian who would bear him sons instead of daughters.

✖◈✖

They were a match of opposites, Tomasz and Olena. Where he was deeply curious about the world and the way things worked in it, needing to discuss ideas as he needed air to breathe, Olena had always to be doing something useful with her hands, something to keep herself from thinking too much about the hardness of life, the way things had to be. Without Olena, Tomasz would have fallen even deeper into the hopelessness that seized him now and again, moods far grimmer than melancholy. Olena's powers of endurance were extraordinary, but she also possessed a kind of quick-fire, something that makes me think of matches struck, over and over, in the darkest rooms.

When my godmother speaks to me of my grandparents, I sense that her respect for Olena is enormous but that it is Tomasz she loves. For his sheer generosity: stopping on the street to talk with strangers, offering his shirt to anyone who needed it more than he. Olena, on the other hand, had a wryly judging eye. In Staromischyna, when the village women brought her shirts or sheets to hem on her miraculous machine, she'd ask favours in return, keeping an eye on the washing of dishes, the sweeping of floors while she sewed. Often the woman who brought the sewing would be dismayed when Olena gave it back to her: "It's only half-done," she'd cry. Olena would point at the floor half-swept, the pots half-scrubbed, and then they'd both set back to work.

Her practical side, her pragmatist's flair for steering between recklessness and paralysing caution, so perfectly expressed in the purchase of the Dovercourt house—this was one of my grandmother's banners. But the other was a complex and exacting pride, a legacy from her own iron-hearted mother. "People are always watching you," Olena would tell her daughters. "Waiting for you to fall in the mud, to drown there. Don't you ever give them that pleasure." *Proud—too proud*, I've heard it said of Olena. To my mother such a remark makes no sense at all—it's like criticizing someone for keeping her house too clean or her children too healthy.

Two stories about the shape such pride can take, one told to me long ago and one I've learned only now. The first concerns Olena's mother, who refused to attend church in the village of her new husband—he of the corduroy pants—and insisted on hearing mass at her home parish of St. Nikolai. Every Sunday morning Melania would walk to the house of her younger, cast-off daughter and put on the church-going clothes she kept there: a severely cut black blouse and a woollen skirt, a funereal waterfall of folds. The blouse and skirt hang in the *svitlytsia*, safe from dust and disturbance. Except when Natalia takes it into her head that the doll she's conjured up from a potato masher needs a dress to keep it from turning back into a lump of wood.

She steals into the *svitlytsia* one afternoon when everyone else has left the house. Spreading the huge black skirt over the floor, she finds an innermost fold from which she can cut a square large enough to wrap round the potato masher. What name does she give her doll? Something opulent like Roxolana, after the priest's daughter captured in a Tartar raid in the early 1500s, sold from a slave market in the Crimea to the Sultan Suleiman the Magnificent? Or Yaroslavna, Solomea—names that can carry off a dress of best black wool? She's already parading herself in the streets of Ternopil', this doll, inquiring into shop windows with a regal stare as Natalia returns the skirt to the hook on the door, puts back the scissors, picks up every last thread that could give her away.

It's God who undoes her—her grandmother's immense pride before God. For next Sunday at St. Nikolai, when Melania kneels before the pictures of God and his mother set on the small table before the icon screen; when she makes her deep, dramatic bow so that her forehead touches the cold clay floor, her skirts fan out and a loud whisper comes from the people massed behind her. *Melania, Melania, cover yourself, everyone can see.* The glare from her cotton drawers, a white square the exact length of a potato masher.

When my mother tells this story, there is laughter and equal acceptance of two events: that she was beaten for shaming her grandmother, who never again showed her face in any church, and that she'd found her vocation. She would become not just a seamstress, but a magician who could turn limp cloth, faint lines on tissue paper into dresses that would transform their wearers into arabesques of elegance. All of which Olena would dismiss with a *ta deh*. To my grandmother, dressing well meant dressing respectably, in clothes that were perfectly cut and sewn and would last almost forever. To be able to dress well was a source of pride, and pride was the way to put yourself beyond the reach of those who could hurt you with their hands or tongues.

All through her pregnancy with Vira, Olena works in her fields, even on Sundays, when she should have been at church. A woman in the next village has done the same thing and given birth to a child with a cleft lip. When Vira is born, Olena is too frightened to look at her. Tomasz has taken charge of two-year-old Natalia and been banished from the house; Olena's only companion is the midwife. She holds out the newborn to its mother, who stretches out her fingers to the baby's face: it's covered with a membrane like the skin that forms on heated milk. The features underneath the caul turn out to be perfectly formed, but the child has to fight for each breath she takes. The midwife runs off to fetch the priest and Olena waits alone, listening to her daughter's tortured breathing, staring at the floor. A floor that, if not dirty, is hardly clean enough for a priest to walk on, a priest who tells everything to everyone. And so, partly from pride and partly from terror, Olena leaves her bed and gets down on her knees to scrub the floor, barely finishing before the priest arrives.

In this story told to me by the woman born with a caul and a perfect face, I can see two things. One is my grandmother's gift for disabling fear, forestalling grief. But the other is the kind of pride that digs its own pit and tosses you inside. You know as you scrub the floor that your newborn child may be dying, alone, in the bed still warm from your body. You know how hard you're driving that body, already punished by the labour you've just come through. And yet you go down on your hands and knees, which by some bizarre alchemy has become a position of pride, not abjection; you scrub at the yellow clay as a child's wrenched breathing fills the room and a priest comes running down the lane. And you pull it off, one more time you pull it off, not just in your neighbours' eyes but in your own. You never look too closely at what you've accomplished and what might have happened instead. For pride—despite its endless care for what others might see when they steal their envious looks—pride is blind.

⁂

Was it as penance, divinely assigned, or just the physical cost of such passionate pride that Olena suffered so badly from migraines, an affliction both her daughters would inherit? A violent sensitivity to light and sound, extreme nausea, pain so acute, so unstoppable, that the sufferer calls out for someone to please, please put a pillow over her head and smother her. To be reduced to helplessness, to be lorded over by pain—what could have been worse for this woman responsible for running a farm and household, singlehandedly? The caul that Olena had so gingerly lifted from her daughter's face had been dried and stored away. When her headaches were so fierce that she had to take to her bed, Olena would call one of the children to get out the caul, soak it in cold water, place it on her forehead. Once, when her pain was unbearable, the children watched their mother tear the soaked caul from her face and hurl it against the wall. They let it hang there until it dried and dropped off, too terrified to touch it.

But at other times, Olena would try to sing the pain away, and that is how Vira remembers her best: singing and sewing at the black and gilt machine:

> My brow aches, my love is far away—
> how can I tell him my pain?
> I'll bind up my head, send him
> a grey dove, a silk ribbon.

❈❖❈

A studio portrait, like a thousand others, taken by a second-rate photographer in a sub-provincial town.

Tomasz and Olena's family, as death, but not distance, has compacted it: the parents at either end, their two daughters between, all four bodies vanishing below the waist. The children wear white sailor suits that Olena has stayed up half the night to sew for them. Natalia's hair is wrenched to the side; Vira sports a white-blond cap created by the blacksmith's shears and a pudding basin. At Vira's side stands Olena, with a chignon and curled bangs and a dark, elegant afternoon dress. Next to Natalia, Tomasz, in a suit and tie, his expression a little severe, abstracted.

For years I thought this portrait was taken when my grandfather returned to Poland. It was only when I began to add up ages and dates and distances that I discovered the photograph tells a lie, or at least only a would-be truth. Looked at closely, the print reveals the seam that has permitted the solitary image of my grandfather, taken by a Toronto photographer, to be joined to that of his wife and children in the studio at Pidvolochys'k. Though the tinting has been done by a skilful pair of hands, it can't disguise the scar between presence and absence.

All my life I've been haunted by this photograph. It used to hang in my grandparents' bedroom, and when I was sent to nap there, I'd lie with my head at the foot of the bed, so I could stare up at the faces over the headboard in their dark, eye-shaped frame. The children frightened me; they were so pale, they seemed to be fading from the paper, leaving their parents like bookends, holding nothing between them but empty air. Sometimes it seemed as if the pallor of the children who'd survived was an act of revenge or pleading by the ones who'd died.

The week before the twins were born it rained without stopping, rain dark and thick as ink, turning the roads into rivers. The day of the birth, Natalia, just five years old, sits huddled in the barn, its roof a huge blank drum: the sound of the rain beating down makes her think that God's in a rage and walloping his angels. Her feet look black against the straw: what used to be earth is a brown soup that clogged her toes until she could barely lift her feet when she'd stepped outside. Natalia has come to the hayloft because she's too frightened to stay in the house. Her mother's lying sick in bed, her little sister is burning up with fever and her father is nowhere to be seen. A strange woman's come in from another village, but she won't explain what she's doing here.

At last there's a cry from the house, sharp and loud enough for the child to notice through the drumming rain. She can't move for fear. She waits for another cry but hears nothing, and suddenly it's worse than seeing her mother dead, hiding here, not knowing. In the moment it takes her to reach the house from the barn, she's drenched to the skin. Her feet leave great clots of mud on the kitchen floor; she's looking frantically for something to clean the muck away when the strange woman comes towards her, holding in each of her arms a red-stained, tight-wrapped package. The red turns out to be not blood, but two squalling faces, so small and screwed-up they don't look human.

"Look what the rain's brought you," the woman says. "It's made a river flowing right past your door. These babies were drowning in all that water. Your mother's a good woman, she's promised to look after them."

Natalia eyes the woman. She looks at the babies in the woman's arms, then turns her back. "My mother," she says, "doesn't need any more babies. My sister's enough trouble. My father's leaving and my mother has only me to help her. Put them back in the river."

Olena must have known they couldn't live long, that the fits they kept falling into would harm them terribly. And yet she fought so hard to keep them alive, her only son, her youngest daughter. In one version of the story Marusia refuses to eat after Ivan dies at the age of eight months. She lies in her cradle with eyes that seem neither open nor closed; she lets go of the slippery red string that is her life. In another telling—the more painful and thus truer one—she dies of the scarlatina Vira has picked up and passed on to her. But the most poignant story of Marusia's death has to do with Olena. A year after Tomasz has left, a night towards the end of winter, she falls asleep at the kitchen table, worn out with nursing Vira and Marusia. She's wearing a nightdress, with a shawl thrown over her shoulders: her fine, fair hair hangs down her back. The lamp has burned out beside her, and in the chill silence, Olena dreams.

Something evil has entered the house, some heavy mist that has to be gathered up and taken outside before it smothers them all. She rises from the table, moving slowly, her arms outstretched, until she finds the place where the fog is thickest and coldest. As if it were a carpet, she rolls it up in her arms and carries it outdoors, wanting only to run and be rid of it; taking great care that she doesn't trip and fall and lose her hold. She staggers across the yard, and just as she tries to throw away this terrible, formless thing, she wakes. In her thin nightdress she is pressed up against the fence, her arms outstretched. Everything is dark and still. And there is snow on her sleeves.

⁑

I have always loved the portrait of Olena as she was, aged eighteen, dressed in Ukrainian costume for her wedding. Weeks before my marriage to a bearded *Anglik*, when I was only a year older than Olena had been when she married Tomasz, I sat in the dining room of the Dovercourt house, looking across the table at my grandmother. I was still pinned within the edges of a dream I'd had the night before: Michael and I dressed in late 1940s clothes, playing the parts Gus and Vira had assumed thirty years earlier, pleading their case to an unyielding Tomasz and Olena. I saw my grandmother's soft skin, its cloudy sheen of pearls. I saw the silvery hair she always took such care of, I saw her small, round, tireless body, but where was the girl who'd defied her mother to marry a man of her own choosing? And as I looked at her, wanting something I could never have, Olena reached towards a small vase of poppies and cornflowers at the centre of the table. She took a few of the flowers and held them against her temples, like remnants of a wreath she'd once worn. And through that gesture she became again a girl of eighteen.

The summer before my grandmother died, I came back from England to show her our infant son, whom we'd named Thomas Solowski. She'd been well enough to play with him in her back garden, just as she'd played there with all of her grandchildren. But after I returned to England, her illness grew much worse, and she spent a long time lying in her bed, unable to do anything but think. Of the Old Place, and how her house had been torn down after the war; how the fields she'd refused to sell were nothing now but pieces of paper. It must have seemed the cruelest of jokes to her that she and Tomasz were so mismatched in their dying. She should have been the one to fall in mid-stride and vanish instantly; he would have wanted to take this lengthy leave, facing his own end, trying to puzzle it through.

Yet in the last months of Olena's life, when she was still at home and her body had not yet become its own ghost, she performed another gesture, as extraordinary as the one that had turned her from a woman of seventy into an eighteen-year-old girl. It was this: when her daughters, who were taking turns making the nourishing soups she could no longer eat, assembling her medicines, washing her nightgowns, would take their leave of her for the night, Olena would hold up her face for a kiss.

7

childhood: no kisses and no toys

Two sisters, aged seven and five, shut up day after day in the small vestibule, or *siny*, whose window is no larger than a prayer book. They must stay there from the first light of morning till dusk. To keep them company they have a jug of water, a loaf of bread, a pail below the rough wooden bench on which they sit. There are no toys, no books, no favourite blankets or pillows— just the two children and whatever stories they can tell each other, whatever songs and rhymes they know to pass the time till their mother comes back to let them out.

"Nowadays, people would call it child abuse," my mother says. She has just watched a television documentary on a young boy whose parents, without lifting a hand, have savaged him with endless dressings-down for his stupidity, his ugliness. The papers are full of stories of parents who grossly neglect, or beat or starve their children; full of earnest essays on how to stop parents from killing their children. And my mother returns, as she has done so many times in the past, to the story of the *siny*.

"We were too young to be left on our own, there were no such things as babysitters. My father was gone, no one in the family would help, my mother had to bring in the harvest. What else could she do?" Enough disasters had nearly happened when Olena had been home with her children. Once Natalia, furious at how long it took the stove to heat, stuffed in so much bundled straw that the door blew open. Luckily, she lost only her eyebrows. It was because of incidents like these that Olena locked her children in the *siny*. I can understand the laws of such necessity. But what I can't understand is that my grandmother, whose songs and stories were the light of my childhood, could lock up her children for eight or ten hours without even a kiss to comfort them.

When my mother speaks of the *siny*, she does so matter-of-factly. Perhaps her deepest memory, the very ground of her being, has to do with another, much earlier, scene, something she's been told of by her mother, but that her body remembers without even knowing: being taken to the fields at harvest time, being nursed by her mother and left, an infant of four months, in the shade of a wheat sheaf. She sleeps, wakes, cries out with hunger—no one is there. By the time her mother comes to her, the baby's mouth is torn and bleeding: in her hunger, she has tried to chew the glass-sharp stalks of wheat.

Vira has also told me the story of being left all day in that small, dark vestibule. Like my mother, she keeps her voice calm, but there are tears running down her face, tears she doesn't seem to notice. "Only once," she confides, "only once in my whole childhood can I remember my mother giving me a kiss. There'd been some terrible problem about the fields, the wheat—she couldn't see her way round it, my father was away, she had no one to turn to. And suddenly I had an idea—it jumped into my head from the arithmetic we were doing at school. When I told her, she stared at me for a moment, as if I'd gone mad or she had. And then she laughed and held me and kissed my hair."

✖◈✖

I used to fantasize, when I was small, that my mother's mother was really Anastasia. I had pored over an article in *Life* magazine about Anna Andersen, the German woman who claimed to be the only surviving child of the last Russian tsar. It wasn't because Olena bore any likeness to the Anastasia of court photographs that I dreamed up this lineage for her; it was because there was a definite resemblance between my grandmother, aged sixty, and Anna Andersen, who would have been about the same age then. Something pulled and worn about the lips and eyes—the same heaviness of body. I suspect that Anna Andersen was from a farming family; that she was closer in social class to the peasantry than any aristocracy. But even as I write that word, *peasantry*, it seems as artificial, as absurd, as an operetta backdrop or a Ruritanian guard.

The culture my family came from was a peasant culture, even if my great-grandparents were literate, and well-off. It was a harsh culture, though it has been sentimentalized by those who know it only through images on greeting cards or on glass paintings suitable for hanging on the kitchen wall. One of the most terrifying stories I have ever read is Chekhov's "Peasants," in which the author, whose grandfather bought the family out of serfdom, records what can only be called a culture of beatings. When Marya is so badly beaten by her husband that she almost loses consciousness, her sister-in-law tells her to bear up, that the Gospels teach us to turn the other cheek. The sister-in-law is lucky: her husband, who is dying of a wasting disease, never lifts a hand to her. But the young daughters of these women have no such luck. Set to watch the vegetable garden on a hot August day, they play games instead of keeping the geese out of the cabbages. Their grandmother runs screeching out of the house towards them:

> She . . . picked up a switch and, seizing Sasha by the
> neck with her fingers, dry and hard as spikes, began
> whipping her. Sasha cried with pain and fear . . . . Then
> Granny proceeded to whip Motka, and so Motka's shift
> was rolled up again. In despair and crying loudly, Sasha
> went to the cabin to complain . . . .

"She's your grandmother, it's a sin to be cross with her"—such is the justice of the cabin. The children go off to their beds, where they nurse the welts on their backs and comfort themselves with thoughts of Granny crackling in hell.

Life in Staromischyna, at least from the stories I've heard, was a far cry from the dregs of wretchedness pictured in Chekhov's story. And yet the Old Place allowed its children just as little room for misbehaviour or mistakes. It was a parent's duty, even privilege, to beat a wayward child, yet whether the blows were dealt with a stick or the flat of a hand, the pain must have been deepened past measure by the fact that the person beating you was the one in whose arms you should have found help and comfort. So that the first, most important object of your love became, as well, the source of your deepest fears.

I know that Natalia and Vira both loved and feared their mother; they also trusted her profoundly. Though Olena's anger could be terrifying, her daughters somehow knew it would never turn into that brute, blind rage that their neighbour showed his son, Bohdan. The boy was the same age as my mother; on the day when he was out helping with the harvest in his parents' fields and did something to anger his father, he would have been no more than twelve or thirteen. Perhaps he worked carelessly or too slowly: whatever the reason, his father took the shovel with which he'd been digging up potatoes and began to beat his son. He beat him so hard that the boy's back made a noise like a branch breaking in a storm. Perhaps the beating went on after that noise was heard—or perhaps the man stopped, threw down the shovel and walked away. But what sickens me most as I try to imagine this scene is the way the boy must have lain on the earth; the look on his face as he tried, again and again, to pick himself up.

"From then on," my mother said, "he could only stand up straight when they propped him against a gate or a wall. He could hobble around a little, but mostly he'd stand propped up against the high wooden gate in front of his house. We'd see him there on our way home from school. I always tried to say something kind to him—I hated it when the others were cruel. But it was hard to look at him. He'd shove his hands so deep in his pockets, trying to stand straight, following us with his eyes."

When she would tell us this story, I'd wait for my mother to add something else. How the whole village condemned the beating, refused to speak with the boy's father or made known to his face the contempt they felt for any man who could cripple his own child. But my mother had nothing more to say. Once, many years later, she talked of a carpenter who'd done some work for her, a man from the Old Place. He used no tape measure or fancy tools, but everything he built was straight and true. She'd asked him how he'd learned his trade—the man replied that his father had taught him everything he knew. "He taught me with his fists. If I didn't learn something straight off, the right way, he'd beat me so I could hardly stand. You learn fast, that way."

⌘

So many stories of love mixed up with fear, the way poison and ointment might mix together, making a salve that burns as it tries to heal.

Natalia in the fields at the edge of the village, trying to help with the harvest. She is still so young that she's clumsy with the sickle; she has scarcely begun to work before she cuts her shin instead of the wheat. It's not the pain but the fear that hurts. Having to face her mother, bring her this new trouble—blood spilling from the bag of her skin. Or Vira, desperate to help Olena, who's been off working in the fields all day. The child sets out to make the cornmeal mush her mother loves. It's nearly evening, she is stirring and stirring the cornmeal over the fire so that it thickens without lumps; stirring, and getting wearier and wearier until she falls asleep, until her hand begins to burn. All evening she contrives to hide it from Olena, the smart of her blisters nothing compared to what she fears from her mother's hand.

Or, worst of all, the story of the *hrybka*, the mushroom-soft pincushion in which Olena's two precious needles are stored. Vira and Natalia, wanting to do some mending for their mother, take the *hrybka* and their sewing into the orchard. Somehow Vira's needle slips from her fingers and can't be found, however frantically she runs her hands through the long, bright grass. She prays for the needle to stab her, to mistake her palm for the *hrybka*, but the needle never surfaces. And though it's still a fine summer afternoon, the children run indoors to hide under the kitchen table, praying their mother will have no time for sewing that night. It's not the physical beating that terrifies them, being slapped and shaken till their ears ring. It's knowing that their mother can't afford to buy another needle, and not knowing how she'll manage without one. They're as much afraid for her as they are of her.

"I would spend long winter evenings," Vira once confessed, "writing letters in my head to my father, telling him how terrible our mother was to us." And yet, she tells me now, it's from Olena that she draws her courage. "I've forgotten every hurt in my growing up, I forgive her everything because I know how hard her life was. How unloved she was as a child, how little she had of the man she loved. She would have died for your mother and me, although she never let on. Proud, so beautifully proud of us—but she could never say it."

❌◈❌

They used to puzzle me, those Bible stories in which blessings are asked or given; the laying of a parent's hand on a child's head, not in anger, not in affection, but in a solemn act of acknowledgement. As if to say, "You exist, you are mine, but you are also your own now, and on your own." Blessings are something children must always claim from their parents, who gave them the one gift no one ever asks for. We may live our whole lives trying to defy or deny our parents—what they are, who they've tried to make us be—but we are always playing to them, whether they sit in a curtained box at the edge of the stage or in the very front row. And when we ask a blessing, we are asking acknowledgement not just of them, but of the past itself. Establishing our right to exist in relation to that past; claiming a place for ourselves in the future, for whatever we make to leave behind us.

My grandparents always opened their arms to their daughters' children; they spoiled us, made us toys and sweets, took us to cartoon matinées and told us endless stories. And yet their love for our mothers was too deep or too painful to show. Tomasz kissed each of his daughters once—when he gave them away in marriage. Only once did Olena speak her pride and love in her daughters' hearing, give them her blessing—and then, only by accident.

At a Toronto cemetery a Ukrainian woman comes up to where Olena and Natalia are digging in chrysanthemums at Tomasz's grave. The woman watches for a while, admiring the neatness of their work, the bronze and deep red of the flowers. And then she calls out to them—she can't get any water for the plants at her husband's grave, the tap is broken. Natalia offers to fetch water from the next tap over, and while she's gone, Olena and the woman fall into conversation. There's a rowan tree planted over Tomasz's grave: on her way back, Natalia stops dead behind that tree, a full bucket of water in her hands. For she can hear her mother speaking, and she cannot believe what she is hearing. "My daughters call or come to see me every day," Olena is saying. "I want for nothing. No one could have better children."

And then Olena catches sight of Natalia behind the rowan tree and calls out as if she's never spoken. "What's taken you so long? Come and bring the water. What are you staring at?"

Natalia answers as a grown woman and as a child, insisting on a truth that must be spoken.

"It's the first time," she says, "that I've ever heard you praise us."

"So?" her mother answers. "Stop talking and start digging."

✖◇✖

> You grew up in a place
> where kisses were rare as money—

The start of a poem I once wrote for my mother, a poem about the sweet tooth for which she's famous. About how sugar, honey and those rare oranges like small suns plucked from a sweeter sky were substitutes not for love, but for the perceptible signs of love: embraces, praise, caresses. It's so easy to see this now, looking at my family with the eyes of an inside stranger, which is what I'm becoming as I write these stories down. Why do we always swallow whole what we most need to speak out loud? And why do we recognize so little of what we see?

Sugar strengthens your bones—an ad my mother remembers from the co-operative store in Staromischyna. Once she managed to buy a sliver of unwrapped chocolate there to take to her mother, only to have it melt away by the time she reached home. My mother's still crazy for chocolate: at Easter or Christmas or her birthday, when she receives too many boxes of Black Magic or Moirs Gold, she'll make caches of chocolate all over the house. Often she won't find them for months, even years.

In the Old Place, when Olena managed to give each of her daughters one small box of candies for a Christmas gift, Vira would hide hers away, taking them out now and then, holding the shiny wrappers up to the light. But Natalia always wolfed hers down, and then searched everywhere for Vira's hiding place, devouring the candy the moment she found it. Perhaps she was simply righting the balance, for whenever Vira was beset by fevers and delirium, the first sure sign of recovery would be requests for candy. In her relief, Olena would buy a few boiled sweets with whatever bits of money she could scrape up.

It wasn't just sweetness Natalia craved, but something like luxury. Though Olena would exchange most of her cream and butter for fabric bought at Helka's store, she would save some of the richest milk for special baking, storing it in an earthenware bowl in the larder. The cream would gather under a thick, taut skin, and Natalia learned how to take a clean straw from the barn, poke it under this skin and suck up mouthfuls. Once, startled at hearing her mother's footsteps behind her, she dropped the bowl on the hard clay floor. She wore the marks of that beating for a long time; they mixed themselves into her craving for cream and sugar, a blue-black line in all that white.

But there's more to this hunger than greed. What I most love about the child my mother was is her defiance of poverty and punishment alike. In one of my favourite stories my mother is sent on an errand to Helka's place. Just outside the shop door a group of children cluster: hot, hungry, barefoot, like Natalia. They can sense the few coins she clenches in her hands, smell the film of sweat over metal. What is it she's been sent to buy? Naphtha to fill the lamps or to be poured over sugar cubes, a cure for worms and sweet tooths together? Whatever it is, she goes inside, hands over the coins, obtains what she's been sent to buy—and orders, on credit, in spite of the beating she will surely earn, ice cream. For herself and all the children lingering outside, digging the dust with their heels.

✖◈✖

Who were your best friends? What games did you play when you were small? My aunt, my mother—they look at me as if the question has to do with some abstruse subject no one could expect them to know. But I press for a response, any old account of how, as children, they spent their rare moments of leisure. Finally they begin to speak.

All their friends were boys: girlfriends were later, girlfriends were Toronto. What was his name, that boy with elephant ears who was sweet on Vira? *Haliu Puliu*, didn't they call him that? And the boys' names for them: *Virka Shkirka, Natalka Kachalka*. I stare at my aunt and mother, shut out by language. They try to explain: *shkira* means "skin," hence Skinny-little-Vira. My mother's round face inspired Little-Natalie-the-rolling-pin. And *Haliu Puliu* is Little-Mike-plucked-chicken. Nothing harder to translate than diminutives; how can you possibly carry over the softness of Haliu into "Mike," or the affectionate *k* in Virka, Natalka? I can see in their faces the remembered pleasure of being teased, and the regret that translation is called for. Not just of the words, but the world contained in them, the host of things they can take for granted but their children have to learn like verb forms in a foreign language studied late in life.

As for games—well, none that children here would think worth playing. There were no sports, no teams or equipment. *Kuchka*— you'd filch a metal can from some adult who was saving it for some proper purpose, beat it with a heavy stick till you'd turned it into some semblance of a ball, then hit or lob it with another stick,

making sure you didn't lose it down a hole—metal cans were hard
to come by. Baseball, field hockey, golf: *kuchka* could have been an
approximation of any of those. It doesn't sound like a great deal
of fun, but I keep my thoughts to myself—I who never swung a
baseball bat without shutting my eyes tight, expecting more from
praying than aiming.

An embarrassed silence sits down at my mother's kitchen table
with this talk of games—as if a guest has arrived unexpectedly and
there isn't enough food to go round. "Weddings," my mother
finally says. "It was our favourite game, dressing up in towels,
whitewashing the chicken coop to be our 'house' after the cere-
mony. I don't know why we played it so much—there were a lot
of kids like us, whose fathers were away."

Silence again.

Then Vira speaks. "Remember the castle game?" My mother
doesn't.

"You'd find a bare patch of earth and draw a circle around
you—it was like black butter, that earth. And you'd stand in the
middle, shouting, 'Who's going to cut it?' The others would come
with sharpened sticks and each in turn would cut a little piece, and
whoever got the last cut . . ." Her voice trails off, as if she's not
sure whether the last one to get a cut of that black, buttery earth
would earn a penalty or win a prize.

It doesn't seem much more fun than *kuchka*. I think of a painting I've seen in the Musée des Beaux Arts in Brussels, the
hundreds of different games being played by the children
Breughel drew. Surely they played tag, or hopscotch, or leapfrog
in the Old Place? Vira and Natalia look blank, until Vira remembers how, sent to take the geese down to the marsh, she'd play
jacks with the other kids, using five small stones, while the geese
wandered off into someone's field, to be seized by whoever found
them. And how she'd get on her knees and pray with her chin
jutting up at the sky, pray for her geese to come back. And some-

how, they always did. Far more important than jacks, this game she played with God.

"A glass bottle," my mother volunteers. "If you found one, it was the greatest treasure you could imagine. Nothing came in bottles at home—only clay pots or dishes. But there was always the potato masher. I'd steal it when no one was looking, try to dress it up."

"What would we have done with the things kids have here?" Vira wonders. "Barbies, Betsy Wetsies, Chatty—what was her name? Chatty Cathy." Slipping back thirty years into the marvels of her daughters' childhoods.

"It's hard," my mother says, "to dress a doll without arms or legs."

I remember another museum in a foreign city, the Museum of Childhood in Edinburgh. A glass display case that preserves the doll of a Victorian slum child. A shoe sole, with eyes and nose and mouth chalked over the heel, and arms and legs devised from tubing. The huge poverty, the need signalled by these dolls fashioned from shoe soles, potato mashers.

※◈※

Perhaps the lullabies express it best, the kind of world in which children grew up without kisses, without toys. A lullaby like this one, which my mother writes down for me, adding, "It's a good thing the babies didn't understand the words":

> *ah-ah, ah-ah, ah-ah, ah,*
> *zily vovky barana*
> *a yahnychku zyily psy*
> *ochka zazhmury*
> *ty dytynko spy, spy, spy.*

It would be sung in a rhythm of rocking and sighing, this concentrated lesson in the way of the world. My mother, my aunt would have learned it with their bodies, their very breathing:

> ah-ah, ah-ah, ah-ah, ah,
> the wolves ate the ram
> the dogs ate the lamb
> close your eyes, my little one,
> sleep, sleep, sleep.

8

---

two sisters: two eyes

Who did they grow up to be, those infants sung to sleep with this lullaby? Sisters different as chalk and cheese; twins who fail to share a common birthdate. This trick of being both alike and opposite: it's there in the photo that used to live on Olena's chest of drawers, a studio portrait tinted in shades of rose and soft turquoise and reddish brown.

Turquoise is the colour of the neatly tailored matching dresses, turquoise the (highly inaccurate) colour of the young women's eyes. The reddish brown is their hair, styled identically, circa 1940: puffed up on top of their heads, long and straight at the sides, ending in the pageboys that are all the rage. The sisters stand back to back, their shoulders touching yet their faces turned to the camera, a pose that seems to produce no strain, for they're smiling happily at the photographer. Natalia is a good three inches taller; she has her father's handsome square-shaped face, while Vira's is oval, with her mother's small nose and shortsighted eyes, though she's taken off her glasses for this photo. So it's not their features as much as something in their expressions, and the curious pose they've assumed, that mark them unmistakably as sisters.

✖✧✖

"I have you like two eyes in my head," Olena would tell her daughters. "I'll share everything with you, half and half—no favourites,
everything equal." What other words could they have grown up
with, given their mother's childhood, how she'd been grudged her
very existence while her sisters and brother enjoyed whatever love
their mother had to give? And yet how could two sisters, born so
close together, not have fought over what share they'd receive of
their mother's love, shown by the clothes she sewed for them, the
food she cooked? How many occasions were there like those
dinnertimes when, sharing a bowl of kasha with her sister, Vira
would sink her spoon into an imaginary line down the very centre,
marking their separate territories, sites of possession? Natalia
would go on eating, the level of food in the bowl going down and
down, till Vira understood that if she wasn't to starve, she'd have
to forget about boundary lines and spoon what was left of the
kasha into her mouth.

The things they didn't share in the Old Place, in spite of living
together in one room, in spite of being sisters: Vira's nightmares,
when she kicked and flung out her arms, touching the sheepskin
tacked to the wall, jerking her arms back, convinced that wolves were
about to devour her. And Natalia, waking in the middle of a night
through which no lights were ever left burning. Lying very straight
and still, thinking, *This is what it must be like to lie in your coffin.* Listening to what had woken her, a sound she'd never heard before but
knew to be her mother's voice. Leaving her bed, walking across to
where her mother lay sleeping and awake, silent and singing.

A dream Natalia never tells her mother or sister or father: that
she only tells her daughter fifty years later, almost by accident.

✖◈✖

My mother was supposed to have been called Nadia, or Hope, one of the cardinal virtues, and a brave choice, given the way her parents had flown in their own parents' faces by marrying at all. But when Tomasz, high on thankfulness and plum brandy, carried off his firstborn to be christened, he sang out Natalia instead of Nadia, after Natalka Poltavka, the heroine of a play he loved. Certainly my mother possessed a heroine's spirit, finding out and taking what she wanted, damning the consequences. For she was the strong one, the tall one, the tomboy who could take on anything. And she was always getting into trouble.

Vira means Faith—at his second daughter's christening, Tomasz got it right. Perhaps the faith in question had to do with the child's very chances of survival. No sooner had she learned to nurse than Vira was struck with an unending series of staph infections that covered her in boils. No sooner had she recovered from these than she came down with a whole parade of illnesses. Diphtheria. Typhoid fever. The scarlatina that left her deaf in one ear and killed her small sister.

And yet the real plague wasn't disease, but the neighbours. "Why do you take such trouble with her?" they'd ask Olena. "Why not just throw a pillow over her face? God will forgive you." Vira's fevers always spread to their own children, they complained; sometimes the whole village would fall sick from what Vira had brought in. But Olena was as stubborn as she was proud, and keeping life in her child's body became a formal fight she undertook with death. Once, Vira's fever ran so high she burned to the touch; her face became so swollen that her lips almost disappeared. Olena sat up with her child, splashing water onto the crimson face, unable to get any of the liquid near her daughter's mouth. Until she began to slap her. She slapped her sick child, harder and harder, till Vira's gummed lips burst into a wail, just wide enough for Olena to slip in a teaspoon of water.

If Natalia was driven by a craving for sugar and the will to have what she wanted, whether a square of black wool or a gulp of cream, Vira's passion has been curiosity—as if, born with that thick, blank caul over her eyes, she must spend her whole life tearing it away. The midwife had predicted she'd be wise and full of learning: Vira proved the midwife right, becoming a scholar, a doctor and diagnostician and, more importantly, a connoisseur of curiosity. She tells me of how, while visiting her daughter's farm, she met a vet doing his rounds and used his instruments to peer down the ear canal of a dairy cow. Her awe could not have been greater if she'd looked through a telescope straight into the eye of Saturn. This delight in a world that's a constant source of wonder, is it a gift she was born with or something she learned in order to justify her very right to be? *Why not throw a pillow over her face and have done with her?*

Two sisters, survivors in a world where not only lambs but grown rams are eaten by dogs and wolves.

❈❖❈

After the deaths of the twins, they have to be everything to one another, for better or worse. On Sundays, they set off for mass in their homemade sailor suits, their barely worn patent-leather shoes pinching their feet. "Hold hands," their mother says. "That way you won't get into trouble." That way when Natalia trips on a rock and flies headlong into a puddle, Vira dives after her, and they sit together in the shallow bowl of mud, hands still firmly clasped. Once Natalia, set to mind her little sister, swings her over a stream made by the spring runoff, swings her back and forth by the shoulders of her dress as she talks to one of the neighbours' sons. Back and forth, back and forth, until she realizes that the weight has gone from her hands—her sister has slipped out of her dress and sailed off downstream.

Or later, much later, in a world where everything is different except for the givens of family life: Natalia is setting Vira's fine, straight hair, stabbing the pins against her sister's scalp. Vira is always studying for exams, never to be disturbed, so it's always the older sister who must bake, wash, cook, clean while their mother works shifts at the factory. Though later still, when Natalia's children are born, it will be Vira she calls at all hours of the day and night, when they cut their heads so that blood blankets their faces, or when they burn and shiver with fevers. And it will be Vira who sits with her in the ambulance, stalled in traffic, as Natalia bleeds out the baby she's carrying, and the siren wails.

I have you like two eyes in my head. When Olena died it was as if the continents had lost their outlines, as if the stars had fallen from the sky, so that her daughters couldn't orient themselves except by being sisters. Now that their own children have grown up, Natalia and Vira have become as close to one another as they once were to their mother. When they meet to talk with me about their childhood in a place that no longer exists, this closeness between them is perfect. As if, remembering together, they have become that yolk and white of the same egg which Plato describes as the symbol of human completeness.

Listening to them in my mother's living room, her Canadian equivalent of a *svitlytsia*, the differences between them emerge in their voices. My mother's is deep, formal, with a gravity lacking in my aunt's. Vira is more likely to laugh or make a joke when she describes the past, Natalia to weep. Yet though Natalia remembers far more details, sounds, colours, it's only Vira who can speak of the pain of their past. Despite and because of these differences, I can't help remembering how, when one fell into the mud, the other had only one thought, one act: to join her.

I think of a game my sister and I used to play when visiting our grandparents on Dovercourt Road. Walking down the sidewalk in front of their house, or along the narrow ribbon of cement that ran the length of their garden, we would weave an arm tightly round the other's waist and press our heads together. Seeking out passersby to jostle, narrow doors to squeeze through, we'd walk on and on, falling or stumbling or sometimes running, never once letting go. Stick-together-girls we called this game. I have only to close my eyes to feel the joined pressure of our arms, the panic and delight of this pastime we put behind us years ago, when we grew up into our differences. Moving away, pulling apart.

Departures, Arrivals:
Staromischyna—Toronto

"Travel": same word as "travail"—"bodily or mental labour,"
"toil, especially of a painful or oppressive nature," "exertion,"
"hardship," "suffering." A "journey."

Bruce Chatwin, *The Songlines*

blue stones, bananas, the immigrant shuffle

Towards the very end of 1935, just before her thirty-third birth-day, Olena receives a letter bearing Polish, not Canadian, stamps. It contains a notice that three third-class prepaid tickets from Gdynia, Poland, to Halifax, Canada, have been secured by one Mr. T. Solowski of Toronto, Ontario, for three adults (children are defined as being under ten years old). The notice includes the price for the family's "Total Ocean Fare"—$384.00—and Canadian rail-road fares—$53.88—between Halifax and Toronto.

The receipt for the tickets looks a little like an old-fashioned theatre bill:

THE POLISH TRANS-ATLANTIC SHIPPING
COMPANY, LIMITED
owners of
GDYNIA–AMERICA LINE
Polskie Transatlantyckie Towarzystwo Okretowe, Sp.
Akc. Linja Gdynia–Ameryka
NOTICE TO PASSENGERS issued in connection with

Prepaid ticket No. 07173

Date of Issue Dec. 10, 1935

[Not good for Transportation]

The GDYNIA–AMERICA LINE will furnish all necessary instructions and will deliver a ticket from the port of embarkation for transportation.

Passengers MUST NOT leave their homes for the port of embarkation until advised to do so by the Line, but whether or not such notification has been issued, the Line assumes no responsibility as to the length of time passengers may be delayed prior to sailing, nor as to expenses for maintenance or otherwise incurred by passengers because of such delays.

Which must have left the mass of soon-to-be passengers— emigrants who'd spent their life savings on tickets for themselves and their families—in an anxious mood. Those booked to enter the United States were also warned that their rights were subject to "the act of Congress approved May 19, 1921, entitled 'An Act to Limit the Immigration of Aliens into the United States.'" The instructions are reprinted in Polish, Ukrainian, German, Finnish, Lithuanian, Latvian, Roumanian, Czecho-Slovak [sic], Serbian and Croatian. There's also a text in Hebrew letters, labelled "Jewish." So no one could possibly claim they hadn't understood the conditions; could demand reimbursement for expenses incurred due to the regrettable necessity of having to eat and sleep all through the days, even weeks, when the ship lingered in port for reasons known only to the owners of the Polish Trans-Atlantic Shipping Company, Limited.

※◇※

When did Olena finally admit that her husband would never come back to live in Poland? After Tomasz left Staromischyna for the second time, in the autumn of 1932, it took her almost four more years to decide to join him. Even then, she set out with an eye to coming back. Looking at her life from the pieces of paper she left behind, the contracts for sale and rental of land, the buff envelope containing a surveyor's map and inscribed with the words *moyeh poleh*—my fields—I recall the depth and endurance of her passion; how on her deathbed she spoke of the loss of her fields with sorrow and bewilderment still. And yet despite this passion for land, despite her neighbours' warnings that she'd perish in the ice and snow of Canada, she sold her house and most of her goods, packed up the rest and left. Perhaps she was moved by fear—fear that she would lose Tomasz forever if she stayed another year in Staromischyna; fear that if she stayed, she would lose herself, that alloy of pride and aloofness that defined her.

What did she bring with her to Canada? The sky-blue can in which she used to carry cream to Helka's store. A handful of photographs, a miniature cupboard with a tilting mirror. Goose-down quilts and cushions; lengths of homemade cloth. Kilims woven with patterns of large and startling roses. A wall hanging of a golden fox, chain-stitched against a black background. And a long, slender *poyas* that she'd woven herself, out of wool dyed in stripes of blue and green and white, against an earthen red. This *poyas* is meant to be wrapped tightly round the waist, marking off the gorgeously embroidered blouse from the intricately woven skirt in which, of course, each of Olena's daughters will be married. And which, of course, are nowhere to be seen when Natalia and Vira sit for their photographs in white satin and tulle and orange blossom.

She took with her, too, a sheaf of documents signed and stamped at a municipal office in Skalat, the *Syndykat Emigracyjny* in Ternopil', a Warsaw commissariat. There's a Testament of Moral Standing, in which the mayor of Skalat attests that Olena Solowska and her daughters Natalja and Wira are known by him to have behaved irreproachably in every way. Certificates of Belonging carefully, even elegantly, signed by Natalja and Wira Solowska, pin them to the most minute of maps: the Republic of Poland, the province of Tarnopol, the region of Skalat, the township of Kaczanowska. There's a marriage certificate, and certificates of birth and death for the twins, Ivan and Marusia. And a notice written in Ukrainian that on March 19, 1936, an agreement was drawn up between Olena Solowska and Myhailo Pankevych whereby he would rent her fields in Staromischyna for a period of five years only, paying the rent in advance and ceding all rights to this property on Olena's return.

Arranging all this must have been a horrendous business: in the photo fixed into Olena's passport she looks sadly careworn, though this may be a trick of the light, of over-harsh exposure. Her daughters stand on either side of her, Natalia a robust fourteen, Vira paper-delicate, her cropped hair and short bangs making her look far younger than twelve. In each face, blankness: a mask tied over fear, confusion, misgivings.

※◈※

Other things are lost forever, ephemeral or expendable by their very nature. There were doctor's forms that must have been surrendered at Halifax, forms vouching for the perfect health of these immigrants, at least at their initial point of departure. For just after they set out from Staromischyna, Natalia's eyes turn red and watery, and by the time they reach Ternopil', her lids have started to twitch. Olena takes her daughter to a physician, who diagnoses trachoma, that longstanding bane of immigrants, as can be seen from the front page of the *Halifax Herald*, April 4, 1903. An article reporting the arrival of over a thousand immigrants on the Hamburg–American steamer *Armenia* declares that of the 160 Canada-bound passengers from Eastern Europe, fifty to sixty were held up for trachoma.

Chlamydia trachomatis is its proper name, the one Vira looks up for me now in her medical books. It's a highly communicable disease afflicting vast numbers of people in the dry, dusty areas of the tropics and subtropics—it is also present to some degree in southern Europe. In endemic areas the disease is commonest in children: Vira says she has never seen a single case in her fifty years of pediatric practice. The problem with trachoma is that it can cause blindness if left untreated—and it often is, since the onset of the disease is "insidious," the textbook says, and may pass unnoticed until the sufferer's vision begins to fail. I think of the steamer *Armenia*, of fifty to sixty passengers with watery, twitching eyes, their corneas already scarred: I think of the Halifax officials, panicking at the thought that with each boatload of immigrants, dozens of people soon to be blind will be loosed onto the streets of Canada. I think of my grandmother's determination to have her daughter's eyes cured so that nothing will stand in the way of their journey. Nowadays a course of tetracycline will easily dispatch a case of trachoma; in 1936 a doctor in Ternopil' prescribed this treatment: rubbing the girl's eyelids with blue stones and a special crayon.

What Natalia remembers of her time in that strange city is that the treatment, however odd and painful, lasted only a day—and that it worked. By the time they made their way back to the railway station to take the train to Gdynia, where a representative of the Canadian immigration bureau would pronounce her fit to travel, Natalia's eyes were clear enough to let her glimpse a marvel in a shop window. A pale yellow fan of oblongs made from some waxy substance she'd never seen before, and which would mystify her for some time to come.

XX

When I ask them what they remember of the months and weeks and days lived through in the knowledge of leaving, they can't respond. In the same way children have such difficulty under-standing what death means, Natalia and Vira couldn't understand all the *never agains* that would have shadowed their simplest, most ordinary acts—fetching water from the pump down the lane, or running to that same pump to press their hands against its icy metal, hands stung by their uncle's bees. Vira has only one vivid memory of leaving: she and her sister sitting on the gate of their house, kicking their heels, bawling their eyes out as their cow, Helka, and her twin calves were led down the road by the man who'd bought them.

On a morning near the end of March, a secular form of reli-gious procession makes its way down the streets of Staromischyna: Olena, Vira and Natalia, the priest and the schoolteachers, all the neighbours—everyone in the village except Yulia and her family. I imagine it as the first fine day after a spell of storms: the buds on all the branches magnified by raindrops, the mud thick as stew along the roads. One of the leave-takers neither walks with the procession nor waves as it goes by. This is Bohdan, the boy with the smashed spine, who is leaning against the gate of his father's house. His eyes never leave the face of the fourteen-year-old girl he has watched walking home from school each day, the girl who'd spoken kindly to him while the others jeered. And because he can only stand straight by jamming his hands in his pockets, he can't even wave goodbye.

When they reach the road leading to Pidvolochys'k, where the train station lies, the villagers say farewell and turn back. Perhaps Myhailo Petrylo has loaned Olena his cart to carry her baggage: the driver helps the woman and her daughters up, secures their bundles and then sets off to town. He finds nothing to say to his passengers. They no longer need to care about the planting or harvest in this small corner of Poland; though he's seen or talked to this woman and her children nearly every day of his life, they've already become strangers. It's a relief to them all when they reach the station. The train pulls in so quickly that there's barely time to load their baggage before the whistle blasts their ears and a whoosh of steam carries them away, perhaps for five years, perhaps forever.

※◇※

Five hundred miles or more between Ternopil' and Gdynia. On their way to the coast they would have passed through Lwow, Lublin and Warsaw before the train headed north through a string of small towns to reach the sea. They'd have had German names then, these towns today called Swiecie, Tczew. But my grandmother and her daughters travelled without the luxury of maps; neither Vira nor Natalia can recall the places through which the train passed, or which lay along the coast skirted by the MS *Pilsudski* once it left Gdynia. Past Copenhagen and round the tip of Denmark; perhaps a stop at Bremerhaven and again at Rotterdam; through the English Channel, with a last call at Le Havre, and finally the open Atlantic.

It's impossible to keep romance out of this reconstruction. Perhaps I shouldn't try: Natalia and Vira would have breathed it in along with the stink of vomit and overflowing toilets down in steerage. For while Olena, tortured by seasickness worse than any migraine, lies in her bunk the entire voyage and prays to die, her daughters run the length of the ship, dance to the sailors' accordions, devour the oranges served up in the enormous dining room. That these oranges are woody and tasteless hardly blunts their pleasure. For this is the first time since their infancy that every moment of their day hasn't been burdened by household or farmyard labour, by school or churchgoing. The only hindrance to their freedom is the shoes on their feet, shoes they must wear every day from now on, instead of just on Sundays. Each morning they wash their mother's face, offer her a few sips of water she can barely swallow and leave her to the care of the women who haven't succumbed to seasickness. Then they bolt up the iron stairs to the decks outside, standing at the railing with their mouths open like sails to catch the fresh, salty air. A boy from Warsaw offers them the first mints they've ever tasted; they name the candy *whirlwind*, for the delicious storms it makes on their tongues.

On April 6 they catch their first glimpse of the Newfoundland coast. *Kanáda, Kanáda*, they cry out, as if expecting their father and the great city into which he's vanished to rise up out of the rocks and trees. When they reach Halifax Olena staggers up from the berth she's lain in for the full nine days of the crossing—she's been too ill to move even for the ship's obligatory fire drill. Freshening the clothes they've worn day after day, clutching their hand luggage, they totter down the gangway into what looks like a gigantic barn. They're deloused and bathed, their clothes fumigated, their bodies intimately searched for signs of communicable disease. Men in one section, women in another—all of them naked. Natalia stares at the older women huddling as far as they can from the tables of doctors and officials. At first she thinks they've hidden their nakedness with pale leather aprons, and then she understands: the aprons are their breasts and bellies, sagging after years of childbearing. She takes her turn shivering at the table, being pushed and prodded, until she's finally permitted to put her clothes back on. Vira, being younger, seems less shamed: to the doctor examining her, she blurts out her only words of English: "wan, too, tree!"

The train on which they endure the journey from Halifax to Toronto has bare wooden benches. At first they watch everything that flashes past them through the windows: cars, roads, dingy towns, then evergreens and rock cuts making a blur of green and grey. But long before nightfall, when the windows give them nothing but their own drained faces, they've had their fill of something too strange to call scenery. Vira strikes up a conversation with a man sitting across from them, a Polish man returning to Toronto from Lwow, where he's been visiting his family. When Vira tells him of the puzzling yellow objects they'd seen hanging from hooks in a Ternopil' store, the man calls to a porter passing by and buys for each of the girls one pale, unspotted banana. He explains how to twist the stem and peel back the skin, and watches as they take their first bites of a fruit far more exotic than oranges. Because he's watching, they can't make a face as their lips go numb; they must eat every inch of the unripe fruit that furs the insides of their mouths and chills their stomachs. When I first read Colette's description, in one of the *Claudine* novels, of how her heroine is initiated into sensual delights by eating the blackest of bananas, fruit so ripe its flesh has gone murkily translucent, I couldn't help thinking of my aunt and mother. Eating green bananas, smiling at the gentleman who'd treated them, and the gentleman beaming back because he'd authored this tremendous pleasure.

The train jolts on and on; the children fall into a tense, smoky sleep. They wake up next morning and endure another full day's ride until finally someone calls out, *Toronto, Toronto next stop*, and they push down the aisle with all the others, through the open door and into the night. The man walking up to them on the platform is not their father, or at least is not the same father they'd last seen four years ago. He limps under the pain of a wrenched back—only days before he'd been in hospital, in traction. They see the worry climbing back into their mother's face; they keep their heads down, stumbling behind their parents, sweat covering them like a clammy bandage.

Only when they step outside the station into the street do they stare up at the one thing that has stayed the same throughout this whole astonishing journey. But instead of being packed with stars, the sky is blinking out Polish words they've never seen before: *Tsotsa-Tsola, Tsotsa-Tsola.* Letters they'll learn to pronounce differently in English, turning them into the name of a dirt-coloured drink that scrapes and fizzes their mouths. The taste of sweetness here, this harsh soft drink called Coca-Cola.

※◇※

Tomasz had come to Union Station with a friend, Mr. Moroz, who'd offered to drive the Solowskis home in his beat-up Ford. To the children, for whom rides in lumbering wooden carts had been a treat, that Ford racing along Front Street to Spadina, past brilliant-coloured lights and glinting sparks from streetcars, must have seemed like the chariot of an angel.

Home, the first home, was Antler Street, one small room that Tomasz had furnished with two beds, four chairs, an enamel-topped table and the indispensable orange crates. Later they found better lodgings on Queen Street West, with another Ukrainian family. Somehow they all fitted into an apartment over a store—on hot summer nights the children would sleep on the roof, watching the stars rise or the sun come up through grids of telephone wires. "Which store was it?" I ask my mother. She can't remember: besides, it changed hands long ago. Walking back and forth along Queen, I try to guess which of these tall, narrow houses it might have been, houses at whose gingerbread gables I used to stare when having my teeth drilled in my father's office. It's hopeless. The street has changed so much even from the time I knew it best, working for my father as a teenaged receptionist, trying to interpret the Ukrainian and Polish of his patients, many of them old men with stooped shoulders and cloth caps, women bundled up in shawls and kerchiefs, a fragrance of poppyseed and dill about them.

Hopeless. Yet one day, only months ago, walking along Queen past Bathurst, past fashionable cafés and punk clothes boutiques, I happened to glance down a side street to find a large sign saying Charles G. Fraser Public School. This was the very school my aunt and mother had attended more than sixty years ago. I walked down the side street and inside the school's front doors. The buzz of lights, the intimidating height and width of the corridors—this my aunt and mother would have recognized from 1936. These stained glass scenes of children having tea parties or flying kites— they would have been here, too, their content as opaque to Natalia and Vira as the lessons they were sitting through.

It's the end of the school day, most of the children are gone, there's nothing for me here. But still I walk inside the office, making my way past teachers, telephones, newspaper articles pinned to the wall praising the school for its success in acculturating immigrants—Asian, these days, rather than Eastern European. It cheers me to see these clippings and the photos that accompany them; they're a connection to my family's past. But when the secretary at the desk—a woman who wouldn't have been born when my aunt and mother first were students here—responds to my question by pulling out file cards from a cabinet, I am astounded. They are dated 1936, and they give me the very information that I need:

Solowska, Nataljia. Solowska, Irena Vera. Last School Attended: Poland. Present Address: I. 716 Queen Street West. II. 29 Manning Avenue. III. 94 Manning Avenue.

✕◈✕

The immigrant shuffle, moving from rooming house to rooming house, apartment to apartment, each in a slightly better neighbourhood, with fewer roaches and more and more gestures towards gardens—pots of geraniums, even a patch of rank grass outside the front door. After Queen Street, two rooms on Manning, and then two larger rooms on Shaw. Tomasz and Olena, Vira and Natalia used the hallway as a kitchen and shared the house's one bathroom with half a dozen other families. Olena would take her turn lining up for the bathroom with the other women, lock herself in—it was the only room in the whole house where she could be alone—and cry her eyes out for the five minutes or so before a timid knock would signal the next woman's turn to go in and weep.

From a thatched and clay-floored cottage to a downtown rooming house; from the quietness of carts and horses to the screech and slam of city traffic—how do Olena and her daughters survive these sudden, stunning leaps? How do they know who or what they are anymore? Nothing here gives them back their true reflection. To those who own this place they are incurably foreign; if they're overheard speaking to someone in their own language, slurs like *bohunk* will be tossed their way. Not the colour of their skin, but the width and slant of their cheekbones, the very shape of their tongues mark them out as different, dangerous—why else would English people—the *Angliky*—go to such lengths to keep clear of them as they walk down the street? "It will pass," Olena's neighbours tell her. Or else, "You'll get used to it."

But for a long, long while they think they'll never get used to anything here. The first time Vira sees her father come home with a paper bag holding eggs, milk, bread, she feels a shock that sixty years haven't stilled. The shock that money must be paid out for the food you put into your mouth each day, money that's always been so scarce you're terrified to spend even a little of what you've struggled to save. At home the only things you needed to buy were what you couldn't make yourself: sugar and salt, coffee and tea. Soap you brewed from ashes and fat, oil you got from hemp seeds pressed at the mill. Even when paying the hired man after harvest, you gave him sacks of wheat, not money.

Not just at night, but all through the day, Vira dreams of home, the cow whose warm, frothy milk her mother would squirt from the teat straight into a glass for her to drink, the walnuts shaken from the trees, the deliciousness of sour cream dribbled over lettuce pulled tender from the garden. The fourteen fragrant loaves of rye bread her mother would bake each month, pulling them out of the oven with long-handled paddles; the *kvas* that was their version of a soft drink, made from fermented buckwheat flour. The pigs slaughtered after Christmas, every inch of their shaved, skinned bodies boiled or salted down to make sausages, blood pudding, headcheese. Home is the place where she never went hungry. But here, if her father's back doesn't heal, if her mother's eyes stay so inflamed from sewing that she can't go to work, what can they do but starve? The government offers relief in the form of free oatmeal for something called porridge, but Olena is too proud and too fearful to claim it: she's heard that those who sign on for relief are shipped right back to where they came from.

And so Olena walks her mile and a half each day to and from the shirt factory: partly to save the fare to buy bread, and partly because the jolting of the streetcar reminds her too much of her ocean crossing. Mr. Rosmaranovich, a neighbour who works at a dairy, brings them outdated milk, cream and butter for their table. Tomasz finds temporary work at a bakery, rescuing whatever's too stale to sell—I imagine the family sitting down to dinners of soured cream and three-day-old chocolate cake and wonder what Vira and Natalia made of this new, forced luxury. Later, they'll live off soup bones and rhubarb; they'll even be able to laugh at things. Like the family downstairs, whose six sons play—most of them hopelessly—the violin. For exactly half an hour, each boy practises, handing the instrument to the next brother down as if it were a piece of chewed-out gum.

At first Natalia accompanies her mother to the shirt factory, but by the end of the summer Olena starts to earn enough—$3.50 a week—for Natalia to join Vira at school. This improvement in her wages Olena owes to the Russian woman who's the only person on her shift with whom she can communicate. "They're paying you less than anyone else," the Russian says. "They know you can't talk with the other women and compare wages. Don't let them get away with it—don't let them stick you with all the big sizes that take so long to sew." Somehow Olena makes herself understood, and the foreman, reluctant to lose such an expert seamstress, pays her the paltry sum per shirt that's considered fair. It's a small victory, but enough to give Olena the assurance she can hold her own here, just as she'd done at home.

It's the kind of assurance Tomasz lacks, by temperament and by experience. He had to borrow money to prove to the authorities that he could support his family once they came to Canada; now he's disabled and in great pain. If his back doesn't heal, he may never work again, even if by some miracle there's work to be had. He wanted to welcome his family to Toronto with a whirl of presents; all he can manage is to swear off cigarettes, after having chain-smoked all the years he was alone. But he quits cold turkey and manages to keeps his temper, too, the best part of the only gift he can offer his wife. As for his back, Olena contrives to save up the price of a chiropractor. After one appointment Tomasz comes back dancing; finding Olena sewing in their room, he swings her round as lightly as he'd done when they first met. Instantly his back gives out and Olena has to help him into bed. He returns to the chiropractor, who effects a more permanent cure, but never again does Tomasz trust himself, or fate, enough to dance up a set of stairs.

Nights are Olena's bête noire, literally. Of the four of them it's she who wakes at two a.m., covered with red, swollen bites. After airing the mattresses, they carry the iron bedsteads out into the yard, pour gasoline over them and light matches, listening to the bedbugs pop in the flames. But the next night the bugs are back, as bad as ever. Tomasz suggests his wife sleep on the wooden table in the middle of the room, but when they switch on the light the next morning, bedbugs are massed on the ceiling over the table; the hardier among them have, of course, dropped down during the night onto Olena. It's only when the Solowskis acquire a home of their own that Olena can sleep through the nights once more.

What was it like living all together again? My mother once told me that her parents' reunion, after all the years apart, had been saddened by something that was other people's doing. In Staromischyna Olena held her head high in the midst of talk that Tomasz had abandoned her; in Toronto she held herself back from her husband. The signs of such holding back—how obvious and yet intricate they must have been in those conditions, husband and wife and children in one small room, haunted by other rooms unreachably distant and yet always there. Finally Tomasz persuaded his wife to tell him what had gone wrong. Again, as in the orchard sixteen years ago, his tenderness embraced her pride, disarmed it. But something, my mother says, was spoiled in her parents' first days together: a joy refused, to return only slowly, and in altered form.

There were no arguments, no scenes. Perhaps my grandparents were so busy trying to survive each day that they had no energy for shows of emotion. Except once, when a letter arrived for Olena. A letter from the Old Place, a rare enough event, but the handwriting on the envelope, the mere fact of the letter's having been written at all, makes it all the more conspicuous. Olena's at work when the mail's delivered. Tomasz accepts it from the post-man's hand, takes it inside to their room, where Natalia's trying to make some kind of meal out of stale rolls and rancid butter. There's a look on her father's face she's never seen before, even when his back was causing him most pain. She sees the letter he doesn't open but keeps turning over in his hands. She, too, recog-nizes the handwriting, and only a fast wire of courage lets her keep her head when her father asks her, softly, what she knows. She shakes her head, and he, too, shakes his, leaving the room, the house, still grasping the letter in his hand.

When he returns, long after Olena has come home, he makes no mention of what has kept him, where he's been. He's as gentle as ever with his wife, his oldest daughter, who knows enough to keep the letter, and the wordless conversation she's had with her father, a secret.

※◈※

Community is the one luxury they possess. In this sense, despite electric light and automobiles and department stores, Toronto becomes an extension for them of the Old Place. Among Ukrainians, hospitality is a religion: even those just scraping by will offer guests a cup of tea, a spoon of sugar, advice on where to buy fruit at a good price, which butchers to avoid. One of the first things Tomasz does once his family joins him is to buy an enormous enamel pot. To repay the many meals he's been given here, he explains to Olena. Somehow, without telephones, without specific invitations issued or answered, up to thirty people come by after church, or after sleeping in on the one day a week they can do so. All Sunday morning Olena labours over two burners set up in the hallway, dropping the *varenyky*, for which her daughters have peeled and mashed endless potatoes, into the vat of boiling water. Lifting them out with a slotted spoon, dropping them into a pan glistening with buttery onions, and onto plates that empty faster than she can fill them.

Ten years later, in her own kitchen on Dovercourt Road, she will cook these meals for the classmates my aunt brings home from medical school, among them Amala Ramcharan from Trinidad, who'll invite Vira back to her place for an initiatory curry dinner so strongly spiced that Vira will sleep with a pail of water by her bed. But now Olena repays the hospitality shown to her husband. And with sign language she shows Natalia's first friend in Canada, the daughter of the one black family in the neighbourhood, how to make *varenyky* and *holubtsi*. But something goes wrong in transmission: the girl, when she cooks these dishes for her family, ends up baking what should be boiled and boiling what should be baked. I say "the girl" because my mother, sadly, cannot recall her name, only that for this one black family, things were even harder than they were for her own. "They were fine people," my mother says; yet their neighbours, who should have seen this fineness, made life so unhappy for them that the family quickly left the area, never to be heard from again.

But Natalia still talks of Stella, whose mother finally allowed a crew of immigrant girls into her home each week to listen to Lux Radio Theatre—if they took off their shoes and sat, not on the sofa, but in a semicircle on the floor. She talks of Mary, the pale girl with a tumour on the brain, whose neck was so stiff she could only walk with great pain and effort. Mary and my mother would creep the few blocks to and from school each day, their conversation as slow as their footsteps. Yet Stella and Mary, and the classmates Vira met at school, became something unknown in Staromischyna: *girlfriends*.

Even now, talking of women in their seventies or dead long ago, this is the word Vira and Natalia use in a way that seems so brimmingly sweet for them, and so foreign to me. I'm remembering my 1960s adolescence: how any girl who showed she had brains would be spurned by the prom queens, the cheerleader corps. And if you did find someone with whom you could talk about other things than Maybelline or miniskirts, someone who, like you, had vowed never to learn how to run a washing machine or iron a Brooks Brothers shirt, then you did your best to forget the fact that you were girls at all.

Looking at my mother's and my godmother Anna's albums, all

the photos of girls and young women, heads crowding together, laughter and whispers still on their lips, I'm filled with nostalgia for what I never knew. In Anna's albums there are even more pictures—some small as postage stamps, others full-sized studio portraits—of girlfriends. Sunbathing on Centre Island, baking themelves, cooling off, baking again, so that at night their skin was puffed crimson and sore to the touch. Or sitting out in small back-yards in the two-piece suits that seem so chaste today, in the sunlight that once seemed so healthy. Girls talking together, the future in their eyes like a flotilla—which boat will come to carry you off? Will you board it, or at the last moment hang back and let it sail on without you?

And then the albums change: breezy snapshots give way to the formal spell of wedding photos, in which the girlfriends out on double dates metamorphose into bridesmaids. Hordes of them, sometimes eight or ten at a go—sometimes girls the bride hardly knows but has to include in the wedding party because they're going out with her brothers. Sometimes a girl and boy coming from different places out west meet in Toronto and decide to marry: "They couldn't afford to bring their sisters and friends from Saskatchewan, so you'd be asked to join the wedding party just for the look of it," Anna tells me. "I was always in great demand as a bridesmaid," my mother laughs. "I worked in the rag trade on Spadina; I could get the material for bridesmaids' dresses wholesale."

What happened to the girlfriends who never became brides? The beautiful girl no one will name for me, the one whose father beat her so badly she was always hiding out at a girlfriend's house. She ended up on the streets, my mother tells me, alcohol the slow fuse that burned her alive. I think of a song I learned almost on the sly at summer camp: "*Mala Ya Muzha Piyaka.*" About a woman whose drunken husband does nothing but beat her; how she threatens to leave him with the children and run off, clear across the Danube. We used to sing it laughingly, tauntingly, over illicit campfires. Never once thinking of the song as a lament, as anything that could touch our own lives here.

What happened to the brides themselves, the radiant young women with their pompadours and platform shoes? They walk inside the whiteness of their wedding gowns and vanish, like trees in mist.

schooling: thread and ink

Tomasz and Olena had their educations cut short by disease and war; they were determined their daughters would fare better.

My mother started school when she was seven—the village school in Staromischyna. To this day she finds reading not difficult, but largely unnecessary. The poems and folk songs she loves she knows by heart; she is fluent in all the lines and textures cloth can assume, and she can design, cut out and sew a complicated dress or coat faster than most people can leaf through a pattern book. Vira, on the other hand, was a born scholar, quick at sums and letters. Because she was so small, her teacher made her sit at the very end of a classroom bench crammed with a dozen or more children. A huge, hefty boy would sit in the very centre, a boy who could never answer the simplest question. He would shake and wriggle, causing a general jellyquake that ended by tossing Vira clear off the bench and onto the floor. This would always happen during religion class; the priest would haul her out to the yard, grab her by the collar and hit her with a switch. But she'd always twist and pull away so that her skirt and not her backside took the brunt of the beating.

Somehow money was found to send her, aged eleven, to a *gimnazium* or high school in Pidvolochys'k, where the town children made fun of her country ways, and where she was seated among the Jewish children with their perfectly straight, perfectly black, chin-length hair. It must be at this school that Vira's given a poem she doesn't understand, a poem that the older children order her to copy out and pass to someone in the row ahead of her. She finds the words impenetrable, despite her fluent Polish. The teacher intercepts the note; recognizing the handwriting, she tells Vira she expects to see Olena at the school that evening. And so Olena, after a full day's work, dresses in her Sunday clothes and walks the few miles into town to meet with the teacher. When she returns at last, she picks up a galvanized tin pail, lifts it high over her head and flings it so hard against the floor that it squashes flat. Nothing more is said about the incident, and it's not till the next day that Vira learns, from one of her schoolmates, what the note had been about.

"And—?" I ask. Vira is seventy-three and I am forty-five; for the longest time my aunt can't answer me. And then, half-blushing, half-laughing, she answers. "It was about a painter who used his penis for a brush."

But Vira got her own back at that school she must have both loved and hated. Not long after, she stood up and announced to her class that the king had died. "What king?" the teacher asks scornfully. Poland, after all, is a republic. "King George the Fifth," Vira replies, proud of this knowledge she alone possesses and that has come to her from across the sea. "We are going to Canada," she continues, "because the king is dead, and now life will be so much better." She sits down with a flourish, having summarized the anti-royalist sentiments expressed by her father in his last letter home; not knowing how greatly Tomasz has underestimated the colonial mentality of Canada. How the teacher responded, I don't know—the point of this story is this: for the first time in her life, Vira didn't have to care.

※◇※

As for their Canadian teachers, Vira and Natalia fell in love with them, entirely, eternally. Not at first sight, but over the first few weeks and months spent in the company of the maiden ladies who taught them at Charles G. Fraser Public School. Miss Ferguson, who took charge of Vira; thin, tall, fine-boned Miss Sinclair, who became Natalia's mentor. I remember being taken with my sister on visits to Miss Sinclair's house on Duplex Avenue; sitting in her sunroom, playing with a matrioshka doll and being so good it hurt. African violets on crocheted doilies, a silver teapot and porcelain cups, the smell of winter light—a smell not of dust, but starched lace—from these few memories I try to understand what they were like, Miss Sinclair and the other spinsters who taught my mother and her sister.

What must they have been or done to earn the devotion of those silent or stammering immigrant girls, terrified by the enormous school with its harshly lit halls, coached by their schoolmates in four-letter words they'd proudly repeat as proof they were finally learning English? The true courtesy they possessed, Miss Sinclair and Miss Ferguson, invited to the clean, bare room on Shaw Street, sipping tea from enamel mugs and not once betraying surprise or disgust that, as a mortified Natalia noticed, small beads of fat were floating at the top. She'd had to use their only pot to boil the water, the pot in which soup had been made that morning, and no amount of scrubbing had banished the traces of chicken fat. But the teachers sipped their tea till it was gone and even asked for one more cup.

What I take to be cruel, arrogant behaviour on the school's part, my aunt and mother see as normal, necessary. Natalia, at fourteen, put in a kindergarten class, feels like a goose among goslings. In the classroom the teacher draws a picture of a rooster on the blackboard. Rapping it with his pointer, he demands that the big, shy, foreign girl tell him what the creature's called—something anyone out of diapers must surely know. And Natalia, who could have answered him in Ukrainian or Polish or even Russian, is laughed down when she comes up with the only answer she can manage: "Chicken's father." As for Vira, she goes crimson when asked questions in this language she can't understand; she crawls under her desk until the teacher finally persuades her to come out again. Vira ends by staying after school each day to practise her English: so great is her longing to learn that after only a year she jumps up six grades.

School helped them forget the enormity of what they'd left behind, of what they'd come to; it also helped them to understand that their lives were full of entrancing possibilities, not just worries and dangers. Their teachers did far more than point out these possi- bilities. Miss Sinclair, who taught home economics, gave Natalia her old clothes to make over into dresses for herself. The fabric was excellent, my mother recalls, Liberty prints, but the styles hope- lessly old-maidish. Natalia restyled them with Peter Pan collars and puffed sleeves. Her teacher was so impressed that she loaned her the fee for a couturier's course at the Toronto School of Design. "If she hadn't taken an interest in me," my mother insists, "I would have ended up with a factory job like my mother's."

Miss Ferguson, Vira's science teacher, took her aside shortly before her Grade Eight graduation to ask which high school she'd be going to. Vira, trying to fold herself into the coats hanging in the cloakroom, answered, "Central Tech." She was going to do what so many immigrant children did: learn the clerical skills that would get them an office job—one step up from the meat plants and sweatshops where their parents worked, if they were lucky. "You ought be be going to Harbord Collegiate," Miss Ferguson announced. And she gave Vira the then-considerable sum of five dollars to help her buy the textbooks and supplies she'd need for such a venture. It was Miss Ferguson, too, who took Vira on her first visit to the Royal Ontario Museum; she had to pry her away at closing time, so intent was the girl on seeing, knowing, everything the "castle" contained. A cup of hot chocolate at Diana Sweets was the inducement to leave, and Vira still can't tell which of the two experiences she savoured most.

Abiding affection and endless gratitude, this is what Vira and Natalia feel towards their teachers, those fabled names I heard throughout my childhood: the names of empresses in countries of the mind and heart. Miss Ferguson and Miss Sinclair.

✖◈✖

i. Natalia. The Story of a Dress

A soon as her firstborn was old enough to thread a needle, Olena sent her to learn the art of sewing from a village woman living near St. Nikolai's. My mother can't remember the name of this woman with jet-black eyes and brows and hair, the most beautiful person she had ever seen. The most beautiful and the most mysterious, for although she was well past girlhood—twenty-five, even thirty—she let no man near her. The teacher lived with her widowed mother, who did all the household chores while her daughter sewed by hand. Delicate work, feather and satin and cross-stitch, drawn thread and fringe work for the embroidered towels or *rushnyky* indispensable to weddings and christenings and funerals. In the afternoons she'd sew by the window; at night by a lamp with a large glass shade, painted with flowers and fine ladies.

All the time her teacher threads the precious needles, or separates the long silk of embroidery thread, or as she straightens up from the table she's been leaning over, gently tugging the edges of her jacket so they hang just so, Natalia is falling in love. This passion is different from the curiosity that drove her to fiddle with sticks and string, inventing for herself the art of knitting, unknown in Staromischyna. It's connected to the cutting of her grand-mother's black skirt, for which she was so severely punished. It has to do with something you could call style, flair—appearances. The way her teacher looks, walking so elegantly down Staromischyna's thin, muddy lanes, transforming them into something her pupil hasn't got names for yet: avenues, boulevards, promenades.

※◇※

Only a few months ago I asked my mother something I'd never wondered about before. "What kind of clothes did you wear in the village?" I hadn't been curious because I'd always known that people in the Old Place dressed in some simplified form of regional costume. Youths in hemp trousers and cross-stitched homespun shirts; maidens with flowery ribbons in their hair, bril-liantly embroidered blouses, heavy strands of glass beads or else *koralyi*, strings of fleshy orange corals. Now I discover that I'd dressed up the whole village in a lie. For except at Easter, when they put on a child's version of their regional dress, Vira and Natalia wore the low-waisted dresses of the twenties and, later, simplified versions of 1930s frocks.

Plain cotton or woollen dresses sewn on Olena's machine, with plenty of tucks and pleats to be let out over the months these dresses had to last. To soil, never mind rip, a school dress was a disaster. How then to explain what happened when, one morning on her way to school, Vira climbed the plum tree, the one with the branch half-broken off? Shimmying up the tree after one especially fat and gleaming plum, she slips and finds herself suspended, her skirt caught on the splintered branch. For a moment she hangs immo-bile until, inch by inch, the dress lets go of her, pitching her bottom-first into the nettles. Overhead, the perfect circle of the skirt, impaled; by her side, holding a broom, her mother. Inexplicably,

Olena keeps the broom to herself and merely chides her daughter. "You've still got your eyes, you've still got your legs. What are you wailing for?"

In Toronto Olena and her daughters had to dress in whatever they could find, until a neighbour, a woman from Staromischyna, loaned them her sewing machine. In my mother's album there's a photograph of some social gathering, perhaps an anniversary party held shortly after she came to Toronto. At either side of a phalanx of adults stand Vira and Natalia, wearing matching dresses of some pale, filmy, ruched material, with sleeves like little clouds and slender belts drawn through shiny buckles. They may have been eating stale bread and sour milk, but they look, as one of those Depression sayings goes, like a million dollars.

In a memoir of life in working-class Carlisle, novelist Margaret Forster writes of the significance of dress in her own "respectably" poor family. Describing the custom of "getting dressed for Easter," on which families would spend their last penny, Forster explains the importance of having smart as well as decent clothes. "They showed the world you respected yourself and had made the effort to be as immaculate as possible. They showed that however hard your circumstances, you could rise above them." And one of the most moving chapters of the book has to do with her mother's outfitting herself for a brief return to the clerical job she'd had to give up in order to marry. The pleasure she took in buying new clothes so as to arrive appropriately dressed for the work she delighted in—brain work rather than bruising physical labour. The guilt she felt at buying clothes for herself and not her children.

At what point did Natalia outstrip her mother, making suits and dresses for herself and Vira; sewing Olena's clothes? Was there never a moment when she doubted her talent, mistrusted her ambitions—or simply wished she'd been born for something else? It's not a question a child can easily ask a parent, and for answer I can only go by something she told me once, when I was thirteen, fourteen. Arriving home from school one afternoon, I found my mother sitting in the living room we so rarely used. I waited for a moment, then joined her on the sofa, under the painting of an English countryside she'd never seen but that reminded her, a little, of the land round Staromischyna.

She sees my school bag, picks up a botany textbook, thumbs through it looking for the diagrams. She tells me how, in her last year at public school, she'd been asked to make a whole set of botanical drawings. How she'd spent the happiest hours of her life choosing the colours, designing the placement of seed and flower and fruit on the page, deciding how words and text would fit together. It took her months to complete them, but the pictures, she tells me, hung for years and years on the classroom walls. My sister may be sitting with us as well that afternoon, my sister who already knows that when she's through with Grade 13, she will not follow our mother's urging to study something practical, but will go on to art school. The battles about how Karen expects to support herself, about what she will wear to her studio classes—not the ladylike dresses my mother has sewn her but *jeans*—lie a few years into the future, yet my sister's vocation must have been sitting with us, too. For suddenly my mother's confessing how she'd always longed to be a painter. How, if there'd been money for art school, to buy her equipment, to cover the time it would have taken to establish herself, she'd have—

The telephone rings, and by the time she returns she's someone else. Not the fifteen-year-old, drawing dozens of botanical specimens; not even a woman who remembers with her whole heart a longing that she'd had to surrender even as she formed it. But our mother, who needs us to peel potatoes and carrots, to run the vacuum cleaner before our father comes home. The wife and mother who knows how painful, how dangerous it is to untie her apron and step back, even for a moment, into that most Cinderella-like of ball gowns, her former skin.

XOX

How does she do it, what elixir turns the pudding-faced girl of the Polish passport photo into a young woman so slender that people tell her not to stand sideways, lest she disappear?

Just before I turned sixteen, when I still had a moon-shaped face and a chubby, blundering body, I left home for the first time, fell in love, had my heart broken and forgot to eat. The girl who returned at the end of a summer in Winnipeg was unrecognizable to her family, her friends, even herself. I'd lost twenty pounds and my hair had grown long enough to change the shape of my face, which, having shed its puppy fat, was acquainting itself with its cheekbones. Sixteen-year-old Natalia didn't have the luxury of living away from home, or of heartbreak, for that matter: she was too intent on helping her family earn a living. But she must have gone through a similar crash course in possibility, learning she could alter the shape of her body as she altered the cut of Miss Sinclair's Liberty prints.

What are the stages in this journey Natalia makes from immigrant schoolgirl to independent working woman? Fourteen when she arrives in Toronto in 1936; fifteen by the time she acquires enough English to get a Grade Six diploma and enter the Toronto School of Design. Sixteen when, in the fall of 1938, she starts work as a designer. Eighteen when she begins the most dazzling and demanding part of her career: travelling to New York City, staying at five-star hotels, window-shopping on Fifth Avenue, sitting dressed to kill at fashion shows. Memorizing every flare and flounce, every detail down to the number of buttons on a sleeve.

I think of her on that first trip to New York, this girl who has never spent a night away from home, never slept in a room by herself. It's late at night, she's sitting at a table by the window of her hotel room, overlooking the brilliant lights, the traffic roaring far below. She has kicked off her skyscraper heels and changed into pyjamas; she's sketching everything she's seen on the runway that day. Once or twice, when there are noises in the corridor—a woman with a champagne laugh, a waiter wheeling a trolley past— she glances up at the door. It's locked, of course, and the chest of drawers she's dragged across the floor to make a barricade is still in place. *Men are like that.* Like what? She still doesn't know.

One other, less glamorous, point in this journey. It has to do with a joke told, for once, by the immigrant instead of the oldcomer, a joke at the expense of all the givens of "English" culture. Natalia is shopping at one of Toronto's better department stores whose windows she hardly dared glance at only two years ago. She buys a great many outfits, the design and cut of which she'll pore over before sending them back and making her own improved versions. She asks for all these purchases to be delivered to her home. "Of course, madam," says the shopgirl, deferential to this stylish young woman with her elegant hat, her soft leather gloves and her good shoes (all of them bought wholesale, through contacts, though for all the shopgirl knows they come straight from Sak's Fifth Avenue). "What name?" she asks.

Natalia's so tired of spelling out S-O-L-O-W-S-K-A; of hearing, "What kind of a name is *that*?" So she tells the shopgirl, "Sloane." Thinking nothing more of it till the next afternoon, when she comes home from work and finds her father shaking his head over the huge package someone tried to deliver to their door, a package destined for the zoo. It takes Natalia a moment to catch on to what's happened: that when her father read the delivery slip, what he saw wasn't Miss N. Sloane, but *slon'*—the word, in Polish and Ukrainian, for elephant.

※◇※

The sixteen-year-old girl is nervous, spotlit, stranded in front of all these people; when she tries to smile, the cold sore she'd woken up with—the bloom of panic—bursts, and blood spills down her chin. She and a model supplied by Simpsons, along with the material and a seamstress and presser, share a satin-draped stage at one of the ersatz palaces at the Canadian National Exhibition, illustrating what is billed as "The Story of a Dress." In front of packed rows of watchers, without a single error or wasted movement, she sketches a design, makes a pattern out of brown paper, cuts out the slippery, shining cloth and hands it to the seamstress. After a whirr of basting, the seamstress hands the cloth to the model, who, retiring into the wings, emerges with the idea of a dress wrapped cloudlike round her. And now the designer deftly, swiftly, continues her work, so that the cloud, bristling with pins, can be sewn up on the industrial-sized machine and handed, limp as a fainting child, to the presser. Who does her part, steam gasping from the iron whose pointed nose she expertly guides along this line, that fold. The presser hands the dress to the model, who disappears once more, then pivots round the stage, her skirts shimmering as she links hands with the designer and seamstress and presser to receive a rapture of applause.

Natalia is far from rapturous—she's faint, and furious. When Mr. Sinden, the teacher who'd chosen her from all his students at the design school to put on this display, comes up to congratulate her, she turns on him. "If *he's* here tomorrow, then I won't be!" "He" is the man who sat front row centre, never taking his eyes off her hands, and at every stage in the "story" calling out questions, interrupting the plot. "He," Mr. Sinden explains, handing her a Dixie Cup of the coldest water he can find, "is one of the few designers who's hiring these days, and he wants to give you a job."

The Toronto School of Design, once at 1139 Bay Street, no longer exists: its function has been taken over by Ryerson University. To my mother it had been a little hothouse heaven: she'd passed the course in half the time it was supposed to take. A young model named Gay was her partner in the design course;

to honour that friendship, my mother gave my sister the middle name of Gay, despite the disapproval of her father-in-law. (He found the baby's first name, Karen—chosen by my father— equally impossible: Carrots, he thought it was.) To me, it's one of the freest acts of my mother's life, this naming of her first child after a state of happiness.

Going to work for Harvey Webber, on the other hand, was far more than heavenly. The paycheque Natalia earned went straight to her parents, to help buy groceries and medicine, and, later, to pay off the loan for the house they'd bought on Dovercourt Road. If she'd failed, if she'd simply been let go—and in 1938 designers were still a dime a dozen—it would have meant disaster. Yet she never faltered; she was even strong enough to hold her own against a group of zealous Baptists when Mr. Webber sent her, along with his daughter Margaret, to a Muskoka Bible camp. "Come, you sinners," called the preacher to the row of girls sitting on the rustic bench before him. Before anyone else could reply, a voice with a Slavic accent yelled, "No way!"

Once through the door of the huge brick box on Spadina Avenue, Natalia had nothing like an office to herself—she worked at the end of the shop where enormous rolls of fabric were piled. She was one of forty or fifty people employed by Mr. Webber: cutters, steam pressers, seamstresses, finishers, examiners, ship-pers, office staff—a lot of the work was contracted out for trans-Canada sales, for the big chains. Natalia designed evening jackets exclusively for Simpsons, and later casual outfits for Alton Lewis, discovering there really was an Alton Lewis, "a true gentleman," who'd take her out for lunch from time to time.

In designing clothes, my mother explains, you've always got to outdo the competition. You follow the line, whether it's pleats or flares, V-necks or princess collars, but then you have to add some-thing different, you have to gussy things up. At a shop along Spad-ina, a sewing supply wholesaler's, she finds boxes of specially finished nailheads in all kinds of colours. She buys handfuls from each box, taking them home, experimenting, and showing up a week later with evening jackets and crepe de Chine tops on which the nailheads, gleaming green or red or blue, cluster into peacock feathers, fireworks of leaves and flowers. Mr. Webber is ecstatic, taking them home to show his wife and daughter. They beg him not to take them back to the office, they are so beautiful. The jackets and tops sold, my mother adds, like hotcakes—business picked up in spite of hard times, and her career was made.

By the time my mother left Harvey Webber Designs to get married, she'd been offered a line of her own. She always said she turned it down because she hated the name of it—the "Nat-line." Her boss took her out to lunch the day she told him of her engagement. "Don't do it," he pleaded. "You're just about to make the big time. You can have a house in California, a house in France. You can have everything you want on your own—why do you need to get married?" A question that must have rung in her ears a few years later, when she was lugging round pails of dirty diapers, cooking enormous meals for in-laws, sitting up all night with a feverish child. Or later still, when her children were all safely at school and she suddenly had time on her hands in the large house in a quiet suburb away from all the grit and hustle of downtown.

She was often asked to go back to work; once she toyed with setting up a small design company of her own. But none of it came to anything. She sewed for her children, her mother, her sister, for friends who had "challenging" figures. Later she worked on theatrical shows, designing costumes for Odessa sailors and market women, or for a Poltava wedding. Making the rounds of wholesalers, renewing acquaintances in the rag trade after so many years away, my mother bloomed, despite the long hours, the frequent obstacles and frustrations and—of course—the fact that she was being paid for all her work in nothing but applause. She didn't expect anything else, and yet after the show was over it must have been hard to go back to being just a wife of long standing, a mother of children well past the tractable charms of infancy.

We had arguments all through my last year of high school, arguments only superficially to do with what I'd study when I got to university. What was really at stake was whether I'd become a mirror to my mother, or a door. I chose to be a door, thinking, perhaps, that doors can swing open after they've been slammed. My mother wanted me to study dental hygiene: she wanted me to marry a dentist, to have a life as safe and solid as she'd made her own. But I was in love with lost possibilities, and the closest I could come to what my father might have been if he'd run off with his violin to New York all those years ago was to study literature. Metaphors would be my guiding stars; through them I could trace connections between the most painfully disparate things, peel back the cloudy skin over my eyes, become real, at last.

The heated kitchen debates as to what I should do with my life were finally resolved by my father: "Let her study what she loves." I moved away to university; two years later I was married—not to a dentist, but to a graduate student in English literature and, what was worse, an *Anglik*. When we moved into a shabby downtown apartment, gloriously our own, my mother came to visit. All she could say to me was, "This is the kind of place we had to live in when we came to Canada. Don't tell your Nana—it would kill her."

Twenty-five years have passed since then: my mother and I have come to accept one another, the different lives we've fashioned for ourselves. And yet I want more than acceptance, the bread and butter of family love. I want to cut the stitches that keep my mother and me from knowing each other as equals and as strangers, too, the way all our friends were once strangers. I want to meet, in my mother, that sweet-toothed child so full of mischief and need, that young woman, hardly out of girlhood, setting off for New York to mingle with people who'd never guess in a million years that she grew up in a place where women soaked flax and dyed wool with onion skins. And I want her to see me as more than a daughter, known and named long before I could speak a single word for myself.

The closest I can come to any of this is listening to and telling stories. One I learned for the first time only months ago, though it's a story for children: bright and urgent. When she was eight years old, walking through Pidvolochys'k with her mother—it wasn't a pleasure walk, they had cream and eggs to sell—Natalia passed a girl her own age. This girl was carrying a small green purse, a toy and thus doubly desirable. "I wanted that purse so badly," my mother sighs. I see her following the child with her eyes, memorizing the exact shape and shade of a purse that seems like a leaf plucked from a rare and lovely tree. Years later, my mother tells me—when she was working on Spadina, or perhaps after she'd married—she saw in the window of a shop downtown a small green purse, walked inside and bought it.

It stops there, the story. And for once I don't want my mother to tell me anything more. I'm remembering how, when I was eight years old, I wanted nothing else in the world but the dog I wasn't allowed to have. Praying every night for two years, making count- less bargains with a God who'd obviously forgotten that his name spelled backwards was the object of my longing. It would have made all the difference in the world to me, then, if I'd known about my mother's helpless passion for that small green purse.

When my mother was finally able to buy herself a green purse, when I finally bought a dog, not for myself but for our two sons, neither the dog nor the purse meant what they once had. I never came across the green purse in my childhood, although my mother tells me she still has it in a drawer in her sewing room, filled with buttons. It has come to remind me of how desire tarnishes. The dog I bought for my children is beautifully sweet- tempered, but I hold myself back from him. I can't wrap my arms around his neck, confiding all my dreams and griefs as I'd longed to do when a child. Just as my mother, a grown woman when she bought her child-sized purse, could never walk round with that bright green flag signalling from her shoulder.

Hope deferred maketh the heart grow—I can't remember the end of the adage. But desire deferred can turn the present moment, with all its possibilities for joy, into the smudge of ashes. We may know our true selves at the last by what we long for and can never have, but we must, just once, receive the objects of our longing—a dog, a green purse—if only to discover their insufficiency, and thus the true nature of desire. How it overflows the most precise outlines, the most lavish contours we can make for it. And how it stays with us a whole life long, the immense destination of our small, stubborn hearts.

✄◇✄

ii. Vira. Aches and Pains: The Time of Her Life

When did she know she'd become a doctor, stitching up not taffeta and silk, like her sister, but split skin? Back in Poland, when she nursed dozens of goslings she'd found bleeding through their beaks? Or when she was given a precious orange to take to her sick grandmother, an orange that Melania refused, wheezing so badly from asthma she could barely breathe, moaning, "Eat it yourself, eat it yourself." And Vira did, her guilt and pleasure intermingling so that even now she can't peel an orange without hearing her grandmother fighting for her next breath. Or did her vocation find her long before, when she learned that her infant sister had died from the scarlatina she herself had brought into the house, and somehow survived?

Shortly after starting her last year at Harbord Collegiate, Vira gets a weekend job shelving cans at a corner store. One afternoon she overhears a conversation between the shopkeeper and one of his customers, a Mrs. Karmulska whose daughter Lilian has just been accepted into medical school at the University of Toronto. Mrs. Karmulska pronounces the ten syllables as if they refer to some vast, celestial empire. Vira stands clutching a tin of pitted cherries, saying over and over to herself, *Lilian Karmulska, Lilian Karmulska.* A girl with a Slavic name like her own, going on to medical school.

On the last day of Grade Thirteen Vira Solowska, wearing the box-pleated plaid skirt and matching waistcoat her sister has sewn for her, walks down Harbord Street to King's College Circle, where University College is laid out in all its splendid sham-Romanesque. She pauses in front of Convocation Hall, catches her breath and walks inside that grandly columned building echoing with its own importance. For it's here that decisions are made as to who will be allowed to enter the University of Toronto in this year of God and War and Study, 1944. Vira locates the Admissions Office, and finds herself before the desk of a maiden lady like the ones who taught her English and who came to her rooming house to drink tea poured through a film of chicken soup. But when this woman takes the application form and reads the name printed on it, she loses all resemblance to Miss Sinclair or Miss Ferguson. "Solowska?" she asks. "I hardly think so." And she hands the application back without reading any further.

In spite of Lilian Karmulska, Vira has scarcely dared believe she could become a doctor. How would her parents find the money to pay for her tuition and textbooks, how could they afford to keep her in school so long when she could be earning a salary, as her sister does? At the most, she might become a nurse, since the hospital would pay for her tuition. Or perhaps she could study pharmacy; she has often daydreamed about Tomasz and Olena working with her in her own shop, soda jerks in fresh white uniforms. When she'd revealed how expensive medical school would be, her parents told her to fret about her marks instead. She has those marks rolled in a tight cylinder in her hand, and somehow she finds the courage,

Tomasz Solowski

*a dignified man, in possession
of whatever words he will
or will not speak*

Toronto, 1930s

Olena Levkovych
dressed for her wedding

Pidvolochys'k, 1920

Melania Levkovych, née Sikora

*a starved nun, with
a beaked and hooded face*

Pidvolochys'k, 1937

Adela, Vira, Natalia and Natalia's sewing teacher
Pidvolochys'k, 1936

Ivan, who proposed marriage to
13-year-old Natalia offstage and on

Pidvolochys'k, 1936

Hannia, Tomasz's sister,
with her daughter-in-law Olga, and grandchildren
Wroclaw(?), some time after World War II

Grade six class, Charles G. Fraser School
Natalia is seated directly in front of her botanical drawings, in the back row

Toronto, 1937

Natalia and Vira
unmistakeably sisters
Toronto, 1940

Natalia and Anna
girlfriends
Toronto, 1940s

Natalia, Vira and Anna
Vira's graduation from medical school

University of Toronto, 1949

Joseph Kulyk in captain's uniform
Natalia vowed she'd marry him when he came home from the war

Leaving the Dovercourt house: Natalia's wedding
Back row: Vira, flanked by bridesmaids
Front row: Tomasz, Natalia, Olena

Back row: Natalia, Olena
Middle row: Tomasz, Vira
Front Row: Janice, Karen

White satin and tulle and orange blossom

Pandora's Parcel to Ukraine,
Natalka Husar, 1993,
oil on linen, 224 x 274 cm,
(from the series *Black Sea Blue*),
Collection of the National
Gallery of Canada

Olena, Vira, Natalia, Tomasz
the scar between presence and absence
Pidvolochys'k and Toronto, 1928(?)

after that icy, authoritative *I hardly think so*, to unroll the cylinder across the woman's desk.

Thirteen firsts on finishing Grade Thirteen. The woman reads through the figures twice, as if searching for something that doesn't add up; she stares at Vira no less haughtily than before. Yet this time she nods her head ever so slightly: Miss Solowska will be admitted to this year's class, one with a noticeably higher number of women, since so many of the men who would have enrolled are off fighting in Europe. A fact the professors will not let their women students forget. "Why are you here?" these men will complain. "You'll only marry and have babies and never use what we're letting you learn. Why are you wasting our time?" It was a question Vira answered by going on to practise full-time as well as marrying and raising three children. At the age of seventy-three she still sees patients, is still brought in for consultations by the large, prestigious hospitals.

When it comes time for Vira to be interviewed for that stark necessity, a bursary, she dances her way through the questions, until the key one comes round, the one on which her whole future hangs: *Why are you going into medicine?* She forgets about her hospital for sick goslings, the grave illnesses her mother somehow pulled her through. Instead, she blurts out a story of how, when she was very small and very ill in the Old Place, a doctor had come from town to see her, a doctor in a fine grey suit. He'd made her pee into a glass, and the pee, instead of being clear, was the colour of strong tea. That mixture of the fine and strange—this is why she wants to take up medicine.

She did get the bursary and plunged into her studies. It was the first ex-serviceman's year, and they crammed six years of learning into five: there was no time for holidays in the summer, no time even for a concert or a film. She graduated tenth out of a class of 178 in 1949. "So I must have done well," she tells me. "I don't know why—I just loved it so much." The fact that she was a brilliant student never enters the equation, it means nothing next to the warmth she still feels for her classmates, the gratitude to her early teachers. They attend Vira's graduation, two pale, proper ladies admiring an enormous bouquet of red roses given Vira by a young Irishman, who'd disappeared as soon as her parents came into view.

Even with the roses, the diploma, the borrowed mortarboard and robes, the stunning graduation gown confected by Natalia, the hurdles stay in place. When she is interviewed for a job at Toronto Western Hospital, one of the doctors on the interview committee—a certain Dr. Feesby—takes Vira aside to a window overlooking Bathurst Street. He's a well-built man in a pinstripe suit: his hand as it cups her elbow seems to be made of something far more durable than flesh and bone. He points to a building at 300 Bathurst Street, the Labour Temple to which Vira's father belongs and where she'd played mandolin on the concert stage until medical school swallowed her every moment.

"*That* is where you grew up," Dr. Feesby says. "*That* is where you belong."

How he'd found out about her family's being Labour Temple, Vira never knew. But just as she'd found the courage to slap down page after page of glowing examination results at the Admissions Office, so she now detaches her arm from Dr. Feesby's grip. "I wouldn't work in your hospital," she says, looking straight into his eyes, "if you begged me on your knees." Later she'll tell the doctors who want her to join their pediatric practice in the Medical Arts building, the tony one at St. George and Bloor, that no, she will not change her name from Solowska to Smith so that her patients' parents won't have to know their children are being handled by someone from *that* part of the world.

(A few years later, at the hottest moment of the McCarthy era, my father, who had also refused to change his name to something more Anglo-Saxon sounding, will be denied entrance to the United States to attend that most subversive of all activities, a dental convention. The grounds for this refusal are these: as a boy, he played violin in the Labour Temple orchestra. Soon afterwards my sister, who has always spoken Ukrainian with her family, will be sent home from kindergarten with a warning note: if she keeps speaking "Russian" in the schoolyard, the authorities will have to be alerted. My parents stop speaking Ukrainian with both their daughters, and by the time it's politically safe for us to be sent to Ukrainian school—the one run by the cathedral on Bathurst Street—we have become strangers to the language, and will never find a way to make it home.)

❈

In the Old Place there were no pharmacies, no hospitals and no doctors, unless you were on your way to dying. The small child who peed into a glass for a grey-suited doctor had no hint of the world of grotesque and beautiful wonders to be opened to her by anatomy and physiology textbooks, by long hours in dissection rooms. All she knew was that aches and pains were cured with herbal teas, with massages performed by women skilled in the preparation of special oils, women with massive arms and shoulders.

To try to cure Bohdan, the boy with the cracked spine, the women of the village gathered twigs, needles, amber-coloured ants from the floor of the nearest pinewoods and steeped them in boiling water; a bath would then be readied for the boy from that same pungent brew. For bad coughs, for pneumonia, a woman would come round to the house with a special set of glass cups, a bottle of alcohol, a roll of cotton. She'd swab the inside of the glass with alcohol, then heat it over the flame of a candle, putting the rim down over the place where the pain was worst. Vira would watch the skin rise inside the glass like a thick, tender bubble; watch as that skin took on the colours of a different kind of rainbow: yellow, green, purple, black.

Once, Olena developed a painful sty; from the river she procured a fat, black, slimy *piavka* to put on her eyelid. It was supposed to suck up the infected blood, relieve the swelling. But the leech, moving its powerful mouth back and forth, inched from the lid to the eye itself, the painfully sensitive cornea. Olena screamed; her daughters froze until, remembering the jar of precious store-bought salt, they ran to their mother with fistfuls to throw at her eye, making the *piavka* shrivel and fall away.

If you stubbed your toe in the woods, you'd look for a puffball, stick your toe into it, and immediately it would feel better. And should you be tormented by boils or a bad cut that wouldn't heal, you could salve it with any number of leaves, from nettle to cabbage. Band-Aids were unheard of—once, gathering clover from the field by the cemetery, Vira cut her finger so badly that the blood streamed. As she ran home, a woman, seeing the red glistening down her arm, grabbed her. She tore a strip from her underskirt and bound up the finger before Vira fell through the black pushing into her eyes.

※◇※

We use the knowledge we gain in the present to visit the past, to puzzle through its mysteries. Vira has no sense of smell; when she was only a baby, she was told, a group of boys playing *kuchka* had hit her in the face with the can. Her mother's mother could never distinguish between a cut onion and a rose thrust under her nose; people said she'd been bitten on that nose by a horse when she, too, was very small. In her first year of medical school Vira learns of an extremely rare condition called anosmia, a minor congenital defect passed on through the female line that robs its sufferers of any sense of smell. Vira, but not her sister, suffers from anosmia: of Vira's children, the youngest will inherit the condition.

Though the horse bite makes a better story, there's a fascination in the existence of, the very name, *anosmia*. But no such Latinate precision marks the fate of one of Vira's aunts, Olena's sister, the second daughter of Melania Sikora and Ivan Levkovych.

Sometime during the First World War, on a raw November morning, Russian soldiers march into Staromischyna. Everyone is ordered out to the fields to dig trenches. Olena's sister, tired out with digging, sits down on the freezing earth, her legs and arms numb as stones. The soldiers leave her there until the other villagers have finished the work; then she is allowed to stumble home. That night the girl is made to sit with her legs in a pail of the hottest water she can bear. Melania keeps topping up the water so it stays just below the scalding point; the next morning her daughter's legs are swollen and discoloured and she starts to run a fever. By evening a doctor has been fetched from town. He prods the girls' legs with the tip of his finger as if they are mottled sausages he has second thoughts about buying. And then he turns to Melania and says—he is not a man to mince words—"The legs will have to come off at the knee, or she'll die."

For a moment no one replies: neither Melania, nor her husband, nor any of the neighbours who've come by to see what so important a person as the doctor is doing in Staromischyna. Olena watches her sick sister, who is staring at the floor and doesn't see the instruments the doctor's taking from his bag: the small saw, the many different knives. Olena's fifteen-year-old sister speaks clearly and slowly, just three words: "Then I'll die." The doctor waits for a moment till the girl's mother nods her head. She knows the truth of what her daughter's thinking: who would want a wife who can't walk, can't work, must sit in a chair all day? Who would feed, never mind marry, her? Perhaps the doctor knows this, too—perhaps it was only a little show he put on, taking out the polished instruments that he puts back now, wiping his brow with his handkerchief as if he's just finished the operation. He leaves with the proper number of zlotys in his hand; the priest is called. Some days later he buries Olena's sister in the cemetery of St. Nikolai.

It was the shock, my grandmother always said, that killed the girl—her near-frozen legs being forced into the painfully hot water, kept there till they turned the colour of beetroot. What she implied, but never said out loud, was that her mother caused this death, as much as any Russian soldier. But when I ask Vira, she tells me that what killed her aunt would have been blood poisoning, followed by gangrene. When the girl was digging, she must have grazed her legs with the edge of the shovel; when she sat down in the trench, she'd have gotten dirt in the wounds, contracted an acute infection. As simple as that.

Simple and appalling. Not so much that the girl would be allowed to die in a world without artificial limbs, rehabilitation centres, training programs—without the very concept of "handicapped." But that no one in my family remembers her name; that all we can call her is "the girl," the fifteen-year-old I imagine to be fair-haired like her younger sister, and delicate of build. So delicate that she would tire easily and, becoming clumsy, scrape her legs with a shovel so the blood ran down into the earth.

✕◇✕

All through her twenties, despite the fierce pressure of study, the lack of anything like free time, and the absence sometimes of sleep itself, Vira had what she describes, in her seventies, as the time of her life. She and her friend Dorothy Shepherd were the first two women interns taken on by St. Joseph's Hospital; later they were joined by Hilda Vierkarter, daughter of the man called "the black shark" for having swum the English Channel. At two a.m. the three of them would make snacks with the toaster Hilda's mother had given her, only to be told off by the nuns, whose patients, fasting before major operations, were driven crazy by the smell of toasting bread. At other times the girls, as Vira calls herself and her fellow interns, would stagger to their room at four a.m. after finishing in the emergency wards. They'd be so tired they'd collapse onto their beds, shoes clunking to the floor. At breakfast the priest from the room below theirs would joke about how glad he was the girls weren't centipedes.

Gus, the young Irishman who brought Vira roses at her graduation, would come to see her at St. Joe's—a more welcoming place, just then, than the Dovercourt house. They would walk down to the lake, whose sunstruck waters could be seen from the hospital windows. Down to Sunnyside where they'd feast on doughnuts and hot chocolate and maybe go for a swim at the pool. "We would always take Dorothy along, my dear, dear Dorothy," Vira says. "She adored Gus, and he would never leave her behind—so you can see how romantic these dates would be. But anyway, we had a ball." *We had a ball*—the happy slang showing how much she's come to feel at home in her third language: the distance she's travelled between necessity and pleasure.

Vira was advised to finish her training in Detroit, under Dr. Wolfgang Zuelzer, a pathologist and hematologist at the Children's Hospital of Michigan. So off she went, aged twenty-six and on her own for the first time in her life. Her internship, it turned out, was mostly in gross pathology—there were so many dead children to deal with. When she came back to Canada and went on to the Hospital for Sick Children, she was prepared for things that doctors who'd done all their training in Toronto had never seen.

But it was intoxicating being in a new place, doing work that, however grim, endlessly intrigued her. For her work at the hospital she received the queenly sum of fifty dollars a month, out of which she bought for her newborn niece a lamp shaped like a duck. And she cajoled a fellow intern, Reuben, into taking her along on one of his home deliveries in one of the poor, black neighbourhoods. No sooner had Reuben spread newspapers over

the floor than the baby shot from between its mother's thighs and
straight into his arms—he almost hit the floor, catching it. To the
grandmother frowning in a corner, her hefty arms crossed tight,
Reuben stammered, "At the hospital we always jump up and down
with them at least six times—it clears their lungs."

When Vira got her fellowship in 1954 and set up her own practice in pediatrics, she cleared exactly fifty dollars her first year
after she'd paid the cleaner and the rent on the office. Sometimes
her patients gave her cheques that bounced; at other times, when
the ones who never had ready cash would ask, "How much,
Doctor?" she'd feel like crawling under her desk. How could she
charge a child for being sick? When she married, she set up a
practice in her home, and her children learned to deal with a telephone ringing, day and night, with demands that the doctor drop
everything to attend to this or that sick child. And the doctor
always did. It was her way of answering those mustachioed men
in their grey suits who had frowned from their lecterns at all the
wasteful young women who'd only go off, get married and have
babies.

11

happy endings, border crossings

For the first three years after coming to Canada, Natalia and Vira spent their summers on a farm southwest of Toronto, picking strawberries (three cents for a quart basket, one and a half cents for a pint). In the evenings they would cook, bake bread and boil up the berries they'd picked that day to make vats of jam, boiling and boiling till the colour and very taste of the fruit seemed to foam away. They earned almost nothing, and soon stopped cramming their mouths with fresh-picked fruit, but their real profit was relief: at being back in the country; at lessening the strain on their parents, who'd be alone together with only two mouths to feed.

Of all the photographs I've seen of my grandparents, there is only one showing just the two of them together, a small, milky snapshot in which they stand, arms loosely linked, their faces blurred, impossible to read. Since they'd married against their families' wishes, they'd had no wedding photo taken; the pictures of them in Canada always show them with friends or with their daughters. The best of these is a studio portrait that must have been taken just after Tomasz resumed work at General Electric and Natalia entered the Toronto School of Design. In this photo

Tomasz is seated, Olena stands behind him with her hand on his shoulder, and at his other side are grouped Natalia and Vira. They are dressed, all of them, in good, dark clothes. Tomasz sits with his legs crossed, and the light catches the crease of his trousers, a crease that says *success* even more strongly than the good cloth of his suit. Everyone's shoes gleam: behind them hangs a scrim of dense leaves. From the shadows of this background the faces of my family shine like four beautiful planets, only just discovered.

Here, then, is the happy ending of the courtship in that moon-lit orchard seventeen years ago; here is the answer Olena and Tomasz can give to their dead or lost parents, the families who cast them off and folded their arms to watch the disaster this marriage would bring. The answer they speak to their own hearts, which have endured so many years of separation and wanting and loss. The war that will change the Old Place past knowing, turn it into a home of horrors, will bring them something close to prosperity here. Soon they will buy a house of their own and start a garden. They will live together for another twenty-four years, see their daughters well married, all their grandchildren born. They will reconcile themselves to their Irish son-in-law, who will awe and enchant Tomasz by taking him up over Toronto in a Cessna 150, pointing out to him the minuscule house and garden that are 494 Dovercourt Road. In the end they'll have lived more of their lives in Canada than in Poland, and this in itself may stand as proof of that supreme fiction of any life, the happy ending.

With that ending the stories stop—that is, the stories stop happening and start being told. With the births of their grand-children, Tomasz and Olena must have felt that the deaths of their infant son and daughter were cancelled out, or made good. Our being over here, safe and sound, showered with toys and kisses (so, at least, say those supplanters of stories, the endless reels of now-disintegrating home movies)—this is what makes up for the loss of everything that once meant home. Our never knowing hunger or separation from our parents, our having, from the very start, a world of comfort and safety—a future.

Except that we had that other world as well, whatever we chose to make of it. That world where all the stories came from, a world of cracked spines and suicides as well as clay stoves and nesting storks. A world too complex, its energies too violent, to be contained in the contours of an Easter egg.

❧

I keep this gift my mother gave me in a glass-fronted cabinet, along with other rare and fragile things. When I was much younger, I attempted the art of painting Easter eggs: drawing on the blown shell with melted beeswax, trying to avoid blots and spills, to orchestrate a complicated pattern by dipping the egg into dye after dye, from lightest to deepest. I could never have made anything as jewel-like and intricate as this image my mother's friend has crafted, that eighty-year-old with his perfect eyes and touch. This icon of home I hold in the cup of my hand: lost home, remembered.

Memory is a house we may visit again and again, as long as mind and body last. We move from room to room, along corridors and stairwells, our eyes shut, seeing with our hands. For me, the stairs in memory's house lead not up but down. To a place where terror and treasure are heaped in equal measure. Is terror too strong a word? I look again at the egg in my hand, the brightness of the green walnut tree drawn beside the house, the glowing white of the house's walls and the stork's plumage. And find, for the first time, a way of reading the peculiar background to all this brilliance. Under the spoked orange sun to which the stork lifts its head, the sky is deep brown, so dark as to be almost black. The colour of the earth from which the root cellar's dug, fourteen steps into the ground. Although there's no image of the *lyokh* drawn among the sunny shapes of house, tree, bird, I see now that its darkness captures and contains them all.

❌◇❌

I dream of going underground.

To the basement of my parents' house: long, narrow, dark, with a small room at one end holding things to eat or drink. Jars of *borshch* and cabbage soup; cobwebbed bottles of Bright's wine that our abstemious family never drinks, but keeps, forgotten, for special occasions. Around the time of the Cuban missile crisis, when the American family across the street was building a fall-out shelter, my sister and I talked of taking pillows and books and flashlights down to this storeroom and living there for the weeks it would take before the all-clear sounded. It's in this small room that the old refrigerator's kept. Each time you open its door, a buzz slaps through your hands right up to your ears. Something's wrong with the wiring. But no one makes any move to fix the fridge or throw it out, as I'd once dared to throw out a jar still holding an eighth of an inch of jam.

After the storeroom there's the large, dry room where the furnace roars and where, on a shelf above my father's workbench, lies the miniature cupboard whose mirror never gives me back the face I think is mine. In the furnace room are racks and racks of clothes gone out of style; they hang there like headless, footless phantoms. The *Illustrated American Encyclopedia* that Loblaws gives away with every purchase over twenty dollars is shelved here, too, along with the Nancy Drews and incomplete games of *Monopoly* and *Clue* my mother has preserved, not out of some fetish for the past, but out of her belief that possessions make a bunker round you, something better than a fall-out shelter, keeping nothingness away.

Storeroom, furnace room—these aren't what I'm searching for, not food to eat or books to read. I have to go down the corridor and turn into the long, wide space that's been filled, top to bottom, with bolts of material, stacked odd chairs, corner shelves with Bavarian beer steins, wooden carvings of deer and fawns picked up on summer holidays at northern resorts, old desks, their drawers jammed tight with our schoolwork from kindergarten on. Records, tapes, copies of yellowed fashion magazines smelling sharply of the chemicals used to manufacture them. And at the very end of this room, a wall behind whose curtains a never-used dartboard waits, like a Cyclops' eye.

Against this wall is the upright piano my parents bought at an auction, during that time when my mother was discovering antiques. She has stripped and refinished it; the dark grain of the wood waves like seaweed through murky water. I hate the piano's being in the basement—I want it to be upstairs, not in the family room, where the windows are just level with the backyard, but in the living room where it's always light during the day, and where the lamps don't cast crazy shadows when they're lit. Every moment I spend here trying to practise, I'm waiting for a murderer to slide hands like empty rubber gloves over my mouth and eyes before I can finish even the shortest piece. I've confessed my fears to my sister, who has long since given up the piano; one day, in revenge for some misdeed of mine, or simply to see what will happen, she hides behind the sofa. While I have my back turned and exposed, while I'm playing arpeggios, she creeps up silently, clapping her hands round my eyes and jerking my head back.

I don't struggle to break free or even cry out. I'm looking into the black behind my eyes, the black that's made by my not screaming, not seeing the outside anymore. I'm looking into a space inside me and yet under the ground, a place full of objects that I've only to hold out my hands to grab onto. Not outgrown books or clothes or old-fashioned furniture too good to be given away. For I'm in the *lyokh*, the magic place of that faraway house and vanished land, more secret, more mysterious, than the *svitlytsia* where the dead are laid out. A place of safekeeping, a hiding place, where things aren't lost but found.

✖◈✖

They play their favourite game in secret, down in the *lyokh*.

But how can they see to play? Among the boxes piled in the deepest, farthest hollow of the cellar, they find candelabras shaped like wide-branched trees; they fill them with beeswax candles filched from church. Lighting candle after candle, a forest blazing over gilt-edged dishes painted with grapes and roses, through teacups thin as flower petals. Using the packing crates as tables, draping the rough wood with fine white linen unearthed from tissue paper, linen appliquéd with lace that makes them think of white spiders, the webs they spin between piles of softening onions and carrots.

Sometimes they crawl as far as they can into the maze of boxes and crates and towelled-up goods, unearthing a silver-backed brush, a music box with a broken spring. Once, they pull into the tiered candlelight a picture of a girl in a blue cloak with a baby in her arms. She's sitting on a donkey that her father leads by the bridle into a desert place. The stones are like small, puffed buns under the donkey's hooves. They make them think of their father, who has journeyed so far away from them: they wonder whether he has enough to eat where he's living now, whether there are rolls lying on the ground there, waiting for you to pick them up and stuff them in your mouth. The candles burn down and the children pretend a feast out of the air—oranges and cherries and white bread. Just before the last light goes they put the treasures under the cloths, into the crates, so carefully that nothing is chipped or torn. And then, when nothing's left but the dark, they stumble towards the stairs, the younger one clutching her sister's skirt. Both of them blinking their eyes as if to clear mist or earth from them when they open the door into the noisy light of day.

XXX

Once when I was in London and spending an afternoon in the British Museum, I chanced upon a treasure trove in the medieval section. A sign was tacked to the length of maroon cloth on which the objects were exhibited: *Part of a jewellery hoard from Kiev, Ukraine, found in the street of the Three Saints, opposite the Michael Monastery, in July 1906.*

The Metropolitan Museum in New York, the sign went on to say, holds similar gold and silver from this find, although the many coins that originally formed part of the treasure have disappeared. It seems that many such hoards were discovered all over Kyiv—they may all have been buried during the period of Tartar invasions, perhaps during the sack of the city in 1240. The items on display behind the glass are subtly, beautifully worked. Pendants to a high, stiff headdress; nielloed backgrounds on which animals—possibly griffons—race through geometric motifs. There's a scattering of what look to me like jingle bells—they're really silver globes that would have hung from the hoops piercing a lady's ears. An armband lies on this length of cloth the colour of old blood; beside it are two silver ingots pitted with craters like the surface of the moon. I find rings incised with family signs or *tamgas*, and best of all, a bracelet engraved with arches holding birds and leaves. It's the one object in the whole display that conjures up for me the warmth and softness of the skin that wore it.

Kyivan treasure hoards, root cellars, basements. Just as with the rings and pendants buried during the sack of Kyiv, no one ever came back for the treasures hidden in the *lyokh*. Perhaps their owners, like my father's parents, made it safely across the sea and decided that their lives were the only possessions worth looking out for now. Perhaps they were caught up in the storm of the war they were trying to flee and perished in strange places, without friends or the means to acquire them, without shelter or hope. The man to whom they entrusted their porcelain and lace, their oil paintings and silver candelabras died not long after, in one of the typhus epidemics that raged through his homeland after the war. His daughter kept the treasures safely stored in the root cellar, when she might have used them to buy land. Her daughters played there in secret, by the light of scavenged candles. And his great-granddaughter dreams of playing a set of black piano keys, a skein of music leading her down to that place where she comes from, where she's never been.

Could it still be there, the *lyokh*, though the house with its carved door, its walnut tree is gone? The children who played in that cool, dark hollow under the ground, did they ever cross the borders between desire and need, placing on a Limoges plate an onion or whiskered carrot, joining two different worlds in that one act? Will I cross the same kind of border, now that this stage of my journeying's done? This sorting and setting down of stories; this mapping of the Old Place as it has emerged for me through memory and imagining.

Borders take you under as well as over. Into places where the past is stored; into the present that's made up of this past, in the way valleys are made up of the rivers that once rushed through them. The past I venture into now is that larger public world holding my family's private stories. In them, this larger world possessed the transparency of ghosts, their visible elusiveness. I must look for it now on a different kind of map, one that will show me the places my family's stories skirted as if they were chasms. Places in a world where history and politics are a thick tangle of embroidery, with blood, not thread, stitching the pattern.

Here I am, at the border between story and history, personal desire and a shared reality over which I have no more power than I do over my dreams.

III

Journeying Out

How does the old country live on in the citizens of the new? How may I understand these people and their extraordinary history—my blood relations, as it were, from whom I was separated by the accident of being born . . . in Canada? . . . What is their claim on me? Mine on them? In other words, what has this part of the world got to do with me?

Myrna Kostash, *Bloodlines*

12

Eastern Galicia: war and "peace"

For as long as I've known there's an Old Place, I've known that it lies by a river. But where does that river lie on the map beyond memory?

The documents in my possession place it in the Polish province of Tarnopil, now called Ternopil' in Ukraine. I've been told that the Old Place was part of a region the Poles named Kresy, which means "on the edge, far away" and which referred to the whole eastern borderland between Poland and Russia. But Staromis-chyna was also part of a geographical and political entity called Galicia. In an edition of the *Encyclopedia Britannica* published when Tomasz Solowski was ten years old, I find Galicia defined as a crownland, indeed the largest province, of Austria. When Tomasz turned eighteen, Galicia became part of a newly resurrected Poland. The capital of western Galicia remained the medieval city of Krakow; the principal city of eastern Galicia, the Austrians' Lemberg, reverted to its Polish name, Lwow. Twenty-one years later, when Hitler and Stalin carved up Poland between them, eastern Galicia became part of the Soviet Union, its capital rechristened L'viv or Lvov, depending on whether your sympathies were Ukrainian or Russian.

This intricate politics of naming, this succession of rulers and empires meant nothing to me for many years. Galicia—Halychyna in its Ukrainian guise—was only a distant province of what my Saturday School teachers mapped as the heart of my being, the ancient city of Kyiv. Yet every one of my ancestors, on both my father's and my mother's side, came from the hills and river valleys, forests and fertile plains of eastern Galicia. During the middle Paleolithic period this landscape was settled by agricultural tribes who managed to survive the onslaughts of varied armies, sharing a language, a range of gods and legends, and crafts such as wheel-turned pottery. Later, in what the *Encyclopedia of Ukraine* calls "the princely era," civilizations arose that left behind more substantial traces:

> . . . fortified towns, settlements, burial grounds, architectural remains . . . and the Zbruch idol. Evidence of foreign in-migration can be found in various localities: eg. ancient Magyar burrows near Krylos . . . caches of Varangian arms. . . .

Magyars and Varangians mean nothing to me—what I want to know about is the Zbruch idol: what was its shape and size, was it made of gold or silver or stone? Could the peasants or archaeologists—whoever actually found the idol—have come across it in the marshes close to where Natalia and Vira took the goslings each spring? Was it discovered somewhere on the riverbank where soldiers fished out the bodies of drowned students in silver-buttoned capes? Or could it have been the children of any of the villages along the Zbruch who unearthed the idol while playing their castle game, cutting the chocolate-coloured soil with sharpened sticks?

Galicia was once joined to the medieval principality of Volhynia. It was to Galicia that the rulers of ancient Rus' escaped after the fall of Kyiv in the mid-thirteenth century, when the Mongols thundered through the Golden Gates, sacking and burning three hundred years of churches and palaces. One of the chronicles records that when the Kyivan nobility and their retainers fled the slaughter, a child-princess was forgotten in a labyrinth of richly decorated rooms. It gnaws at me, the legend of this small, abandoned girl. It speaks too closely of the fate of my father's two older sisters, left behind when their parents, fearing the approach of war and Austrian recruiting agents, fled Galicia for Canada in 1914. The children were ill with diphtheria; the older one died; the two-year-old survived, to be met at Union Station eleven years later by the parents she couldn't remember, and a new brother and sister whose existence she had never imagined.

There are facts enough in the encyclopedia and history books to constitute a kingdom of knowledge: how will I ever find my way home here? How far back can I imagine the people I come from? Six hundred years, when, after the last of the Romanovych dynasty was poisoned by his boyars, Galicia was "acquired" from Hungary by Poland, and the vast estates were established through which lords or *pans* would viciously exploit the peasantry, both Polish and Ukrainian? Two hundred years or so, to the Partition of Poland, when Galicia was absorbed into the Austro-Hungarian empire? Or little more than a century: to 1887, when Stanislaw Szczepanowski wrote of "the Galician misery," a phrase that sums up the centuries of lethal poverty and backwardness to which the region's rulers and landowners had condemned it?

They weren't wholly passive in their misery, the peasants of Galicia. Between 1490 and 1492 they launched an uprising that was brutally suppressed. Those who survived fled eastward to the Steppes, finding temporary freedom from forced labour barely distinguishable from slavery; from gross interference in their everyday life by those who came to see themselves as owners of their souls as well as of their bodies. But what of the peasants who stayed behind when the others fled, the ones who bowed their heads and bent their backs—my ancestors among them? They'd have breathed a little freer when their part of Poland came under Austrian rule: it was thanks to the Empress Maria-Teresa that the draconian laws concerning peasant marriages were relaxed, so that lovers no longer had to secure their *pan*'s approval of the shape and ventures of their very hearts.

Under her son's rule—that same Josef II whom Peter Schaffer's *Amadeus* portrays as an arch buffoon—the "personal subjection" of the peasantry was abolished and serfdom introduced, "whereby," the *Encyclopedia of Ukraine* explains, "the peasantry received certain personal and property rights"—*certain*, in this context, meaning minimal. Even when the serfs of Galicia were emancipated in 1848, their poverty remained acute, since they now had to pay the *pan* for the right to graze their cattle and cut wood on what had formerly been common land. They also had to pay the cost of building and maintaining schools and roads, which may explain those notoriously rutted, mucky roads that so infuriated my grandfather as late as 1931. It may also account for the fact that in 1900, the year of Tomasz's birth, there was "only one elementary school per 1,500 inhabitants as compared to one tavern for every 220 Galicians." The 1911 edition of the *Encyclopedia Britannica* describes Galicia's distilleries as producing nearly 40 per cent of the total output of spirits in Austria.

As part of their strategy to maintain imperial control over eastern Galicia, the Austrians extended certain rights to the various groups they ruled, but they played these groups off one another expertly. The Poles were struggling to regain, the Ukrainians to achieve, a nation of their own; one reason for this region's blood-black skies is that Poles and Ukrainians fought so bitterly against each other. That they intermarried as often as they did seems astonishing; whether such unions testify to the exaltation of love over nation, or simply the urgent need to put survival—the amount of land a couple could scrape up between them—before loyalty to *ethnos*, is difficult to tell. But my grandparents, having married across the barriers separating Poles and Ukrainians, were lucky to leave Galicia before the Second World War. Is "lucky" an adequate word to describe an escape from a killing field? Can any history book, any encyclopedia, furnish the right words?

※◇※

Tomasz Solowski was too young to have been conscripted into the Austrian army at the outbreak of World War I; too young to have set out for Canada before that war, joining other hungry men of his region who, because of their nominal Austrian nationality, were branded enemy aliens and shut up in forced labour camps at Fort Henry near Kingston, Spirit Lake in Quebec, in Brandon, Manitoba, and Castlefield, near Banff.

Tomasz's father must have taken ship for the United States shortly after his son's birth: exactly when he left, no one can tell me. Perhaps he was still in Galicia in 1902, when a series of agrarian strikes broke out to protest the Polish nobility's opposition to even the mildest agricultural reforms. Perhaps when Tomasz was a small boy, he was told stories of the father he never knew taking part in these strikes: this refusal of ordinary men to go on working their scraps of land to feed the rich, while never making enough to buy shoes for their children or to educate them past grade school. For the social and agricultural reforms that Josef II had attempted to push through more than a century before had been largely sabotaged: the arch-conservative policies of Franz Josef I, whose spectacular moustaches my aunt had worshipped as a child, fixed Galicia in the role of Austria's backward, broken breadbasket.

It has been calculated that in 1902—the year of Olena's birth— over 400,000 peasant holdings in Galicia were so small "that they could only supply food for the average family for three months of the year." Between 1911 and 1914 as much as a quarter of Galicia's population was forced to emigrate—a figure comparable to the number of Irish who died or had to leave for North America during the potato famine of 1840. Well into the 1930s Galicia was overpopulated; land was far more expensive here than in other parts of Poland. My grandparents were among the thousands who left the region between 1918 and 1939, before the war that so brutally decreased the surplus population.

In 1914 Tomasz Solowski, destined for the priesthood like so many bright boys from poor Galician families, goes blind. Though the blindness proves to be temporary, he never returns to school: his eyes remain so inflamed and delicate that any kind of print tortures them for years to come. For the first months of his illness he lies in a narrow bed with poultices bandaging his eyes. Later, when the days grow longer and the air is warmed by spring sunlight, he sits out on the *pryspa*, that clay version of a verandah, sorting out courtyard sounds—water being tossed from a basin onto the onions, the jabber of geese and chicks, men calling to their horses as they plough. Someone—perhaps his stepbrother Mykola—takes him to the *chytalnia* to hear the newspaper being read aloud and politics discussed. For it must be during the shock of this disorienting illness that Tomasz's passion for new ideas is born; that he decides against spending the rest of his life as peasant or priest. Listening to the news read out by the reeve or the schoolteacher—news of war declared between Russia and Germany and Austria; of forced enlistments, and the requisitioning of animals and foodstuffs; of a Russian scorched-earth policy that turns Galicia into an official disaster zone—he begins to translate catastrophe into possibility.

When Tomasz is seventeen, he learns that Tsar Nicholas II has been forced to abdicate his throne; when he is eighteen, he hears that the last of the Habsburgs has fallen. There's a revolution in Russia that's turning the whole world there upside down. And the war? It doesn't end so much as collapse, the way a fire can burn down to smaller, radiating piles of coals. Perhaps the most astounding event of 1918 is the resurrection of Poland as a nation after its erasure, for the past 150 years, from the map of Europe. But something far more dramatic occurs in that year the war collapsed—more dramatic, at least, to the young man who will become my grandfather. One evening in early winter, when the village air is thick with buzzing rumours, he is able to run to the *chytalnia* and read, with his own eyes, an account of the declaration of a Ukrainian People's Republic in L'viv, and the formation of an army to defend it, an army crying out for volunteers.

※◇※

Was he Polish or Ukrainian, Tomasz Solowski? When I was a child, I felt the question hovering in the air like a bird that beats its wings so fast they can only be seen as a blur. At Ukrainian school, it was understood that the Poles were our enemies; they had forced many of our people away from the Orthodox faith into a hybrid religion, Greek Catholicism, to make them ripe for Polonization. Although my mother had been baptized a Greek Catholic, she married my father in the Orthodox Cathedral on Bathurst Street; when I was a teenager, it was the stuff of scandal for a Greek Orthodox boy to date a Greek Catholic girl, as if these romances kept re-enacting the plot of *Taras Bulba*, that tale of a Ukrainian cossack selling out for the love of a beautiful Pole. So they would both fascinate and alarm me, the Polish newspapers I occasionally saw my grandfather reading; the small, holy pictures tucked into the corners of my grandmother's bedroom mirror. Not the rigid Byzantine icons of Virgin and Christ I knew from churchgoing with my parents, but the long hair and soft faces, smooth and pliable as icing, that spelled out *Catholicism*.

My grandfather's name as it appears on official documents is perfectly Polish: when I ask my mother about her father's nationality, she says the question doesn't make sense. Tomasz's mother was Ukrainian, his father Polish. Did Tomasz feel himself to be both, or did he have to throw away the Pole in him to marry a Ukrainian, adopting her language and culture as his own? If his father hadn't disappeared when Tomasz was so young, would the boy have ended up in a Polish regiment? Was it his instinctive sympathy for the underdog, the oppressed and put-upon, that drove him to fight against Poland for the establishment of a Ukrainian state in eastern Galicia?

In histories of Poland it doesn't merit much of a mention, the Polish-Ukrainian war. It lasted from November 1918 until July of the next year, and Poland's victory over the badly equipped forces of the Ukrainians is declared to be of far less importance than its miraculous defeat of the Red Army in 1920. But the Ukrainian-Polish war is, for me, one of those crucial places where private and public history, family memory and public record, intersect.

I need to go back to those November days of 1918 when the teenaged Tomasz, identifying with the cause of his mother's people, devours the news of revolution and resistance reaching his village. In Kyiv, where so many wealthy Russians have fled, champagne flows freely; florists and jewellers and cakeshops do a roaring trade. At a decent distance Reds and Whites engage each other, slaughtering, starving, burning out the peasants caught between them. As they do so, a hastily assembled government takes advantage of Tsarist Russia's collapse to declare the creation of a Ukrainian National Republic in Kyiv. The Bolsheviks set up a rival state, its capital in Kharkiv, farther to the east, closer to the Russian border.

What follows is chaos, with six different armies in the field and Kyiv changing hands five times in under twelve months. When the German army drives out the Bolsheviks, who had briefly seized power in Kyiv, it sets up a puppet government for the Ukrainians. In the spring of 1918 Tomasz may have seen, in the newspapers at the *chytalnia*, the same picture of its leader that I stared at some forty years later in my history book at a Bathurst Street Ukrainian school: Hetman Pavlo Skoropadsky, boasting a magnificent bandolier and wearing an astrakhan hat on his aristocratic head. He fled Kyiv with the Germans on December 14, 1918, after a Ukrainian insurrectionary movement had successfully challenged him.

My grandfather would have cheered Skoropadsky's downfall, creating as it did a vacuum in which an autonomous Ukrainian government, the Directory, took control of Kyiv. But the news that grabbed fiercest hold of him was the announcement, well before this coup, that on October 31, a group of Ukrainian officers, some no older than himself, had seized key government buildings in L'viv. A Council or *Rada* was formed shortly afterward, and a Ukrainian state declared. Street-fighting broke out in L'viv, with the Poles forcing the members of the *Rada* to flee to Ternopil'. In December they moved again, this time to Stanyslaviv, and, in January 1919, they joined forces with the Directory in Kyiv in an attempt to avoid that ultimate exile, extinction.

※◇※

Did Tomasz run away to a recruiting office in Ternopil', hitching rides on farmers' wagons, sleeping in frozen ditches? Or did the recruiting agents gallop into his village and fire his patriotism, reading out proclamations published in newspapers with names like *Republic* and *Ukrainian Voice?*

> *To the Ukrainian People:*
> *We proclaim to you the news of your liberation from ages of oppression. From now on you are masters of your land, free residents of the Ukrainian state. From the nineteenth day of October, with your will, the Ukrainian state and its supreme power—the Ukrainian National Council—is*

organized on the Ukrainian lands of the former Austro-Hungarian Monarchy.

The fate of the Ukrainian state is in your hands! You will become a stone wall around the Ukrainian National Council and protect it from all enemy attacks.

Until the bodies of State Power will be organized in the lawful way, Ukrainian organizations in cities, hamlets and villages must gain power over state, regional and civil governments, on behalf of the Ukrainian National Council.

L'viv, first of November, 1918.

Tomasz joined the Ukrainian Galician army and marched against his father's people. The Poles, under General Haller, had the benefit of troops seasoned in the First World War. Against these soldiers in their blue, French-made uniforms and with their state-of-the-art weaponry, the Ukrainians were forced to pit an army of volunteers, many of them teenaged peasant boys, badly shod, ill-armed and even worse fed. After a nine months' struggle to hold their ground, the Ukrainians ended pinned against the river Zbruch. "On 16 July 1919, with Polish artillery hammering at their backs, the Galician army and thousands of West Ukrainian civilians crossed the Zbruch into Eastern Ukraine." There they joined Semyon Petliura's forces in their attempt to wrest control of Kyiv from the Bolsheviks.

Did Tomasz cross the Zbruch that muggy, blood-soaked day in mid-July and march into Kyiv with the Galician army? Would he have been disgusted by this army's refusal to engage an advance guard of Denikin's White Russian troops, and thus secure control of Kyiv? For the city fell to Denikin, and soon after to the Bolsheviks once more. Petliura made his way to Poland and later Paris to set up a Ukrainian government in exile. Those of his men who'd survived a savage typhoid epidemic made their own way home, starving, ragged, penniless.

I want Tomasz never to have crossed the Zbruch, never to have seen Kyiv. During the period of total anarchy in which eastern Ukraine became a handy killing field, it was not only soldiers who died but civilians, among them between 35,000 and 50,000 Jews, victims of a false but frequent equation, made by those who opposed the revolution, of Jews with Bolsheviks. If Tomasz did join Petliura's troops, as my mother says he did, he would have entered Ukraine after the worst of the Ukrainian-authored pogroms—the Russians, White and Red, carried out their own killing sprees against the Jews. If he ever spoke of this carnage, I never heard it. But one of the immigrant men my grandfather knew in Toronto had a story of those brutal times that I've never been able to forget.

A young soldier has by some miracle provided himself with that most rare necessity, a horse. One rainy afternoon he rides his prize up and down the road outside the small village that his unit's camped beside. He's a comical sight, with his uniform in shreds, his swollen feet bare except for the dirty rags he's wound around them. What a fine thing it would be, he tells himself, if he could find a pair of boots, soft leather with thick soles that would last him through the war and take him safely home again. And as he rides his horse up and down the road, he catches sight of two Jews coming towards him, Jews in warm coats, wearing soft, new, leather boots.

I remember this story of a story passed onto me by my mother, but I can't distinguish anymore between what I've imagined and what I was told. As for the ending I'm about to relate, I've been informed that it couldn't have happened, that it's a physical impossibility. What must have occurred would have been far worse, an act of butchery. But this is my "choice of nightmares" or, at least, the version I can't shake from memory:

The two men run into a field of rain-soaked grass, the earth so soft beneath their feet they can hardly keep from sinking into it. They run and run, but they're no match for a man on horseback, a man with rags wound round his feet and a sabre in his hand. It cuts through the younger man's legs as if they were butter, cuts just above the top of the boots. The man falls, but the boots stay upright, planted in grass that's drenched red now, instead of green.

✖◈✖

Some weeks before Tomasz and Olena marry on November 18, 1920, the leaders of the Western Ukrainian National Republic go into exile. Some head for Vienna and others to Paris, where they begin a fruitless campaign to win recognition for their country. But the Entente Powers use the League of Nations to confirm Poland's rights to eastern Galicia, which the Poles rename "Eastern Little Poland." The same year that my grandparents marry, with only a few scraps of land between them, Poland passes a law making it possible for the vast estates of the nobility to be broken up and sold to landless peasants and impoverished farmers. Polish war veterans and ethnically pure Polish settlers "imported" to Galicia are dramatically favoured in this reform: Ukrainians penalized.

In order to control the Ukrainians, who are seen as inherently subversive, the Polish government launches a campaign of forcible assimilation. Ukrainian-language periodicals are shut down, Ukrainian social and cultural organizations are outlawed, and Ukrainians are denied access to any kind of employment in government. Most Ukrainian-language elementary and secondary schools are converted into Polish-language institutions; hard-won Ukrainian lectureships and chairs at the University of Lwow are abolished. Ukrainian students find it almost impossible to attend university, unless they have the means to travel to Prague, where a college has been established for Czechoslovakia's Ukrainian minority, or unless they're willing to risk attending the secret "underground" university set up by Ukrainian teachers and professors in Lwow.

This campaign of forced assimilation is launched by Poles newly liberated from 150 years of colonial rule, Poles who themselves had suffered under foreign powers that had banned the teaching of the

Polish language and attempted to eradicate any expression of Polish culture. I try to see things from the Polish side—the extraordinary difficulties faced by the new republic, hastily pulled out of the top hat of Allied diplomacy, and sandwiched between a newly defeated Germany and a newly emergent Soviet Union. Both these countries had been devastated by war, yet both possessed alarming capacities to recover and threaten their newly reborn neighbour. To call on all people living in Poland—whatever their ethnic derivation, mother tongue, religion or culture—to build a strong and equitable nation proved beyond the powers of those who led the Second Republic. They defined their country's true citizens as those who spoke the Polish language and practised the Roman Catholic faith. What followed were perversions of justice and denials of human rights. Extremists organized boycotts of Jewish businesses and viciously harassed Jewish university students. And in the autumn of 1930— three years after Tomasz Solowski left for Canada—a "pacification" campaign was launched against Ukrainians in Galicia—*pasifikatsia*, to give the word its Polish name.

❈❈❈

> The "pacification" of Ukraine by means of these "puni-
> tive expeditions" is probably the most destructve
> onslaught yet made on any of the national minorities
> and the worst violation of the minorities' treaty. Indeed,
> it is a whole civilization. . . that has been wrecked. . . .

> *The Manchester Guardian Weekly*,
> Friday, October 17, 1930

This worn booklet I hold in my hands my grandfather may also have held. *Western Ukraine Under Polish Yoke: Polonization, Colonization, "Pacification,"* its title proclaims. Published in New York in 1931 by the *Ukrainian Review*, it describes Polish brutalities against Ukrainians in eastern Galicia, brutalities that a special committee of the League of Nations would soon be investigating. At first I shy away from the rhetorical surges, the imperfect English of the booklet's authors, who make no claim to be impartial. And then I find myself arrested by their arguments. Marshalling statistics from Polish government sources, they describe a campaign of violent harassment directed at the largest ethnic minority in eastern Poland. The threat of violence from members of an underground Ukrainian nationalist organization; sabotage of Polish property, especially a wave of fires lit by arsonists throughout the country, not just in Galicia—these formed the rationale for pacification. Yet the booklet makes an intriguing suggestion as to why so many fires were raging: Polish law decreed that all buildings, even the most useless and dilapidated, must be insured through government agencies, often for large sums of money. Arson may thus have become an attractive means of collecting on one's investments in a Depression-plagued Poland.

Whatever the reasons, city and farm buildings, houses and haystacks went up in flames. And Polish militia units were sent in to search villages with large numbers of Ukrainians—villages like Staromischyna.

※◇※

My mother remembers only one visit by the Polish militia, when Olena happened to be off in town. There must have been advance warning of a raid, for everything Ukrainian in their house has disappeared. Olena's father's books, all the embroidered cushions, blouses, towels have been stuffed in a sack and hidden up the chimney. But even so, the children are terrified; they crawl under the bed, listening to horses galloping, shouting, cries. And then, an even more terrifying silence.

When they force themselves to go outside, they see something they can't believe is happening. Their cousin, a boy of thirteen, lies face down on a wagon, and where his buttocks should be is an ooze of blood, cloth, muscle. Whatever skin there was is gone. Neighbours are taking the boy to Pidvolochys'k, the nearest place where a doctor can be found. Perhaps this cousin was one of the boys who'd stolen out one night, collecting pailfuls of manure to paint the village's newly dedicated statue of Poland's national hero, Jozef Pilsudski. Perhaps the soldiers needed a dozen boys to beat, and he was taken to round out the number.

A mess of red jelly, crusted with flies.

❈❖❈

Miss Mary Sheepshanks. I have heard the name before—that of a prominent early feminist, one of those formidable Englishwomen possessed of limitless energy and efficiency. Mary Sheepshanks, secretary of the Women's International League, its headquarters in Geneva, "who personally investigated the situation in Eastern Galicia" and described it in a comprehensive report on *pasifikatsia*. I don't like to admit it, but Miss Sheepshanks gives the booklet I'm reading more authority, all because of her very English surname, the instant credibility it carries.

Miss Sheepshanks's report is admirably concise and dispassionate, despite the photographs that accompany her text: image after image of flayed human skin, always the buttocks, always the same raw lesions, the size of a pair of hands, hollowed like lunar craters.

> In each case the general plan followed was similar and showed clearly that it was ordered by headquarters. In some cases the attack on the village was made by cavalry, in others by police squads; the time chosen was

generally night; the village was surrounded, machine guns set up. Some soldiers were detailed to levy contributions in livestock, grain and sometimes cash from each household. Others forced the villagers to wreck their reading room, library and cooperative store, and for those operations were not allowed tools but had to use their hands which were often torn and bleeding, in fact used to the bone. [T]hey were then made to sign a declaration that they had carried out the demolition on [sic] their own free will.

A third detachment rounded up the leading men of the village, especially the keeper of the cooperative store, the custodian of the reading room and others including the schoolmaster and the priest. These men were then driven into a barn, stripped, held down and beaten with the thick sticks used for threshing. The beating was continued until the men lost consciousness; they then had cold water poured over them and the beating was resumed. Very often 200 or 300 blows were inflicted, so that the flesh was horribly torn, and in the case of the man we saw, the wounds were still unhealed and raw after two months.

. . . One terrible feature of the whole procedure was the refusal of medical treatment to the victims. Doctors were forbidden to go out of the towns to the villages, and peasants attempting to come into the towns for treatment were turned back by the police. In many cases the wounds have gangrened, and either death or life-long injury has resulted.

If Tomasz had acquired a copy of this booklet, if he'd been able to read the English, or found someone to translate it for him, what would he have felt reading the list of "Pacified Towns and Villages

by Counties" and finding under "County ZBARAZ," listed alpha-
betically between Skoryki and Suchowce, "Staromiejszczyzna"?
Finding the very name of the troops who'd beaten his nephew's
buttocks to pulp: "22nd Regiment of Ulans."

It may have been the news of *pasifikatsia* that spurred my grandfather's return to Poland in the late autumn of 1931. Knowing
what I do of Tomasz, I am certain that, had he never left Staromischyna, he would have been one of the two thousand Galicians
arrested during pacification. He would have challenged the
soldiers whom he'd fought against the year before his marriage;
he would also have helped to rebuild what the villagers had been
forced to ransack: the reading rooms and the co-operative stores,
whose records were reconstructed from the memories of debtors
and creditors, so that some kind of normal life could resume in the
pacified villages.

I wonder again at the transgression of my grandparents'
marriage—a Ukrainian marrying a Pole, even a half-Pole and
Ukrainophile, as Tomasz Solowski was. And I wonder, too, what
Tomasz's half-sister Adela will have to tell me—about pacification,
about the borders in her own heart between Ukraine and Poland.
Adela, who, ever since the war, has made her life in Poland, and
who writes to my aunt and mother in a Polish they find increas-
ingly difficult to understand. Writing back, Vira calls upon a
Polish émigré patient to help her, so that the language is correct,
the proper formalities observed. Is there more than the forgetful-
ness imposed by time and distance in my aunt's loss of Polish—
does it have to do with the terror she knew as a child, hiding under
the bed while the 22nd Ulan Regiment rode by? Witnessing what
happened to that young boy, who may or may not have reached
the doctor, the cart jolting along the dreadful roads, avoiding the
police who were ordered to turn it back.

※※※

Despite international pressure the Polish government never condemned its pacification policy; in January 1932, the Council of the League of Nations agreed that Poland's actions could be justified on grounds of the threat posed by Ukrainian saboteurs. Relations between Poles and Ukrainians became more and more impossible. On June 14, 1934, a member of the Organization of Ukrainian Nationalists assassinated Poland's minister of the interior, Bronislaw Pieracki, in Warsaw. The Polish government responded by withdrawing its promise made to the League of Nations to protect the rights of its minority groups and setting up a concentration camp at Bereza Kartuzka, where it interned Ukrainian nationalists and other activists opposed to the regime. Though a rapprochement or "normalization" was later reached between the government and representatives of the largest political party of Ukrainians in Poland, important sectors of both the Polish majority and the Ukrainian minority remained pledged to a policy of violent confrontation.

The atmosphere in 1930s Poland was embattled and extreme: "Social distress in the countryside was acute. Unemployment in Polish industry during the Depression reached 40 per cent. Intercommunal antagonisms, and rising anti-Semitism, caused great anxiety." When World War II broke out, the Red Army crossed the Zbruch once more, into eastern Galicia. After a show of tolerating, even encouraging, Ukrainian language and culture, the Russians cracked down against "bourgeois nationalism," deporting hundreds of thousands of people—Poles and Jews as well as Ukrainians—to their deaths in Siberia. And then the Germans advanced and the Russians fled, leaving Galicia to be recolonized, this time by the Nazis. A maze of different movements formed among Ukrainians; many collaborated with the Germans in the hope of establishing, at last, a free Ukraine. The Ukrainian Insurgent Army emerged, fighting both Nazis and Soviets, and in some areas, members of Poland's underground Home Army. The result was

> a murderous struggle—often encouraged by the Germans and provoked by Soviet partisans—between Ukrainian and Polish forces for territory and to settle old scores.
>
> Tragically, it was the civilian population that bore most of the costs. According to Polish sources, in 1943–44 about 60,000–80,000 Polish men, women and children were massacred in Volhynia by Ukrainians. . . . Ukrainians claim that massacres of their people began earlier, in 1942, when Poles wiped out thousands of Ukrainian villagers in the predominantly Polish areas of Kholm, and that they continued in 1944–45 among the defenseless Ukrainian minority west of the San River. In any case, it is clear that both Ukrainian and Polish armed units engaged in wholesale slaughter, bringing to a bloody climax the hatred that had been increasing between the two peoples for generations.

※◇※

There's no clean cut between old and "new" worlds, Eastern Europe and North America, the luck of those who emigrated before the war, and the fate of those forced to live through or die in it. More and more, my mother tells me, she falls to wondering what would have happened to her had she stayed behind in the Old Place. And while my mother wonders what kind of life she might have had, what sort of husband and children, I, too, fall prey to curiosity. If Olena had waited too long to join her husband in Toronto, or if Tomasz had finally returned to the fields his wife found so difficult to leave—how would the hatred, the bloodshed, that erupted between Ukrainians and Poles at the end of the war have touched my family? How can I understand what they escaped without listening to another family's story, told me by a woman born ten years before me in a village on the river San?

In this small village, Pavlokhoma, Poles and Ukrainians had intermarried for as long as anyone could remember, without there ceasing to be Poles and Ukrainians. There were many marriages like my grandparents', and although the events of the 1930s must have cruelly sharpened the edges of difference, people managed to live together. But wartime—this war, its release of violent hopes and obscene energies—changed everything.

In March 1945, Katrusia was four years old. She had never known anything but the chaos of war, and so it didn't seem strange to be woken in the middle of the night by her brothers. They told her they were off to their grandmother's house by the church, taking with them their youngest brother, a boy of seven. After they left, Katrusia's father came and carried her out to the barn, where her mother was waiting. They had a hideout there, a room with one small window and a door that could be locked from the inside. It was cold and dark: the child became terribly thirsty, and her father left the hiding place to fetch her a cup of milk. Ice crystals had formed on top of the milk—she remembers this distinctly. "It's so cold," she told her father. "Can't you warm it for me?"

Katrusia is sitting with me in a Toronto café; she has been stirring and stirring a cup of black coffee, as if the clink of the spoon allows the words to come out of her mouth. She lifts the coffee to her mouth, then puts it down without drinking; she says she can never forget the look on her father's face when she asked him to warm the cup of milk for her. That long, sorrowful look, and then everything happening at once: noise, light, familiar voices made strange by the sudden hardness in them, the hate. People beating with their fists at the door of the shelter, screaming at them to come out before they toss in a grenade. Suddenly Katrusia's mother is shouting, too, calling and calling the name of her youngest son. And then the men burst in, and one of them shoves the butt of his rifle into the girl's small face, the very tip of the rifle at her nostril, as if forcing her to smell her own death.

Katrusia, her mother and father—they are marched with their hands high over their heads, past the cows and horses, their breath clouding the dark inside the barn. The child would like to warm her hands on the horses' flanks, but the men shove at her with their rifles till she's left the barn and anything resembling shelter. They're marched through the churchyard, the mud between the graves, the bodies lying face down in the mud, all of Katrusia's brothers, even the youngest. His mother moves to lift his corpse out of the mud, but a rifle shoves against her back; it's as much as her husband can do to help her to her feet and into the church where the armed men are pushing them, women and children to the right, men and boys to the left.

A Polish man, dressed in long johns with a cross cut out on his chest, barks at the men to leave the church, single file, and wait outside. Shots ring out all through the night. Children under five are spared, and their mothers and grandmothers. Once, they hear the priest shout to the killers, "Come to your senses, we are all the children of God!" But the shooting goes on and on, they hear it long after the silence starts, silence that means there is no one left to kill. At last the forty women and children are marched off to a neighbouring village. Not a single one cries or cries out as they walk away. They know even then that their sons, brothers and husbands have been killed—by their own uncles and cousins.

They wandered towards the west, Katrusia and her mother. A Jewish man who lived in a place called Bilava sheltered them, Katrusia remembers: how he'd survived all his own would-be killers, she never learned. In Bilava she went to the local school, learning the Polish alphabet and Polish songs and poems; she was even shipped with a busload of schoolmates to Warsaw, on Stalin's seventieth birthday, to see the Great Leader and pray to him for candies. She never knew she was Ukrainian, she tells me, until she and her mother were aboard a boat headed for Canada in January of 1950.

To obtain the papers she needed to emigrate, Katrusia's mother, like my grandmother, had to produce death certificates for those in her immediate family, documents she could only obtain in her home parish of Pavlokhoma. And so she returned to the village she'd left at sunrise one March morning, the year the war ended in Western Europe. Not far from the village, she met the cousin who'd helped murder her children; he invited her aboard his wagon, offering to drive her to the village—she must have come a long way, he said. She never looked at him but kept on walking until she arrived at the office of the village clerk. There was no new surge of wooden crosses in the cemetery—nothing to mark what had happened to the Ukrainians of Pavlokhoma.

When the clerk asked her how her husband and sons had died, she looked him straight in the eye and said, "Bandits." He wrote down "Partisans," meaning the Ukrainian insurgents who, after the massacre at Pavlokhoma, had come to the village by night, setting fire to several houses. Villagers had shot at them, and one was killed when the insurgents shot back. The fires were put out, the insurgents captured and, in what seems an astonishingly civilized measure, merely sent to jail.

She obtained the papers from Pavlokhoma, then set out for Warsaw; her nine previous emigration applications had all been refused, and this time she was determined to succeed. She made her way to the office of the president of the republic and first secretary himself, Boleslaw Bierut, and somehow managed to talk to him face to face. She told him she would not leave his office until he'd personally signed her papers. He did, and she returned to her daughter, packed up their handful of possessions and set out for Canada.

Katrusia smiles at me—her face is pale, her eyes very dark. She waits for a while, and then tells me something that is obviously painful, perhaps more painful than the account she's given of the massacre. "Years later," she says, "when I was at university, I was talking to my mother about something that had nothing to do with Pavlokhoma. Suddenly I was telling her how much I hated Poles. She grabbed my arm—my quiet, gentle mother. 'Don't you ever say that,' she told me. 'Don't ever think like that. It wasn't a nationality that killed your father and your brothers. Remember that. You have Polish blood in you: remember that, too.'"

✖◈✖

Hearing Katrusia's story, I think of how lucky my grandparents were to escape from Poland when they did. As far as I know, Staromischyna was spared the kind of slaughter that happened in Pavlokhoma, but partisans were fighting in the area, and from what my family understands, partisans were involved in the torture of Hannia's son, Tomasz's nephew.

I think of other things as I sit at the café after Katrusia leaves. I think of that part of her story I find as remarkable as her mother's courage. It's the mention of the Jewish man in Bilava, who sheltered Katrusia and her mother when they fled westward. From what I know of the fate of Jews in Poland during World War II, his survival seems miraculous. It makes me wonder how many similar miracles there might have been, and whether Olena's friends might also have found shelter. The friends who ran the store in Pidvolochys'k and to whom she brought cream each week in a sky-blue jug.

13

---

each small hand an open eye

Amid-winter morning, a small meeting room at a Toronto hotel. A friend and I are at the head table, as if this were a wedding. The table's draped in white cloth, so no one can tell whether we're sitting in the calm, ladylike way our mothers have taught us, or whether we're nervously jiggling our legs before we address the thirty women who have come to hear us speak. For this is no wedding but a conference entitled "Jewish Women's Voices." Among the hundreds of women attending the conference—artists and "professionals" and housewives, young, old and middle-aged—I am, if not the only gentile, then the only Ukrainian. Not Ukrainian-Canadian: in this gathering, my carefully gauged identity drops away; I lose the hyphen that has always put time and distance between me and the Old Place, and *what happened over there*.

I am here to make some connection with these women who seem like me, yet come from a culture that my own background has decreed, often in the most violent way, to be Other. Last night I listened with these women to a performance of traditional Yiddish songs, not only lullabies, but verses of defiant hope, expressing how free and rich a woman's life might yet become. It was haunting, this first experience of hearing Yiddish: I knew how few were left of those born in the cradle of that tongue. I had a translation of the lyrics in front of me, but my high school German kept rising up through the originals: out of a twenty years' sleep, words would shake themselves awake, words that moved between both languages, in spite of, because of, history. Listening to this music, I thought of how these women's longings spoke to my own, and to those of other women in my family, now and in the past.

Rhea Tregebov, the friend with me at this oddly bridal table, is from Winnipeg, the multicultural crossroads that writer Vera Lysenko described in her 1954 novel *Yellow Boots*. Part ethnography, part fairy tale, part *roman engagé* (Lysenko was a staunch left-winger from the city's famously political North End), *Yellow Boots* does more than describe the lives of Ukrainian farmers on the Prairies. It shows its heroine escaping the brutality of her peasant father by running off to Winnipeg. There she falls in love with an Austrian-Jewish refugee; the novel ends with their impending marriage on the eve of World War II. In the Winnipeg she grew up in, Rhea has told me, there was a strong solidarity between Jews and Ukrainians, who could speak together in the language of the old country; who ate the same food and often shared the same radical politics. When her grandfather came to visit her in Toronto, Rhea said, he'd complained that the city didn't have enough Ukrainians in it. Talking of her grandfather's fondness for Ukrainians, and of the symbolic marriage in *Yellow Boots*, we asked ourselves why things were so painfully different in Toronto, why our two communities seemed so hostile to each other.

We are here now to initiate some kind of public speech between us, speech based on how ethnicity has shaped our lives. Rhea talks of her family's life in Canada, and of her difficulty in defining herself as a Jewish woman without getting caught in the ethnic trap: a simultaneous sense of exclusion and suffocation. She reads a few of the family poems from her new book, *Mapping the Chaos*. And then, far too soon, it's my turn. I talk of the journey I'll be making to Ukraine to look for traces of my grandparents' lives. I speak a little of the hardness of those lives, the deaths of Tomasz and Olena's youngest children, the long years of separation between husband and wife. I tell of Polish soldiers bayonetting sacks of provisions, embroidered pillows, making a snow of flour and feathers. And I mention my grandmother's friend Helka, the little I know of her and her husband, a tall man named Blumen.

Woman after woman puts up her hand: "You were telling my grandmother's story." "My family came from just that part of Poland." "There's so much that's the same, between us. But the differences—"

There's something in this last speaker's voice that arrests me— not bitterness, or anger, but something like the sharpness of shadow on a bright summer's day. It reminds me of the fate of those Jews who, unlike my family, didn't manage to leave Poland before World War II; it makes me realize that the Old Place I've imagined to be mine alone belongs to others, too. That when I actually travel to Staromischyna, Pidvolochys'k, I must look not just for the ghosts of my grandparents, but also for whatever traces I can find of Helka and Blumen. What comes home to me, as I sit at this bridal table, talking to the women who've come up to introduce themselves, is that I'll have to start exploring for those traces here and now. That this connection I'm trying to make between myself and these women, between Jews and Ukrainians, began a long way back, so long ago I have almost forgotten that it began at all.

※◇※

The Toronto I grew up in was White, Anglo-Saxon, Protestant. Whiteness, in those days, had to do with your skin colour, of course, but also with whether you came from the "right" part of

Europe—the western and northern rather than the eastern or southern parts. It had to do, as well, with whether English was your mother tongue. In our royal suburb of split-levels and swimming pools, to be WASP was *de rigueur*. On the day my family moved in, one of the neighbours, a Clairol blonde with painted fingernails like ten cheerful hemorrhages, came over to say hello. When my mother introduced herself, the neighbour said, "I thought people with names like yours cleaned the houses of people with names like ours." It wasn't meant maliciously; malice requires energy. But my mother could never un-hear the message folded into that remark: *you're not one of us; you don't belong here.* The same warning she'd heard when she lived in dark, narrow houses on Manning or Shaw or Queen Street back in the thirties, when her father lay in bed with a damaged spine and her mother refused to apply for relief, lest the whole family be shipped straight back to Poland.

Growing up Ukrainian in pre-multicultural Toronto meant being part of a community fissured by differences in politics, religion and degrees of foreignness. People whose ancestors had homesteaded on the Prairies in the 1890s often spoke a different language from those who'd escaped Galicia in the twenties or thirties, or had been shipped to Canada from DP camps after World War II. Yet however many internal divisions the community possessed, it united against the *Angliky* trying to assimilate it; we shared a strong sense of what was *nashi*, or our own. *Nashi* was both consolation prize and rallying cry. When I went with my friends from Ukrainian school to the Folkdance Festival at the Exhibition each August, we'd save our true applause for *nashi*— men in red boots, embroidered shirts and ballooning trousers, performing their astounding kicks and leaps. When the Scottish lassies followed with their meek and stilted bouncings, we would sniff, "They call that *dancing*?"

My friend Rhea, who attended a Hebrew day school in Winnipeg, had identified Ukrainians as "people like us"—marginal people who

weren't WASP. But the only Jewish person I knew while I was growing up, the only person I really knew as being "other" like myself,
was Anne Frank. When I was twelve or thirteen I watched, at my
mother's insistence, the film version of *The Diary of a Young Girl*. I
can remember disliking the actress who played Anne—she was
perky-pretty and far too old. But what seized hold of me was one
blurred, grainy sequence in which Anne dreams she hears a friend
calling out to her from the camp the Franks escaped by going into
hiding. I've never forgotten Anne's relief on waking—relief that it
was all only a dream. And, instantly, her shock of understanding: this
horrific dream was her friend's waking life.

When the bookmobile came to our street that week, I searched
for Anne's diary. Later I picked up a paperback copy, the first book
I ever bought for myself. It became my companion: Anne Frank,
my shadow self. Reading her words over and over, I heard her
speaking my own feelings about my parents, adolescence, the self
I wanted to become. Though she was German and Dutch and I,
Canadian; though she was from a Jewish and I a Ukrainian family,
we were the same, somehow: the same age, with the same
thoughts, the same desires. Except for the other voice I heard
when reading her diary, the voice of History with a capital H,
meaning something you can't undo or wish away. When I learned
of what the introduction to the diary called "the Final Solution,"
two things came home to me: Anne had been murdered, along
with millions of other people, just for being. What happened to
the Franks could have happened to us; Anne's death could have
been my own.

This identifying with another is one of the most powerful experiences I have ever had. I might have felt the same on seeing a film
about a girl who perished in the Ukrainian famine of 1932–33, had
such a film existed. But it was Anne Frank whom I met in imagination and in the desolate corridors that were my dreams. I began
to look out for books written about the Holocaust, which I came,

much later, to call the Shoah. Long before I ever set foot in Kyiv, I made a pilgrimage to Amsterdam, going through the restored rooms of Anne Frank's hiding place as if I were finally visiting the home of a best friend. The actual, material house of a friend whose actual, material body had been made, in the most brutal way possible, to vanish.

※◇※

"You don't know how Jews talk about Ukrainians!" I'm told when, aged fourteen, I try to speak up at some youth club meeting or dinner table when the talk turns to the influence or wealth of Toronto's Jews. No, I admit, I don't—but even if Jews do speak badly of Ukrainians, how does that make it right for us to bad-mouth them? I was born in Canada; why should I be bound by the prejudices of the village, the *selo*? What reason have I to condemn or suspect Jewish people?

Two years later I hear something far more disturbing on this subject of Ukrainians and Jews. I am downtown, perhaps by the Greek Orthodox Cathedral on Bathurst Street, waiting for a bus with a friend. Like me, she has an English first name and a Ukrainian surname, but she was born out west, and her ancestors left the *selo* ninety years ago or more. Someone walks up to the bus stop across the street and waits there, just as we are doing, but for a bus going in the opposite direction. A boy our own age, though he seems to have stepped out of a different century. We are in minidresses; he wears a long black coat and a wide-brimmed black hat. Our hair is cut to look like Twiggy's; at the sides of his face hang dark, thick coils. They remind me of the ringlets worn by early Victorian heroines—this is what I'm thinking as my friend says, in a voice I've never heard from her before, "Look at the *Zhyd*."

It's not just the ugly tone of her voice but her use of the Ukrainian word that shakes me; suddenly it's as if we're standing not on a

Toronto street, but in the mud of some forlorn provincial town in
Eastern Europe. I move away from her—luckily the bus is crowded
by the time it pulls up, and I don't have to sit next to her on the
way home. Or perhaps this is how I've refashioned memory,
perhaps we did sit side by side, chatting about schoolwork or fashions. But I've never forgotten that spontaneous expression of
learned contempt. And I make myself remember that I—the reader
of Anne Frank—said nothing back to her. Not even, "What makes
you talk that way?" I said nothing that might have challenged her,
made her think about her own experience with Jews, or lack of it.

When I visit Israel twenty-six years later, I think again of that
Ukrainian-Canadian girl and her compatriot, a ringleted boy
whom I now know to have been an Orthodox Jew. A Belgian
friend, a recent immigrant to Israel who has picked up fluent
Hebrew within a year of settling in Haifa, takes me to Mea
She'Arim, where the ultra-Orthodox Jews of Jerusalem live. As we
walk through streets where there isn't a sapling, a patch of grass,
even an empty flowerpot to be seen, we encounter groups of men
dressed just as the boy at the Toronto bus stop had been. They
look straight through us as they pass us by with contracted,
hurried steps. They look through us, not as though we don't exist,
but as though we shouldn't, such women as we are, in trousers and
jackets, our heads bare.

My friend speaks scathingly about these men and the culture
they represent. "They're trying to tyrannize the whole city—
they'd like every woman off the street and stuck in a kitchen, with
twelve kids under her feet and a ladle instead of a book in her
hands." It's all right for my friend to say these things—it's even all
right for me to feel outraged, simply as a woman, with no particular heritage behind me. And yet I feel, too, how easy it must be
first to fear and then hate what appears to threaten you. I don't
want the power of that ease, its ready energy.

A few days later, when I walk round the Dome of the Rock and look down at the gardens below, things become more complicated still. I see a Palestinian family having a picnic in the shade. My friend had refused to take me into the Palestinian section of Jerusalem—there'd been an incident a few days before my arrival. Demonstrations are going on right now, right-wing Jews opposed to the visit of an Arab leader, a new turn in the endless negotiations that must have been named by Adman Adam—the peace process. So I stand at the edge of a terraced garden, my hands on a block of that golden stone from which Jerusalem is built, observing this family's quiet meal. Watching the women serving their husbands, and then their children before finally sitting down to eat, a little ways apart from the men. As if they were there on sufferance, however tender.

※◇※

At about the time I discovered Anne Frank, my parents sent me to a Ukrainian summer camp not far from Toronto. The girls slept in the old farmhouse and in an oversized garage where tractors and harvesters had formerly been kept; the boys had a special "barracks" set aside for them well down the road. A small tin-roofed church with onion domes had been built for us to attend on blistering Sunday mornings. The farm buildings were torn down long ago; a cultural centre and a cemetery cover the orchard, the fields of waist-high grass we once pretended into steppes.

In those long-ago summers we spent at Camp Kyiv, we'd be gathered into the barn each afternoon for something called *zbirka*. We'd sit in alternate rows of girls and boys, being drilled on Ukrainian history from the days of the princes of Kyivan Rus' to the time of Skoropadsky and Petliura. The heat was stifling; to keep themselves awake, the boys would tease from the long pony-tails or braids of the girls in front of them a single strand of hair. With it, they'd try to lasso the fat, bumbling flies that, unlike us, were free to move the length and width of the barn. Only once did I see a boy actually tie up a fly with a long black hair so that it circled the head of the girl in front of him, a helpless satellite.

Always, we would be asked questions during *zbirka*, questions having to do with the lessons we were being taught. If we answered correctly, in good Ukrainian, candies would be tossed to us. Once, the lecture was on the coming of Christianity to Ukraine. A counsellor, sixteen years out of a displaced persons camp in Austria, shouted the story to us through a megaphone. Long ago, she explained, when the people were still childish in their ways and worshipped Perun, the god of lightning and thunder, the True God put it into the head of Prince Volodymyr to convert his people. Accordingly, the prince sent out envoys the length and breadth of the known world to study the faiths of those who worshipped the One God. The envoys found the ceremonies of the Roman Catholics paltry compared to the ancient rites of the Khazars. Back came reports of magnificent temples, of raised podiums like celestial stages from which the Torah would be read; of the bells hanging from the silver *rimmonims*, named after that most jewel-like fruit, the pomegranate.

All of this nearly convinced Prince Volodymyr to convert himself and his people to Judaism. But before he could do so, the remaining envoy, who'd been kidnapped by Black Sea pirates on his return from Constantinople, burst into the audience hall and dropped to his knees. For a full hour, he sang the praises of the church of the emperor of Byzantium—the clouds of incense, the brilliant mosaics and jewel-encrusted icons, the magnificent singing of the congregation, voices deep as the bottom of the sea. Only these rites were worthy of a Grand Prince of Rus'. And so Ukraine, which had come within a hair's breadth of embracing Judaism, adopted Byzantine Christianity. The images of Perun were beaten with willow switches and thrown into rivers, where the fish ate through their eyes and the dark dissolved them.

I can't help now but entertain impossibilities. What would have happened if that last envoy had been beheaded by pirates, or had failed in eloquence before Prince Volodymyr? If Ukrainians had become Jews, and there was a common faith, instead of eons of ignorance and suspicion between us?

※◇※

To be Ukrainian, or to claim Ukrainian descent, is to belong to what Polish thinker Adam Michnik has described as "the most tragic nation in Europe." Part of this tragedy has to do with Ukrainians having been, for so many centuries, a viciously colonized people. But the tragedy also has to do with an equally vicious anti-Semitism that became an integral part of life, not only in what is now Ukraine, but in Russia and much of Eastern Europe, too. I learned nothing about pogroms and their causes at Saturday morning Ukrainian school—it's not a subject easily taught to children. The hostility between Ukrainians and Jews was something I began to puzzle through much later, after I thought I'd left my ethnicity behind.

When I was a graduate student at the University of Sussex, in the south of England, studying English literature under the shelter of my husband's safely English name, I became friends with a student working in religious studies. He had a stutter that made you think of a butterfly's stagger, and he wrote like an angel with a devil's sense of humour. He asked my husband and me to tea one summer afternoon at the portion of a house he was renting just under the Downs: he asked us to make the tea and carry it to the table when we arrived, as it was *shabbes* and he was strict in his observance. We drank our tea and then went for a walk in the garden. Somehow we got onto the subject of names, and I confessed that under the easy-to-pronounce Keefer was a tricky one, Kulyk. Ukrainian, I explained. He looked at me for a moment, holding onto his wispy beard as if a bee were caught in it. And then he said, "Ah, Bohdan Khmelnytsky. The Great Killer of Jews." I learned then how differently the same story can be told: that Khmelnytsky, whom my Ukrainian school teachers had taught me to revere as the creator of the first autonomous Ukrainian state since the Mongol invasions, as the hetman who'd liberated us from our near-slavery to the Poles, "well-named Bohdan, given by God," was to Jews an archfiend and architect of horrendous pogroms.

I came across Khmelnytsky in another story, many years later, while staying at the house of another Jewish friend who, like me, has Eastern European connections. I had just flown to England from Canada and was plagued by jet lag: awake at three in the morning, I crept downstairs to search the bookshelves for something to read. *Wartime Lies*, a novel by a New York writer, Louis Begley, caught my eye. The book tells the story of a Jewish boy named Maciek, born, like generations of his family, in Poland; it describes his coming of age during World War II. He survives by passing for a gentile in the company of his Aryan-looking aunt. Maciek's entire existence, his past and even his future, all become a lie, the denial of who and what he really is.

I was stunned, as I read, by the pain of lives destroyed or damaged past any mending. I was stunned, too, reading of the part played in all this terror by people Begley refers to as "Ukrainians"—the peasants who, long before the war, murder Jews in village pogroms and then, as members of the auxiliary police, do the Nazis' dirty work for them, rounding up civilian survivors of the Warsaw Uprising in 1944, loading them onto trains for Auschwitz, beating men and children, raping women. "The Ukrainians were like wild animals," Begley has a Polish officer say. Next to them the Germans appear inhuman rather than bestial—they stand still as statues while their peasant henchmen commit one atrocity after another.

It's when Maciek, in his role as gentile schoolboy, writes compositions on the theme of "the long Polish struggle against the Ukrainian invaders," that the ghost of Khmelnytsky appears, and with it an age-old fear and loathing of Ukrainians, on the part of Poles as well as Jews. Raised as I've been on another theme— the long Ukrainian struggle against Polish colonizers—what was I to make of this? For me, the question wasn't academic: in more ways than one, this was a book I could not put down. I knew that many Ukrainians committed atrocities against Jews during the war, but I was shocked by Begley's apparent assumption concerning those Ukrainians he portrays: that they commit crimes against humanity not because they happen to be brutes and thugs, but simply because they're Ukrainian.

I stayed up till dawn with *Wartime Lies*, in a trance of exhaustion and despair. Even though I was sitting safe in a friend's living room on the Sussex coast, I felt dangerously close to the world the novel evokes with such beauty and horror. Maciek is from eastern Poland: the "T" where he lives may even be Ternopil', the city closest to Staromischyna. What I craved on that rainy, blustery morning was more than sleep: I longed for permanent flight and forgetting. What I've realized since is that I can't flee; my feet are locked. Even if I burned all the papers, the passports and land deeds that connect me with the Old Place, even if I tried to hide my maiden name, it will always be there, the deep ditch of nightmare. It is part of who I am and where I come from; one of the landmarks on a journey I can't help but undertake.

❌◇❌

When I attended that conference of Jewish women in Toronto, I understood, for the first time, how complicated my journey to the Old Place would be, and how little I really knew of what I would be looking for. I began to read whatever I could find on how Jews and Ukrainians in Galicia had perceived each other over the centuries, living as they did in a "markedly warped" society where almost all

Jews had to work in commerce or whatever industry existed, while almost all Ukrainians had no choice but to be peasants. What more predictable stereotype, then, than the moneylender who charges up to 250 per cent interest on a loan, or the tavernkeeper who entices the innocent peasant into the *korchma* where he drinks away any money he's scraped up and, as often as not, his house, his cow and his fields as well? And what could be less surprising than the stereo-typical peasant—not innocent but backwards and brutish, tackling pogroms and home brew with equal appetite. Straw-stuffed figures from folklore and proverbs, hand puppets taken apart by scholars who've shown that "the Jews of Galicia were, on the whole, in straits as wretched as the peasants." That, being a "vulnerable, dispersed minority," they sided with the Poles, "indisputably the ruling nation in Galicia," rather than with the Ukrainians. And that the hostility Ukrainians showed towards Jews was a product not of genetics but of economics and empire.

Vital as such knowledge is, I find it almost too easy, or at least abstract. I need to translate "the Jews of Galicia" into my grand-parents' friends, Helka and Blumen; I need a sense of life lived under the pressure of the moment—closeups, not distance shots. I need another kind of guide than historians now: someone who is both intimate with and a stranger to this world that's mine by inheritance and imagination. I find Isaac Babel, who writes so enchantingly and alarmingly of his boyhood in pre-revolutionary Odessa, in a milieu of Jewish merchants, mothers and bandits. Babel, with whom I fell in love in my early twenties: that perfec-tionist among the makers of short fiction, who declared, "No steel can pierce a heart so icily as a period placed in the right place." The scholar who refashioned himself into a cossack who could sleep on the bare ground and run a sabre through a goose to get his dinner. That same cossack who, in the summer of 1920, crossed the river Zbruch into eastern Galicia, skirting the very edges of my family's Old Place.

When Babel deals with the Jews of Galicia, it's as though he were writing with the tip of a knife, nicking not paper, but skin. In the first story of *Red Cavalry*, "Crossing the Zubrich," his narrator describes the night of "frightened misery" he spent in a Jewish home. Dreaming of bullets piercing a man's head, the newly made cavalryman wakes to find fingers groping his face. They belong to the pregnant woman who lives in the filthy chaos her house has become. She tells the narrator that she's woken him because his shouting and kicking were disturbing her father's rest:

> Her skinny legs and round belly rise from the floor, and she removes the blanket. . . . A dead old man lies there. His throat has been torn out, his face chopped through the middle; blue blood lies in his beard like a piece of lead.
>
> "Sir," the Jewish woman says, shaking the feather-bed, "the Poles were cutting him up and he begged them: 'Kill me outside in the courtyard,' he begged them. 'I don't want my daughter to see me die.' But they did it their way and he passed away in this room, worrying about me. And now I want to know," the woman says, with terrible force, "I want to know whether it is possible to find another father like him anywhere in the world."

❈

The pregnant woman of Babel's story, the unborn child who has already been witness to horrors, are members of a community that had been a part of Polish life from the early Middle Ages on. For Europe's persecuted Jews had found a longstanding haven in Poland—a barbed haven, with cities like Warsaw and Krakow periodically expelling their Jewish populations, and pogroms no rare occurrence throughout the country. But Polish rulers extended privileges and guarantees of protection to the Jews, and when Poland was partitioned in 1772, the part of it that came under Austrian rule proved a far safer place for them than the Russian-occupied part of the country.

Did Helka's and Blumen's ancestors come to Pidvolochys'k from Germany or Russia? What kind of world did they live in, as Jews? All I know from my family is that Helka and her husband were fine people, with whom my mother and aunt felt comfortable—people, it seems, very much like Tomasz and Olena. But I want something more than this—I want the kind of detail that has come down to me about my own family's lives. I find such detail in Theo Richmond's *Konin*, with its amazingly rich account of Jewish life in Poland before World War II. But it's a picture book that offers me the most immediate and haunting glimpse of this vanished world, a book given me by my friend in Haifa.

To Give Them Light is a collection of Roman Vishniac's photographs of Eastern European Jews, all of them taken in the late 1930s. The pictures are luminously dark, more black than white. The black of old women's kerchiefs and of the long coats and broad-brimmed hats worn by pious men. The black of miserable basement flats in which whole families managed to live with their cooking pots and bedding and a few sticks of furniture. For there are only a handful of well-dressed people in these photographs: women with smart hats and handbags tucked under their arms as they make their way through an open-air market. Most often you see many-times-mended trousers, jackets with holes like little puckered mouths. They belong to peddlers, milkmen, lemonade and potato vendors, porters, shawled market women presiding over piles of stark white radishes. People possessed by a poverty that drenches them through, from the babies to the ancient men.

My grandmother walked to town twice a week, carrying cream

to Helka's house in Pidvolochys'k. Perhaps Helka lived on a street like this sloping cobbled one, in Vishniac's photograph of Slonim. "Jewish street," the caption reads. Severe facades, their stucco stained, eaten through in many places. Would Olena have gone past children like this pair, one barefoot, the other shod, carrying a huge wicker basket filled with lettuce? Would she have nodded to these thin women, buckets weighing their bare arms, dresses dark as the shadows flooding from the houses? Or would she have found herself in a less solid neighbourhood, a place like this part of Przeworsk, a small town in eastern Galicia: gouged wooden fences, sunlight staggering across cracked stones?

I search through every photograph in Vishniac's book, but nowhere do I catch sight of them: a tall thin man, a woman with hair that I know would show up red, brilliant red, even in black and white.

※◇※

The ghettos of Eastern Europe were each a little patch of desert "where no green thing would grow." Jews were forbidden by their Christian masters to own land or houses; to grow their own vegetables, or practise any trade but usury. And though they were allowed to gather sticks for firewood, they might not saw a plank, in case this led to building.

Bruce Chatwin, *The Songlines*

It is to the immense credit of the Jews, Bruce Chatwin believed, that they are wanderers, not settlers: conceptual nomads possessing what the German-Jewish poet Heinrich Heine called "'a portable kingdom' which could only exist in men's hearts." Yet

Roman Vishniac's photographs show how tenaciously the Jews of Eastern Europe kept house, even in the wretchedest of cellars. The cover of a memoir by Oskar Pinkus, a Jewish survivor of the Shoah, portrays his family's house in the Polish village of Losice, 80 per cent of whose eight thousand inhabitants were Jews, their ancestors having settled there over four hundred years ago. One of the most desolating parts of this memoir describes the work the Nazis forced Pinkus to perform as a "cleaner" of the houses that had belonged to the Jews of his birthplace. He had to throw onto scrapheaps those most personal, least commercial possessions: photographs and books belonging to friends and neighbours. And finally his own family albums, his own small, dearly bought library.

It was the deep-rootedness of the Jewish presence in Poland's cities and small towns that so often inspired fear and hatred. And by the 1930s, as Abraham Brumberg relates in his own memoir of prewar Poland, anti-Semitism was rampant. "Jewish stores were attacked, and their owners beaten up; Jewish students were forced to occupy special 'ghetto benches' in the universities and were preyed upon by razor-wielding bands of hoodlums. The government advocated policies designed to make the country *Judenrein*." Prewar Poland, as Brumberg describes it, was "a poor and fairly backward country where a great many people believed that Jews had killed Christ and used gentile children's blood for baking matzo on Passover."

In a village as small as Staromischyna, where children were taught that they could recognize the devil by his coal-black skin, what did people believe about Jews? "Our parents never tried to turn us away from anyone," Vira tells me. "Polish people, Jewish people—our parents never spoke against anyone for their religion, their culture, the colour of their skin." When she first came to Canada, Vira says, she fell in love with a Jewish girl at her school, a girl named Mali, who had beautiful curly hair. "I told Mali I was Jewish, so that she would be my friend." I remember being told, once, how Vira used to walk home from university with a fellow student, a young Jewish man. They would stand in front of his door or hers, lost in some fine point of pathology, while their mothers watched anxiously from their upstairs windows, finally dispatching an older sister, a younger brother, to break up the discussion.

I believe my aunt when she tells me that her parents never spoke against Jews or any other group of people. I also believe that prejudice can speak such subtle languages that to eradicate it can seem, at times, like those impossible tasks set in fairy tales. Harvesting a basket of strawberries from snowbound fields, picking a handful of millet seeds out of a mountain of barley.

※◈※

In Camden Town, at the London Jewish Museum, I walk through rooms brimming with small children filling out activity sheets, copying down information about the various objects on display. There's a group of older kids with a guide who can be no more than fifteen. He's explaining the building blocks of anti-Semitism, speaking about the blood libel, something the kids find impossible to credit, judging from the puzzlement that creases their faces. We are standing in a room hung with photographs of synagogues from all over the world—India and the Philippines, Paris and Amsterdam. None from Ukraine, and only the ruins of one from Poland. The photographs are filled with extraordinary light—azure, ochre, sea green.

Among the photographs and oil paintings on display in the museum, the beautifully painted marriage contracts, the banners of bakers' unions, I am looking for something that might have belonged to my grandmother's friend Helka. There's nothing—until I enter the topmost room, where I find a glass case, a shelf of small, shining things. Some are shaped like a keyhole arch, a circle on top of a square; others are hands or gloves, cut off at the wrist and delicately patterned with the smallest leaves and branches. They are amulets, I read: Jews in Eastern Europe often wore them to protect themselves against sickness, misfortune and the dangers of childbirth.

I stand by the display case, as close as I can without alarming the guard. I stare at the paper-thin gold and silver hands, thinking of Helka and Blumen. My mother has told me that after the war, someone from the Old Place wrote to Olena, telling her what had happened when the Germans came in 1941. The Jews of Pidvolochys'k, the letter said, had all been massacred. I know that many Ukrainians assisted the Nazis in their butchery and treated their own people with great cruelty. I also know that the majority kept their heads low and tried to survive. When the Jews who'd lived so long among them were rounded up and marched to their deaths, Ukrainians shut their eyes or looked away, as did so many others in Germany or France or Italy. But only in Ukraine and Poland was the penalty for helping Jews immediate execution— your own and your family's.

The amulets stare back at me under their wall of glass, each small hand an open eye, reminding me that of the 3.5 million Jews living in Poland in 1939, one-tenth of 1 per cent survived the war. I want so badly to believe that Helka and Blumen escaped somehow, that they left for North America before the war broke out or, failing this, found shelter on some isolated farm. Did they have parents living with them? Did they have children—if so, how many, and how young were they when the war began? Yet how can I pray that Helka and Blumen and their family survived, and not their friends and neighbours, too? Because theirs are the names I know; they are the people my family remembers, if only slenderly. They are the ones I hope for now.

Not all Ukrainians shut their eyes or looked away when their neighbours were sent to be slaughtered. The head of the Ukrainian Greek Catholic Church, Metropolitan Andrei Sheptytsky, had originally welcomed the Germans as liberators from the Soviets, who had ruled his homeland so brutally from 1939 to 1941. But a year after the Nazis marched into L'viv, Sheptytsky wrote to Himmler, protesting the genocide against the Jews. He also authored an epistle that was read out in all churches under his jurisdiction, including the Church of St. Nikolai in Staromischyna. In this epistle he forbade the shedding of innocent blood, and threatened with divine punishment all who made themselves "outcasts of human society by disregarding the sanctity of man." Sheptytsky did more than this: he organized 500 nuns, monks and priests to save the lives of between 150 and 200 Jewish children, including two sons of the rabbi of L'viv. One of these children has passed down to us what Sheptytsky told him: "I want you to be a good Jew, and I am not saving you for your own sake. I am saving you for your people. I do not expect any reward, nor do I expect you to accept my faith."

It took me thirty years since first reading the diary of Anne Frank to learn about this extraordinary man. It may have been too soon after the war for my teachers at Ukrainian school or summer camp to have known about Andrei Sheptytsky and the children he helped to survive. But surely it's different for children growing up in Ukrainian communities in North America today—surely they now learn about this man, those children, and all the ones who didn't survive in that time and place? And surely Jewish children—like the ones I saw in the Camden Town museum as I looked for traces of Helka and Blumen—learn not only of the cossack leader Khmelnytsky, but also of Andrei Sheptytsky?

Learn so that they'll embrace "the best possibilities for a dialogue that is healing rather than divisive, and for understanding that is genuine and mutual." Imagining themselves past "the ruts of prejudice and hatred"; imagining themselves inside each other's skin.

※◇※

In Poland, Jews were legally banned from owning land, though some could circumvent these laws, and a very few possessed estates on a par with those of the Polish upper class. But most Jews were landless. Some felt this exclusion keenly: many of them left, or dreamed of setting out for Palestine.

One of the most poignant stories I've heard about Jewish emigration from Eastern Europe has to do not with *Eretz Israel*, but with the Canadian prairies. In 1884 the settlement of "New Jerusalem" was founded by a group of Polish Jews in Saskatchewan. By 1927—the year Tomasz Solowski hopped a freight car from Saskatoon to Toronto—these Jewish agricultural settlements had been largely abandoned. This wasn't because Jews were inept at farming, but because the Dominion Land Act, favouring dispersed settlements in the west, contravened the social requirements of Orthodox Judaism. The need for *mikvehs, minyans, shochets*; the need for Jewish schools and a larger pool of suitable marriage partners—these forced Jews off the land and into urban centres. Today, fewer than a hundred Jewish families are farming on the prairies, and yet the presence there of even that near-hundred seems to me a signal flag for dreams and their translation into possibility.

I think of my grandfather, newly arrived in Canada and refusing to be treated worse than the cattle of the farmer he's been sent to work for. I imagine him walking all one moonlit night towards the nearest railway depot, passing the abandoned homesteads of these Jewish farmers, or perhaps seeing a light from one of the windows of a house that hasn't yet been left. Say that he knows it is a Jewish house he is passing; say that the people in it hail from the same corner of Poland, the same district in Galicia that he, too, has left behind to make a larger, freer life. Say that though they are Jews and he half-Pole and half-Ukrainian, he feels a bond with them, as they, watching from their window, feel connected to him. Say that he waves his hand in greeting as he walks past, and that they return the salutation. And make it—story as it is, only imagined, only just possible—a beginning.

IV

Journeying In

What else should our lives be but a continual series of beginnings, of painful settings out into the unknown, pushing off from the edges of consciousness into the mystery of what we have not yet become. . . .

David Malouf, *An Imaginary Life*

14

the imagination of disaster

When I speak of the Old Place I always talk of returning somewhere I have never been. I know I'm not the only one to do so. Ours is an age of exiles, migrants, refugees. How many children have been haunted by the ghost of belonging? By foreign photographs and documents, by names of strangers who are somehow family, by a strange language that would once have been their mother tongue? How many have grown up not in a haunted house, but haunted by another home?

For Ukrainians and their descendants, this haunting has been chronic and acute. Those seven million people who left their stateless country in the past 120 years for places as far-flung as Paraguay and Novaya Zemlya have been driven by something between a duty and a longing to keep alive the idea of a homeland, the possibility of return. During the Soviet regime, many travelled to Ukraine, if their papers allowed them to do so safely. I had schoolfriends, children of postwar DPs or descendants of the first Ukrainian pioneers in the Canadian west, who went "back" in the seventies. They spoke loud Ukrainian in the Russified streets of Kyiv or Kharkiv, and sprayed liberationist graffiti on Soviet-style buildings. Their elders were more circumspect, quietly finding ways to elude the Intourist authorities and visit relatives in villages unreachable except by atrocious roads and heavy bribes.

Well before *glasnost*, my aunt Vira tried to go back to Staromischyna, but though she managed to slip away from her tour group, the driver she'd found to take her home backed out at the last moment. It was too dangerous, he said. The authorities were paranoid about military security: there might be soldiers on manoeuvre nearby, and if foreigners were caught with cameras, or simply talking to villagers, there'd be trouble. Besides, everything had changed since the war: what of the old ways would be left for her to see? Vira spent the day of her homecoming weeping in a dingy hotel room, whether out of disappointment or relief, it's difficult to tell.

✖◈✖

"The wind won't take them, the water won't take them: keep your fields to come home to one day." So Olena's neighbours advised her. They are gone now, these neighbours, but the fields remain, no longer in Poland but in the newly independent nation of Ukraine, where I'll soon be heading with my husband and our youngest son. Knowing that we're leaving for this journey, friends send newspaper clippings they think we'll find useful, or prudently alarming. About the "Vodka Line," a global-market version of the Iron Curtain that separates rapidly westernized Poland from a still stagnant Ukraine. About the horrendous degree of graft and corruption in Ukraine. About a Canadian court that has convened there, in the village of Selidove, to investigate war crimes allegedly carried out by two men who have since become citizens of Canada.

Corruption isn't new in Ukraine; it flourished under the Soviets and their Tsarist predecessors. Nor are war crimes unique to that country. And yet I'm filled with a heaviness I can't shake off. The more whimsical newspaper stories—concerning, for example, the attachment of Ukrainians to *salo*, or rendered pork fat, held to be a cure against Chornobyl radiation as well as a gourmet's ne plus ultra—make me despair: is this the only way the West can see Ukraine? Not as the home of scholars and artists and scientists, but of thieves, killers and pork fat cures?

I have heard of extraordinary changes taking place now in Ukraine: the passing of liberal laws concerning minorities, and the signing of a historic friendship treaty with Poland. Relations between Jews, Ukrainians and Poles seem, in fact, to have improved dramatically since Ukraine acquired independence. The country's Jewish population numbers 400,000: many of its members hold prominent positions at various levels of government. And while there are extreme nationalists to be found in the western part of the country, they have no political power. Their hatred is real enough but quite impartial; they direct it towards all minorities. Of the former Soviet republics, Ukraine, I'm told, is the one "in which Jews have said they feel safest."

I can imagine how difficult it must have been to initiate these changes; how precarious their future must be in an underdeveloped country struggling with the burden of a catastrophic past. Reading of Ukraine in the clippings our friends have sent us, hearing some report of the country through people who've worked or travelled there, I make an involuntary, uneasy connection. For however Canadian I know myself to be, I feel defined in some way by this other country I've hardly set foot in, whose language I can barely speak. It's as though I looked down on a bright day to discover I had two different shadows, leaning in opposite directions, touching only at the base. Neither sketches my true shape. They will never merge into one. But I know that both will always be part of me, and that this journey I'm about to undertake is another way of looking for my shadows.

There are others who must feel as I do, having made this journey, pulled by something tough yet slender as a runner root. Shortly after the collapse of the Soviet Union, a Toronto painter named Natalka Husar travelled to Ukraine with her mother, to the town of Skalat, in the *dekanat* or deanery where Staromischyna lies. They were looking for the house where Natalka's mother had been born seventy years earlier. *Black Sea Blue*, the paintings that emerged from this journey, reveal the confusion of love and guilt that makes up the kind of haunting called *belonging*. A word that's both an outstretched hand and a fist clenched round your heart, a fist that won't let go.

※◇※

Torn Heart

Too much going on and on in this painting. Till everything blurs or is swaddled to death in shiny bedsheet-tablecloths. A Madonna points to the place where her heart should be, but there's nothing under the blood-coloured dress but a heat-pump glow. A huge table is spread for a feast but only a wreck remains: punctured cans, gnawed bones, smeared plates. Two sisters sit at this table, one with smooth-sprayed North American hair, the other head-scarfed, with teeth rotting behind gold caps, and lips painted that same red the missing sacred heart should be. In the middle of all the stained linen, lace curtains, pseudo-oriental rugs, a shadowy blue hand pokes through a hole, the one entrance to or exit from a Niagara of plunder.

White bucks, purple stiletto heels, nail polish, nylon stockings, compacts of beige pressed powder and the striped plastic tote bags out of which they've spilled, the stripes a parody of prison bars. The sister who got away before the war, who made it to Canada and who returns bearing gifts to the sister she left behind, the sister who has become a broken mirror of everything the other abandoned.

�֎֎

How to summarize the history of this country I'm heading for? Centuries of forced submission to one or another foreign power; centuries of betrayals and lost battles. In the last seventy years alone, mass executions and selective murders of political and cultural leaders. The deaths, due to Stalin's famine, of between five and seven million people and, due to Hitler's war, of another six million, so that, by some estimates, "the wars, famine and purges which occurred during the first half of the 20th century cost the lives of over half of the male and a quarter of the female population of Ukraine."

Not history so much as a continuing struggle for the right to keep breathing, and for that breath to emerge as language in one's native tongue. I remember gathering at the flagstaff each morning at Camp Kyiv, my knock-knees prodded straight by the commandant's baton. How we'd sing, "She is not dead yet, our Ukraine," followed by "God Save the Queen," both in Ukrainian. The absence of "O Canada!" wasn't an omission in the eyes of the postwar refugees who led us in song and in daily exercises meant to build us up to fighting form. Canada wasn't their country so much as a place from which we'd all set out one day to reclaim our homeland, *nasha Ukraina.*

A military journey, that's what we were being prepared for at the flagpole each morning: a crusade of sorts, something we owed to history, to all the heroes who had died for their not-yet-expired homeland's sake.

✖֎✖

I travelled once before to Ukraine, or rather to the city of Kyiv, where I spent five days in early November 1993. I flew first to

Frankfurt, then to Borispol, and so enormous were the differences between these two airports—so similar in function, so antithetical in appearance, in the goods and technology they displayed—that they could have been on different planets.

All through the time I was preparing to go to Kyiv, my mother would phone me with messages passed on to her from friends of friends. "Mrs. Z. phoned to beg me not to let you go. Her cousin's just come back from Ukraine and says conditions are terrible—thieves, muggers, rapists. Promise you won't go out after dark." I refrained from asking my mother whether Mrs. Z. and her cousin, both of whom have some acquaintance with downtown Toronto, warn their friends' daughters not to wander there, especially after dark. I also refrained from telling my mother that there are sufficient numbers of thieves, muggers, rapists in Paris, London, Rome, cities where I have spent enough time to learn to be careful.

Before I left for Kyiv, I dreamed I'd received a call-up notice. I was to board a transport headed for Siberia, a labour camp where there'd be nothing but ice to eat, and nothing to keep me from dying of cold. In this dream I phone my mother to tell her the terrible things that are going to happen to me, and she replies, "But you don't have to go. You're in Canada." It's so simple—I am saved. Immediately I find myself in the midst of some wildly festive occasion, perhaps a wedding—perhaps my own. I change my dress four times, and each time put on something richer, finer. I stuff myself with cake and wine; everyone around me's laughing, dancing, whirled from terror into joy.

※◇※

Guilt Quilt

Instead of a severed hand, this canvas offers us a cold, grey dish of fish heads, clamshells, old handkerchiefs brewed to a bruise-coloured sheen. No drowning tablecloth beneath the bowl, but a frantic weather of pleated, shiny bedspread and drenched bricks bending into cobblestones. In what other country does she lie, this sleeping woman clutching the false safety of her bed? In the country of nightmares, inhabited by generals with breastplates of ribbons and medals, grim children with skinned faces. A sliver-sized boat steams from one tunnel into another along a flat, black pool; the woman, wakened now and seized by vertigo, has turned her back to us. Her hands clutch her head in a parody of the headbands worn by small girls. Half-pushed, half-pulled, she starts to fall out an open window, backwards into the dark she cannot see.

※◇※

Do all Ukrainians, or only my mother's family, possess what Henry James called "the imagination of disaster"? Henry James, that arch-expatriate, arch-Anglophile into whose arms I fled at age twenty-two, going off to England to study, abandoning all that it meant to be ethnic and not normal, not WASP. Only to find him name for me so perfectly one of the very things I was running from. In my family, imagining disaster is an act of sympathetic magic; it works to pre-empt the million and one terrible things that can happen to you, every moment. When, on the horizon of your ordinary life, you spy something unexpected, even something promising delight—the visit of a loved friend, the birth of a child—you must imagine the worst to keep that worst from happening: the friend's crippling in a highway accident, the death of infant and mother in childbirth.

Greek myth tells us that, to comfort humankind, Prometheus not only stole fire from the heavens, but also took from us our paralysing knowledge of the time and manner of our death. Yet some of us, at least, have kept a cold trace of that knowledge, anticipating disaster in the hope of diverting it and, in the process, strangling hope as well as despair. For what you feel after the worst has somehow missed your door isn't the bliss of relief, but renewed wariness—you've been spared this calamity only to glimpse something worse dragging in its shadow.

I wasn't born with the imagination of disaster. I learned it, deep as bone, the way a child learns language from its parents. I thought I'd unlearned it in shedding the various skins of childhood and adolescence; in marrying as I did, in having children of my own. Unlearned it or buried it, only to find it flooding back, stronger than ever, as I take the first steps of this journey home.

❈❋❈

Odessa's Tears

A slippery avalanche of satin, kerchiefs, shawls, painting the sleeper's eyes, holding her head under bleeding water. She falls headlong out of bed, this dreamer, jolting with the baby carriage down the endless, monumental stairs from Eisenstein's *Battleship Potemkin*. But the ship's sailed on, the sea is plugged with jetsam: manic scarves, a lidless jar of cherries, bug-eyed dolls with round, tippy bodies and vestigial arms. And an empty pair of shoes, the kind a child might learn to walk in—squashed, spectral shoes, a white gone bad, like the yellowed cucumbers heaped beside them.

❈❋❈

A street of severe white houses in South Kensington, home to the Ukrainian consular office—I happen to be living abroad at the time I need to make a visa application to Ukraine. I walk down a shallow flight of stairs, gathering my courage, remembering how difficult it was to pry a visa out of the Ukrainian consulate in

Toronto four years earlier. But then I recall the two young women I saw on the Tube, crossing London. They were speaking Ukrainian and laughing; they seemed so much at home here, a sign of how everything's changed for the better in their country.

Pushing open the basement door, I walk into a windowless room. Its panelled walls are empty except for a tiny map of Ukraine and a slightly larger photo, in fading blue-green, of the current president. Behind a Plexiglas screen sits an official, no older than the girls I saw on the Tube. I smile at him as if he were a distant relation, an acquaintance—anyone but a perfect stranger. When he looks at my passport, he will see my doubled name, recognize that here is someone with whom he has a bond, however slight. He will speak to me in Ukrainian, and I will make some halting reply, my accent passable, my grammar appalling: it will be all right.

There's a metal tray running under the Plexiglas, and onto it I slide the papers I've carefully filled out, the photographs, the letter of invitation from a bona fide organization in Ukraine— all the credentials I've been ordered to present. The man behind the Plexiglas seizes hold of them. I notice, for the first time, the thickness of his neck, the doughy pallor of his scalp beneath his close-cropped hair. I also notice, carved on the edge of the metal tray, various epithets instructing the official behind the screen on what to do with himself, and how. Preferably as painfully as possible.

The man drags his eyes over my papers, then shoves them back to me. His accent is thick as porridge brewed in vodka: "No! You No Can Make Vee-za. Eez Eem-poss-ee-bul. Vee-za You Get In Your Own Country!"

I point out that I contacted the consulate here weeks ago, explaining my need for visas for myself and my husband and my son. I remind him that the consulate sent me those very forms he is now refusing to accept.

"Eez Reg-oo-lationz. Roolz. We No Can Change For Only You. Eez Up To You To Know. Eez Not My Beez-ness To Tell You No-thing."

If I had a pocket knife, I would scratch some obscenity onto the bit of empty space left on the rim of the metal tray. I would take pains to scratch it in Ukrainian, too, some fitting equivalent of the *dickhead* and *fuckwit* inspired by this official who did not, it is clear, achieve his present position by dint of excellent English or the knack of common courtesy. I take back my papers, photographs, the postal order for eighty pounds sterling; I turn my back on the Plexiglas, the vinyl panelling, the microscopic map of Ukraine. Back outside, the dense, polluted London air seems like a breath of paradise.

Much later it occurs to me that I should have tried slipping an extra ten pound note along with my application form into the metal tray. But all I can think of as I make my way back through the maze of look-alike streets is that it's been a long time—as long ago as childhood—since I've been pushed to the verge of tears. "The incomparable trauma of rejection." If only he'd smiled apologetically or shrugged his shoulders, signalling the stupidity of rules dreamed up by bureaucrats a thousand miles away from South Kensington.

"Please do not take this very unpleasant man in the consular office as typical of all Ukrainians. This voice emerges from a public telephone into which I'm pouring one pound coins to keep the connection going. A young woman's voice, the accent Ukrainian. She works at the Geneva office of an advisory council to the Parliament of Ukraine; she has helped me organize my visa applications and, having called and spoken to the man behind the Plexiglas, tells me I can do nothing now but go home and make a new application. "Believe it or not," she adds, "I met just such an unpleasant person in the French embassy, when I was trying to get a visa in Kyiv." I do believe her; I know how icily intractable

French bureaucrats can be. And I also know that the culture I came face to face with in that South Kensington basement wasn't Ukrainian but generic Soviet, the stuff that doesn't wither away when the empire comes unstuck.

All petty bureaucrats are the same. Anyone with even a flicker of power over someone else will abuse that power, given half a chance. Yet I can't tell her this, the young Ukrainian woman in Geneva who speaks such fluent English. For one thing, I still don't trust my voice beyond "Yes," "Of course," "I see." I'm still shaking. It's not just the rudeness of the man at the Ukrainian consulate, I want to tell her. It's his having locked me out of that strange, ungiving place I so improbably call home.

There's something else, something I can hardly explain even to myself. Though I'm desolate at being shut out, I'm terrified, too, of being taken in. I remember how, thirty years ago, my mother had wanted to visit the Old Place. She'd been advised against it: the border guards would let her in, but they might never let her out again.

Consular officials, border guards, basements, detention rooms—whole banquets to feed the imagination of disaster.

⁜

Each night since my return from London and my abortive visit to the consulate, I wake between three and five a.m. Wake with my head scribbled over by a phrase I heard one sleepless night in Kyiv, four years ago. *Nebezpechni moment*—a dangerous moment, the remark of some commentator at a televised football match.

I sit up in the dark, trying not to disturb my husband sleeping beside me. Why am I driven to visit a place whose language I barely know, where the simple mechanics of eating a meal, finding a bed for the night, making our way from here to there may thwart us at every turn? None of the guides or interpreters recommended to me have answered the letters I sent to Ukraine. I've had endless trouble with the phone calls and faxes meant to start things happening with visas and shots and insurance. Why not stop where I am, all the family stories written down at last? Why keep trying to get to a place that seems, one friend observes, more remote than the Arctic?

Nebezpechni moment. Awake in the middle of the night, no distraction but a Bible-sized book on the bedside table—the *Lonely Planet* guide to what used to be the USSR. Guiltily I switch on the light, begin to read:

> Despite stories in Western media about economic collapse, ethnic strife, escalating crime and deathtrap aircraft, travel in Russia, Ukraine and Belarus is no more daunting than in the rest of the world. . . . To explore these countries, all you need are a sense of curiosity and, when appropriate, a sensible caution, a spot of determination and a little tolerance of discomfort.

It sounds so British, so plucky, that "spot of determination"—no birthmark of mine. How much easier it would be to go to Russia, where I have no family living, no ties of story or language. Or to Belarus, though the contamination by Chornobyl of what the guidebook calls that country's "haunting, old-fashioned beauty" would be far harder to witness than the merely industrial pollution that has ravaged western Ukraine.

I am not an adventurer, as far as travellers go. I've never felt pulled to places that are or used to be out of the way: the Great Rift Valley, Easter Island, Nepal. My experience of wilderness is limited to camping in Algonquin Park, where chipmunks proved a greater threat than bears or wolves. It's not the discomfort, the inconvenience or frustration of travel in Ukraine that is eating me now, but a fear of risk, a craving for the safety that has been such a hapless blessing, closing off in me all that should have opened to things unknown and unforeseen.

Fear of, yet fascination with, risk. Whatever drives me outside on late summer nights, when thunderstorms crack the day's metallic heat, and winds crash through the maple trees. And all the while I sit on the porch, flecked with sulphur-smelling rain, daring the weather—to do what? Not to destroy me, or knock down the house and all those sleeping inside it. But to take me up into something vastly larger than myself, that knot of limitations and untried possibilities.

I know what's at stake here, travelling not through stories but with my passport in a leather case strung round my neck; crossing first one border and then another on this counter-voyage to the one my family made more than sixty years ago. The Old Place I know by heart and carry in a fold of memory—what if I can only hold onto it by staying at the farthest possible remove? What will happen when the actual displaces what I have imagined? I remember a story I once heard of a man who, having miraculously survived his years as a soldier during a long and devastating war, set out on the road home. Passing through bombed-out cities and looted towns, he found the roads still marked, the signposts standing. But when he arrived at the bend in the road leading to his birthplace, when he made his way down into the day of his homecoming, he found nothing left. Every wall and door, every roof and chimney, every gate and grave had vanished. Everyone and everything, into air so thin it held not even a trace of smoke.

It's not only what I might lose that frightens me—my sense of self, the very shape of my heart. I'm afraid of what I might learn. About the war that my grandparents and their children escaped, but that trapped the rest of their family. About what happened to those left behind, among them a cabinetmaker, a woman with red hair, a tall man whose name means "flowers." I'm afraid, and even though Michael is sleeping beside me, I feel utterly alone. On the bedside table are my reminders of what needs to be done, where it is we're heading. Under the *Lonely Planet* guide to Russia, Ukraine and Belarus, another book, thin as the slenderest volume of poems. It's the catalogue to Natalka Husar's *Black Sea Blue*. I turn to the last painting of all, the exhibition's centrepiece, *Pandora's Parcel to Ukraine*. It's a response, Husar writes, to "those zillions of care parcels that Ukrainian-Canadians have sent over the years to families in Ukraine," goodwill gestures "laced with a sort of guilty superiority."

The very first thing Husar set down on the canvas was her mother's house, which she found still standing, "romantic, with big fat peaches against the blue-washed walls." Barely a hint remains of the house in the finished painting, which becomes, the more you look at it, one of those fairground rides that hurl you round and round with no hope of ever stopping. At the centre of the canvas stands a gruesomely gold-toothed woman with badly dyed hair and a corncob heart. She's the manager of an ex-Soviet factory turning out substandard shoes; her dwarfish Howdy-Doody protégé stands peering over her shoulder. Above this monstrous pair stands a row of scarecrows, military men and blue-skinned women merging into a table laid with neon-ripe tomatoes and pale, rose-streaked fat.

Canadian-sent care parcels flood the right foreground of the painting: one of them is impaled with a carving knife. But the truly terrifying part of the canvas is the other side, where the only part of the underpainting shows through: a picket fence, its staves crowned with upturned glass jars and battered pails put out to dry. Tied to this fence by the sashes round their waists, or the ridiculously puffed bows in their hair, are four little girls with hollow eyes and pallid skin. Yet if you look closely at the faces of these children, you see that some of them wear what the painter calls a "folkloric rash"—an overlay of those cabbage roses found on traditional Ukrainian shawls. These are Chornobyl children, their bodies already seeded with disease. They are, Husar says, the future, each one of them possessed by the "ghost of limited possibilities."

Although it hurts to look, I pore over this crazy mirror of my own obsessed imaginings. And gradually that fist inside me, that clenched, blue-grey hand, lets go. I am not, I see, the first to throw myself into a collision between past and present. I know that I'll be raising and not laying ghosts by making this journey at long last. But I'll take the map of these paintings to guide me, this carnival of images: hypnotic, grotesque, heart-piercing and once, just once, radiant. In the last picture I look at, a self-portrait, the painter stands on a shore where ersatz oriental rugs clash with seas of white drapery. But my eyes are drawn away from her to an open door, more glass than wood. Beyond the door, to a space of free, unfocused light.

---

azure eating ashes

The Michelin map of Europe sprawls across a floor cleared for
a moment of spread-eagled suitcases. *Tourism. Roads. Relief.*
Index of Place Names. The map's too big for any table we have, and
yet its definitions are truncated: only the first third of Norway,
Sweden and Finland. Russia ending at St. Petersburg and
Jaroslavl; Ukraine at Dnipropetrovs'k with just the toe of Crimea
poking out from the bottom. At the edges of the map, except
where there's ocean, thin red arrows point to unshown names and
places. Worlds we'll never see, making what we're attempting
more concise, somehow—just barely possible.

We make an X at the village south of Rotterdam where friends
are arranging for us to buy and, most importantly, insure the kind
of car we hope no Slavic mafioso will think it worth his while to
steal. From the Netherlands, we'll head down through Germany,
taking the autobahn as far as we can until German towns with
Polish-sounding names turn into Polish towns once called by
German names. Our first night in Poland we'll spend in Wroclaw;
from there we'll travel to Krakow, that smaller and less tourist-
blighted Prague. A few days later we'll make a predawn start for the
border, hoping to arrive that night in L'viv, the capital of western

Ukraine. Then Ternopil', Pidvolochys'k and, finally, Staromischyna itself.

But there's no "finally" on this journey. After our time in Ukraine we'll return to Poland, a small town called Skarszewy, near the Baltic coast. The place where my grandfather's half-sister Adela was shipped at the end of the war, when the borders shifted. We are to spend a weekend with Adela, her children and grand-children before heading back to the Netherlands, and Canada. This, at least, is the journey we've sketched out on our enormous map, teeming with roads and place names in the west, so empty-seeming in the east.

We've been told we're crazy, taking a car into Ukraine. Spare parts don't exist, gasoline can be scarce and theft is endemic. The proverb heading the chapter on motoring in our guidebook to Ukraine makes no bones about our folly: *he who is going to be hanged need not fear drowning*. On the other hand, the crowding on trains and buses, the impromptu alterations to departure and arrival times have become legendary in that country. And there are three of us to consider: Michael, our younger son, Christopher, and me. Thanks to our Dutch friends we have a car, and thanks to this car we have a refuge, a radically contracted substitute for home, defined in this simplest way: the three of us, together. But the car is more than a refuge: as long as our supply of gasoline holds, as long as we don't forget how to use the tool kit and spare parts packed in the trunk, we can write our own ticket out. If it were only me, I tell myself, it wouldn't matter so much. But with Michael and Christopher along, especially Christopher, who can't shake whatever it is—fear or contrariness—that makes him hold back from the Old Place, I have to be sure that doors, once shut, will open again without a hitch.

✖◈✖

Along with dictionaries, phrase books, foreign grammars, we pack what the guidebooks advise for out-of-the-way places in Poland and Ukraine: tissues and toilet paper, thick bars of soap, aspirins and toothpaste, bandages, antiseptic and emergency syringes (accompanied by a doctor's prescription). We've already had typhus shots; for hepatitis, gamma globulin should do the trick. We bring water purification tablets, contact lens solutions; chewing gum and chocolate and coffee for strangers who do us kindnesses. Dried nuts and fruit for our son who eats neither meat nor fish, and who may lose a good many pounds in Ukraine, since our doctor's warned us to stay clear of raw fruit and salads there. Money belts with Deutschemarks and American dollars in small denominations to be snugged round our waists: the open sesame of currency in Eastern Europe.

We have finally obtained all the necessary visas; they are stamped and glued impeccably in place. On the last page of my passport I've pencilled in emergency contact numbers, so they'll be at hand—unless, of course, our passports get stolen. And in a briefcase crammed with absolute necessities, I've stashed the map of Staromischyna my mother's sketched for me on tissue-thin scrap paper—a Depression-era map. Plus Xeroxes of documents printed long ago—passports with Polish eagles, stamped contracts pertaining to the rental of my grandparents' vanished fields, the very map of those fields, narrow as horses' teeth, as a set of piano keys. Crisp simulacra, journeying back, like me, to the birthplace of their originals.

Among this mass of papers, a letter:

Davenport Works,
1025 Lansdowne Avenue,
Toronto 4,
August 16, 1935.

To Whom It May Concern:
This is to certify that the bearer, Thomas Solowski, has been employed
in the Foundry Department of the Canadian General Electric Company,
Limited, Davenport Works, Toronto, from 1928 to 1931, when he
visited his country, returning to these works in 1933 where he is still
employed and will continue whenever work is available.

CANADIAN GENERAL ELECTRIC CO., Ltd.
Wm. O. Maclean
Superintendent, Foundry.

Why my grandfather obtained this letter, whether he was planning
a last visit to his wife and children, to persuade them to leave Poland
before the war he must have known was coming—these remain
mysteries. But the need for authorization, proof of identity, is the
same for us both: folded into the letter signed by Wm. O. Maclean
is one signed by Dr. Bohdan Hawrylyshyn of Geneva, a formal
invitation, for visa-procurement purposes, to visit Ukraine under
the auspices of a foundation with which he's associated. Perhaps my
grandfather needed his letter from General Electric for the same
reason that I need mine—to take hold of when, in strange beds and
cities, we wake from even stranger dreams. To read ourselves back
from nightmare into sleep; to read ourselves home.

※◈※

Our Dutch friends are magicians: parked in their driveway is the
perfect vehicle for Eastern European travel, an ancient, dented but

mechanically dependable Opel. They furnish all the necessary papers, a tool kit and lessons on everything that could fall out or off the car and how to fix it when it does. They give us their telephone and fax numbers so we can touch base on our travels; should we show no signs of life at any point, they will alert our embassies. And they watch my nervousness increase over the few days we spend with them in their house by the sea, where sheep crop the deep green grass and magpies drag tailfeathers like rulers behind them. Our friends offer to keep Christopher with them, if we think it's best. I don't know, I say; I don't know.

I am miserable with indecision. Our friends' daughters are close to Christopher in age—he's already at his ease with them. He could go sailing, learn rowing, have two weeks by the sea instead of bumping over roads in places where the water isn't safe to drink, making a pilgrimage for the sake of stories he's barely familiar with. I ask him what he'd rather do—he says he doesn't want to disappoint me, he wants to see the village where his grandmother was born. But he's scared—about Chornobyl, however far away it is; about going to places where so many people were murdered in the war. They're not the kind of fears I can easily dismiss. At last we decide that he'll stay with our friends while his father and I go on to Ukraine. When I phone my mother to tell her this, she's not hurt but relieved. "Let him be," she says. "Things are so different there, so difficult. He has plenty of time." After I hang up, I tell myself my mother's right; one day he'll make his own decision whether to visit the Old Place or to stay away; perhaps he'll go with his older brother, who's off at university, not wanting to travel yet—not this kind of travel.

Once we've packed the car to bursting, said our goodbyes, pulled out of our friends' driveway, Christopher begins to run beside us, despite the rain that has started drumming down. He's a fast runner; until we reach the end of the road and turn onto the highway, his long legs keep up with the car. I roll down the window, wave towards our son who is calling out *good journey* in the Dutch he's started to pick up.

Bucketing rain, all the way from Stad aan't Haringvliet through northeast Germany. We plough through small lakes on the highways; in strange hotel rooms we wake past midnight, our eyelids seized by lightning. No halt at the border: Dutch signs slide into German, and then there's only the progressively poorer quality of the roads, the deserted centres of towns and cities to show we've crossed into the former GDR. Boxy Trabant cars, grey, harsh-grained toilet paper and a serious smell of drains in the streets. Graffiti in English, as if that language guaranteed truth or chic: *Greetings Master, Misses, Come and We Fuck.* A taste of things to come, we think, these forlorn, abandoned streets of Erfurt or Alsfeld or Wittenberg, these luxury shops crammed with goods and empty of anyone able to buy the silks and perfume, the computer games and software on display.

Crossing into Poland, we find that nothing's like what we anticipated. I don't need one word of the careful speech I've written out in German to explain away the syringes in our luggage. Six, seven years ago there would have been guns at this border; now we're waved straight through, we barely need to flash our passports. Suddenly we're driving past greeny-blond wheatfields on Hitler's original autobahn, the same corduroy road that began thirty kilometres east of the border.

I want a sign, something like the *Tsotsa-Tsola* my mother saw when she walked out of Union Station and stared up at her first Canadian sky. It doesn't have to say *Welcome Home*, it could even be *Look Out* or *Here Be Dragons*, just something to identify the differences we'll surely meet. But in the brief, blind strokes of lightning, poppies stay poppies, wheat is wheat. *First Video Club, Hard and Soft Ware Service*, say the signs stuck every five kilometres along a road empty but for us.

A small blue car, the kind of blue that looks like azure eating ashes. Our token home, pushing through this landscape like a threaded needle. A thread with our son as the knot at the end.

✖◈✖

Ten kilometres from the border the road abruptly smooths: we can talk without hiccupping, drink water without knocking our teeth out. People with bicycles and baskets of chanterelles appear at clearings in the forest. Sheltering under bridges, men set up stands of berries, yellow plums, pickled things in heavy bottles. Sometimes we sight whole colonies of garden ornaments: miniature Dutch windmills, and giant Disney dwarves ranged on bleachers, as if cheering an invisible soccer game. Then, just as suddenly, the road reverts to petrified corduroy.

The fact that we know almost no Polish beyond *Good day, I can't speak Polish* makes the *Bar Inbiss* signs at improvised snackbars falsely reassuring. My high school German is a child's garden of ungrammatical clichés, though it managed to reserve us a hotel room for the night. Just outside Wroclaw we stop for gas. Lightning snakes through a sky the colour of dark mustard: raindrops fall fat as frogs on the windshield. Plague signs, the only ones we're given.

✖◈✖

A state-run hotel, right at the edge of the highway: cold, extortionate, the kind of four-star nightmare favoured by the Party elite in the bad old days. It's raining too hard to venture into Wroclaw; all we want to do is get out of this ocean that the road's become. We eat the leftovers of the picnic we bought in Germany and watch the news. It's full of uprooted trees, flooded streets, floating cars, all because of sudden heavy storms in southwest Poland and the Czech Republic. If we want, we can switch to dull live coverage of the British handing Hong Kong over to the Chinese, or to a Canadian sitcom where a red-coated Mountie is being drowned out by Polish dubbing—one male voice reading all the parts as if they were the latest figures for steel production.

Michael lies like a continent beside me. He's driven for ten hours, all six feet six inches of him crammed into the tiny Opel; tonight he could sleep through Genesis. I shift the too-small sheet so that it covers him, turn down the TV. He has no reason to be here except for my sake, this man my family called the *Anglik* when I married him, though his father's family came to Canada two hundred years ago. At Ukrainian weddings it's the custom to give the bride and groom not silver trays, but gifts of money to be used towards the down payment on a house or, at the very least, a suite of bedroom furniture. When we married, we took our wedding gifts and, scandalously, spent them on three months' travelling through France, Italy, England. Michael's mother was a war bride: as a child he'd spent several summers with his grand-parents at their home in Sussex, and he took me to visit them on our honeymoon. They were wonderful people: I fell in love with them, just as I fell in love with England. But I never dreamed, then, of setting foot in Poland or Ukraine; of showing Michael where my own mother had grown up, the world she came from.

And now, belatedly, this journey to my family's home, just the two of us, as we'd been on our honeymoon. The difference between that long-ago visit to Sussex and this trip to Staromischyna is that what was comfortable and familiar for Michael, in his Old Place, can't help but be difficult and strange for me. What will he make of where we're heading—what will I be able to show him, help him understand? What would have happened if our sons had come with us; our sons who don't feel split or doubled but just Canadian, and who carry different burdens than my own? I want them to know the Old Place, so they'll have a fuller sense of who they are. But so much of what they'd find there would be opaque, uncontainable; they'd need constant translations, and I can barely speak the language.

A Chinese observer of the events in Hong Kong gives his views in perfect English, making me cringe at my idiot's German, my kitchen-table Ukrainian, my phrase book Polish. My very English has become a coat whose seams are slit by all these languages I haven't mastered and never will. Long after I switch off the set, I wrestle with words, dreaming in half a dozen languages at once, fluent only in sleep, when my lips are still and my ears empty.

✳◈✳

We head for Krakow, on a highway that gives each of our teeth a separate headache, the car rattling like a deranged tambourine. The rain has stopped, but the sky's still armoured with cloud. Flat fields, flowering lindens, rare and tantalizing slabs of new asphalt on the highway—it's like riding on devil's food cake, the few moments they last. Falsely bucolic, this stretch, showing us our first horse and cart: standing up, tensing the reins, a man in a jacket the colour of buttercups.

A jot of colour, erased by the faces of people waiting at rusting bus stops. They must live in these brick houses with soiled, flaking stucco; they must be travelling to the towns we can put behind us—coal-mine tailings, the sooty candelabras of factory chimneys, apartment blocks roofed by forests of TV antennas. I can feel sludge coating my lungs; the stench of exhaust never clears, even when, between towns, we pass a brief stretch of trees or rain-beaten wheat, the blond of a boy's cropped head at the end of summer. It's one thing to read of pollution in former East Bloc countries, another to taste the diffused poison some people breathe in here a whole life long.

Krakow's old city is a jewel rotted by smoke from the chimneys of Nowa Huta, a steel town slapped up to punish the snooty stones of the Wawel castle where the kings of Poland once held court. But there's a cure, it seems, for everything. Scaffolding blooms in

Krakow; museums and galleries close for major renovation, work-men scrape wood and patch plaster. Ancient streets brim with cell phones and plastic telephone cards, Pizza Huts, Adidas, kantors who'll change yen or Deutschemarks or American dollars into zlotys. Ravishing girls in miniskirts and clog heels; boys who wear their jeans, their logoed T-shirts like tuxedos. Hucksters anywhere there's an inch of sidewalk to spare—pale, bowed girls holding out Coca-Cola cups as begging bowls; gypsy mothers sitting with drugged babies between their splayed-out legs, their seven-year-old sons dumped onto street corners with defective accordions, playing over and over the same first bars of the Anniversary Waltz.

All the time I ask myself—will it be like this in L'viv? It, too, is a medieval city, full of grand and beautiful buildings. Over a glass of wine, a professor from the Jagiellonian university tells us how her grandmother, mad for opera, would dress up in her furs and jewels to board the tea-time express between Krakow and Lwow, arriving just in time for the overture to the latest production of Puccini. I've seen pictures of L'viv in a back issue of *National Geographic*, a fine old market square like the one in Krakow, a turn-of-the-century opera house. I make myself at least one promise: we will spend a night at the opera in L'viv.

✖◈✖

The danger of falling in love with Poland, a replay of *Taras Bulba* with cities like Krakow cast as the seductress. I can understand the temptation to defect. Poland, after all, is Europe: Renaissance palaces, Gothic churches, a Latin alphabet, however odd the accents and slashes and clumps of consonants. All the things Ukraine lacks, Ukraine where, our guidebook tells us, some 250 monuments were deliberately destroyed—anything the Soviets could construe as symbols of nationhood: churches, cemeteries, palaces.

At a museum of nineteenth-century art, we walk straight into Jan

Matejko's painting of the Ukrainian prophet Wernyhora, complete with flitting bats, full moon haloing the sage's head, and hurdy-gurdy at his feet. Wernyhora is Taras Bulba's nemesis and arch-enemy: a Ukrainian who doesn't wage war against the Poles, but sings the glories of a Polish state embracing all nationalities and all religions, stretching from the Baltic to the Black Sea. All to the rapture of the Orthodox priest, the fawning peasant woman in a Ukrainian blouse, the Polish scribe taking down the prophet's every word. Not a bad vision, Michael says, when you think of the horrors of inter-ethnic war that this end of the century has seen. I mention the fate of ethnic minorities during Poland's Second Republic; point out the lack of any Jews in Matejko's fiction of the future.

We wanted to wait for L'viv, to go to the opera, but *Tosca*'s playing on our last night in Krakow: doomed love, doomed art, doomed heroism. The music mixes with a now-constant refrain in my head, *What on earth are we doing, where are we going?* Tosca stabs Scarpia and leaps from the battlements after her lover's been gunned down. The laws of tragedy are, after all, only another form of the laws of gravity, and where we're headed for tomorrow is as weighty as things come.

※◊※

By five the next morning we're on the road, driving east; there can be delays at the border of up to forty-eight hours, even for people with perfect visas. It's a grey morning, mist lingering like headache. Close to Przemysl signs start to appear in Cyrillic; some cars have UA stickers pasted on their bumpers. This is getting serious, this is getting real. I need coffee to steady me, but the first café we stop at is padlocked, and the next has been converted to a hardware store. For the first time in years we go to a McDonald's, deserted except for some sombre children climbing up a stumpy plastic slide. In the funereal cleanliness of Mcdowski we drink our coffee, staring past the children at a streak of sun, anticipating the heat that soon will have us boiling in its pot. Out of nowhere comes a memory of my grandfather, scolding my parents for having taken us to the film of *Taras Bulba*—pure Hollywood, he'd lamented; everything silly and simple. Looking round the empty restaurant, I seem to catch a glimpse of Tomasz, shrugging his shoulders, shaking his head at me.

※◇※

Borders aren't places, but emptiness with edges. Concrete, asphalt, migratory flocks of vehicles instead of birds.

We've been here forever: we'll never get out. Our car is one of hundreds wedged between miles of transport trucks and cranky orange buses. Hot, so hot the chocolate we've brought all the way from Rotterdam, slabs with the sheen of polished walnut, melts to cloudy soup. Nothing moves, not even the air, as though we've all stopped breathing but haven't got the energy to die. Next to us a truck plays loud, blurry tapes of rock-accordion; the car in front overflows with giant bags of bleached cheesies. The only smell in the world is diesel fuel; the only gods are these play-police in black trousers and grey shirts, their visored caps supporting crowns as huge as turkey platters.

Craziness, I hear Olena say. *The only reason we left home was so that you would never have to.* I try, unsuccessfully, to banish my grandmother's voice. In an hour, a day, a year we'll have inched up to the checkpoint, surrendered our passports to men in absurd and overweening caps who'll ask us what we're doing, where we're going and why. I speak enough of their language to understand their questions, but how can I answer them? In my fantasies of border crossing it was always midnight, by a river. One lonely, tired soldier and only us in all the world trying to cross over. The soldier would look gravely at our papers, motion us inside a house like an empty school; we'd sit around a wooden table, the three of us, interrogation turning into urgent, common speech.

Only this part is like the fantasy: a young Polish guard, halting us at the last checkpoint before we cross to where Ukrainian border guards are waiting. He looks at our passports and smiles as he hands them back. *Kanáda?* he asks, and I say yes, yes, near Toronto. He tells us that he has family who live in Mississauga. And then he smiles and waves us through, as he might have done anyway, and we're abruptly, formally in Ukraine, though still stuck in the border zone, as stuck as if our tires had melted into the asphalt.

Sha na na na na, a tape plays, with speeding trains and sirens built into the soundtrack. Some of the cars wedged round us are empty, as if their occupants have given up and walked over the small, artificial hills on either side of the road into some warp of distance. Other cars are crammed. Every fifteen or twenty minutes we crawl a few inches forward. Once, when the gridlock loosens for a second and we don't crawl fast enough to fill the space in front of us, the driver of the car behind us presses the horn as loud and long as the last trumpet. Once, when a corridor opens magically to the left and our car stalls, someone waits to let us through, a show of courtesy that takes our breath away.

The heat is making us stupid, quarrelsome. It helps to think of Christopher, leaning out of a catamaran, his wet suit slick with the chill waters of the Haringvliet. There are more and more forms to fill out, all in Ukrainian; the vocabulary stumps me. "Do you have any forms in English?" I ask. The guard just shakes his head. He tells me to put *nema*—none—by all the questions and to write down whatever currency we're bringing in. We do as he says, and he waves us on to another line-up.

Women with black roots under dead-blonde permanents that look in drastic need of watering. Were they in Poland looking for husbands? Or are those their husbands, bare-chested in the heat, their skin sticky as honey? Men and women wave their passports, old dark red Soviet passports, but the guards circling the vans and cars with their walkie-talkies show not the slightest interest. I surrender any hope of motion; I know in my bones we'll never budge from this spot where we've been snagged for hour after hour, cars jammed in front of us, around us, behind us as far as the eye can see. But now comes the most hopeful sound in all the world. An engine revving, then another and another, and finally a collective vehicular shudder. The gates have finally swung open, they are letting us through.

16

L'viv: ghostprints

This isn't play anymore: not tourism, not even travel. I feel the weight of everyone's expectations on my shoulders: our son, with our friends in the Netherlands, waiting for a fax to reassure them all is well; my mother, who's too old now to journey such a distance, to a place where so much is uncertain. My aunt, who wants us to call as soon as we set foot in Staromischyna, that paradise from which she was barred some twenty years ago. My great-aunt Adela, waiting for us in Skarszewy; Adela's eldest son Bazyli, whom I spoke to last night in my crippled German.

I'm as nervous as if I were heading to an arranged marriage with someone I have never seen. I begin to doubt my own reality, knowing that during our stay here I'll be someone other than I think myself to be. A spy, looking for something that doesn't exist anymore. An envoy, making this return voyage for my mother and aunt, and in some ways for my absent sons as well. And a ghost by proxy, standing in for my dead grandparents, who would see things differently, overlaid by memory, not merely story. The ghost of a ghost, a nearsighted voyeur whose vision, even when corrected by glasses, will remain imperfect, only half-true.

The highway's a straight long line to L'viv, passing through towns and villages and along green ditches where old men or women sit with their legs spread out, studying the splendour of their white goat, their spotted cow. Younger people work in the fields, shaping mounds of hay with wooden rakes. People my age, no older, wielding the same tools my grandmother used to work her fields: scythes, sickles, wooden harrows, the most basic of ploughs. What do they make of a car with a foreign licence plate speeding past? Or do they no longer notice the traffic passing them by, those men ploughing with horses, these women bent over their hoes? No stands by the roadside, no mushrooms or berries or Charlie Chaplins for sale, but iron fences keeping poultry in and strangers out.

I'm scouring this landscape for traces of my grandparents' lives—but there are no orchards and no thatched houses: the homes we pass are roofed with corrugated iron, and all of them were built after the war. In the towns, those compounds of sleep and dust, larger, older buildings answer to the names I know from my mother's stories: schoolhouse, marketplace, store. But these outdoor cafés, where people sit at white plastic tables over dishes of ice cream, these parks with statues of Shevchenko sunk in brooding foliage—none of this could have existed in my mother's time. Caught in a traffic jam in Horodok, we roll down the windows and hear roosters crowing. A hay cart in front of us, cars cutting recklessly in and out, a bus, another hay cart where the road bends and you can't see what's coming.

"What are you thinking?" Michael asks me. "What are you feeling, being here at last?"

"I don't know," I say. The heat, the dust, the long monotony of the road have made me drowsy, just as I used to get on long summer drives to my aunt's cottage. And then I realize that I've been thinking of the place Gus and Vira used to own on Georgian Bay. I tell Michael the story that's been forming patterns in my head like one of those glass-walled toys containing sand or oil that you tilt from side to side, or upside down.

The cottage, I say, was the place Vira loved best on earth, the one place she could escape, if only briefly, the endless telephone calls, the frantic appeals of her patients and their parents. To my grandmother, however, cottages were a baffling waste of time and money better spent at home. Still, Olena came up one summer weekend, not to lie on the beach, but to make Vira a vegetable garden. All one morning she dug and hoed the scratchy soil, tugging up weeds and roots with her bare hands, planting seedlings with the finesse of a pianist racing through scales. By evening, her hands were blistered raw; the sores reached up to her elbows like shiny, burning evening gloves.

"It was the worst case of poison ivy Vira'd ever seen."

"Poison ivy doesn't grow in Poland?" Michael asks.

"Not in Staromischyna, and not in the backyard at Dovercourt, that's all I know. Dirty trick, right? The revenge of the wilderness."

The traffic jam unsticks: we leave Horodok, driving on to what we hope is L'viv, since all road signs have disappeared. We pass field after empty field in this country that is part of the metaphoric earth under my feet. And as we drive, a different meaning rises from this story of my grandmother's first and last brush with poison ivy. I'm remembering how Olena's own fields slipped from her grasp and how Vira, after her children were grown, had to sell the cottage, though it broke her heart to do so. Not revenge of the wilderness, but something like a warning—that earth, familiar or foreign, is no more our home, our native element, than fire.

※◇※

On the sloping road by which we enter L'viv, the traffic is weaving round humped-up cobblestones: cars, taxicabs, buses, all like novice skiers slowly working their way through a field of moguls.

It's not a very large city, and we find our way to the Zhorzh (or George) Hotel that's been booked for us through the same foundation that helped us get our visas. There's a note at the desk welcoming us to Ukraine in the politest German: it takes me a moment to realize that my request for an English-speaking guide has been scrambled or else drawn a blank. I speak to Sofia—the author of the welcome note—over our hotel room phone, a plastic box letting in a whole weather-front of hums and whispers. In German I arrange to meet with her next morning at the hotel. *Alles in Ordnung—bis morgen—auf wiederhören.* It hits me, as I hang up, that I won't be able to use my native tongue at all here; my questions and whatever answers I can get will have to be filtered through German or Ukrainian. Like trying to take a stroll in shoes that are far too tight, or else so big you trip on them at every turn.

※❂※

The Zhorzh was once an Intourist hotel, and though the facade's recovered its Habsburg-era grandeur, the inside is one vast shabbiness of faded turquoise paint and peeled veneer. Our room must be five metres high—you could pile three generations of an acrobat family on each other's shoulders and still not scrape ceiling. Even the bathroom could be a temple, though most of the tiles are cracked and the fixtures predate the October Revolution.

Businessmen must have taken their mistresses to the Zhorzh before the war; ladies must have met their lovers in the discreet shade offered by the lobby's potted palms. But with L'viv under a red star instead of a white eagle, what kind of affair could have been conducted here, in these pencil-case beds, their nylon sheets slippery as banana peels? Ghosts of imperial officers, women in ostrich plumes and scented lace watch us circumnavigate our debris: books and suitcases, bottles of Evian, pyramids of western toilet paper. I let the ghosts play voyeur, go to the window and lean out, looking at the people strolling below or into a sky dull as potato soup.

Later, when we walk into the old centre of L'viv, I will look up at grand, dilapidated houses and see people stationed just as I was, at a window: a young woman combing her hair; a stout, bare-chested man, his arm round a gorgeous redhead—an Irish setter with outrageously wavy ears. Later still I will phone my mother, trying to describe through the ghost of my own voice the sadness peculiar to this part of L'viv, the blackened stone that comes away like popcorn in your hands, the grass sprouting from pediments; a tree lunging sideways from the shell of what had once been a fin-de-siècle apartment building. She will tell me not to drink the water, tell me to be careful. I won't mention the cholera warnings posted at the border. I will hang up, then fall into bed and the arms of a dream hatched by the walk we've taken through the evening streets.

Two small girls, sisters. I find them the way you do starving cats or dogs abandoned in the courtyards of condemned buildings. Inside a metal fence, a filthy bed: children lying on a pile of rags. The older girl—she is eight but looks four—calls to me in a language that is not my own, but that I understand perfectly. I ask, *Are you all right?*

Yes, she answers.

Where are your parents?

They'll be back.

Do you spend your whole day like this, lying in the dark?

Oh no, we play down by the fountain in the mornings, we watch the lions waking up.

These are the gypsy children I saw begging in the streets of Krakow, these are the children I will see climbing the ruins of the old city wall tomorrow evening, waving to me from the very top, posing for their photograph. The street urchins we'll see again and again on our walks through this city: thin and smart, moving quick as arrows down packed streets and eyeless alleyways.

These are my aunt and my mother, locked up all day in the *siny*, with only a crust of bread, a jug of water.

><

Our guide, Sofia, has the black eyebrows and hazel eyes, the olive-skinned and delicately oval face Shevchenko gave his heroine Kataryna. But there's nothing submissively tragic about Sofia. She'd give short shrift, you feel, to any love-'em-and-leave-'em hussar: though she's not more than five foot two, and slender enough to make you think of tissue paper, she has enough strength and savoir-faire for the three of us. What do we want to see, she asks, and though I'm anxious to visit a museum where I might find objects like those in my grandmother's house—a *bambatel*, a pyramid of embroidered cushions, a wooden trough for kneading dough—it seems only polite to ask first for a tour of the city. And so we set off together, two women with strong cheekbones and short summer dresses, and a tall, bearded man who is obviously foreign.

A Galician prince founded this city 650 years ago, Sofia tells us. He named it for his son Lev, meaning Leo, which explains the lions you can see carved on fountains and pediments. Over the centuries L'viv has been under royal Polish, imperial Austrian, republican Polish, Soviet Russian, Nazi German, Soviet Ukrainian and now the democratic rule of a free Ukraine. During most of the last sixty years, history's game of musical chairs has been played to brutal tunes: when the Soviets occupied L'viv in 1939, they deported thousands of its citizens to Siberia; others they held as political prisoners whom they shot en masse before fleeing east when the Nazis arrived in 1941. Hundreds of thousands of L'viv's Jews were starved to death or murdered in the city's ghetto and concentration camp. When L'viv became part of Soviet Ukraine, most of the city's Poles, who'd made up 50 per cent of the prewar population, crossed the western border. Ukrainians from surrounding villages moved in, among them, I remember, Teodor Pokotylo's daughter Varvara, the woman who might have become my grandmother had Tomasz not defied all his relations by marrying a proud girl with no land and a shorn head. Varvara must have died long ago; I have no idea where she might be buried.

Sofia's passionate about her city, and she makes us see it through the eyes of love. The buildings of L'viv's market square are wonderfully old and strange: St. Martin on horseback, knights and dolphins, the Lion of San Marco over the doorway of a house built four centuries ago for the Venetian ambassador. We visit marvels we'd barely noticed on our walk the night before: the Boyim chapel, the Armenian cathedral, the Uspensky church. Worshippers spill down the steps onto the sidewalk, listening through loudspeakers to the chanting of the liturgy. Everywhere we go there are bands of young nuns, sixteen, eighteen years old, their coifs little more than black kerchiefs. Sofia sees us staring. "They're lucky," she says, a little wistfully. "Those girls get fed, clothed, educated. Sometimes they end up in Rome."

Compared to Kyiv, L'viv is a staunchly Ukrainian city. Sofia did all her schooling in Ukrainian, though she learned Russian well enough to tackle Akhmatova in the original. Her Polish is fluent—she needs no translation to read *Pan Tadeusz*, and she's spent a good while in Krakow, a city she loves. "Did you never feel that the Poles looked down on you for being Ukrainian?" I ask her. "All that's behind us now," Sofia says. But even so, she tells us, the very day before our arrival in L'viv an ugliness occurred: in retaliation for the Poles' having sabotaged a Ukrainian festival due to take place in the city of Przemysl, where many Ukrainians still live, members of an ultranationalist youth group in L'viv had trampled on a Polish flag. Several Polish monuments in the Lychakiv ceme-tery had been defaced as well.

Among Sofia's generation, then, there are those who trample on Polish flags and those who are connoisseurs of Mickiewicz. But what of the six- and eight- and ten-year-olds, the girls no longer sporting Soviet-style bows in their hair but butterfly barrettes and flowerbands, the boys with American logo T-shirts? Will it be a foreign language to them, this hatred between Poles and Ukrainians? What of the children? I want to know.

Sofia misinterprets my question. She informs us that in Ukraine, now, there are more deaths than births. Because of Chornobyl; because of industrial poisons in the air and earth and water.

※◇※

Memory has a body breakable as any other body. Many of the streets in L'viv, Sofia tells us, are paved with the gravestones of Poles, Ukrainians, Jews. We ask her about synagogues, and she takes us down a side street to an interruption in the stone: only the foundations are left, a foothold of witness. And a wall, bare except for two hollows that would have been windows, and between them what look like eyebrows traced in stone. There's a plaque inscribed in English, Ukrainian, Hebrew:

> *Remnants of the old temple called "Di Goldene Royz." Built during 1580–95 by the Nachmanowitch family in the memory of Rabbi Nachman's wife. The building, designed by the Italian architect Pablo Romano, was destroyed by nazis and burnt in summer 1942.*

Sofia adds nothing to this till the next day, when we're sitting in a tram at the end of the line, waiting for the conductor to return from her tea break. The rain that's been drizzling all morning has become a curtain; it falls through slits in the roof of the tram. Perhaps because we're alone together, or because we've run out of jaunty things to say and silence is soaking us worse than any rain, Sofia tells a story.

Only a few years ago, when she worked at city hall, she'd been asked to go through a list of names presented by a visiting Israeli delegation. Halfway down Sofia found the name and village of her paternal grandfather. The list, it turned out, was made up of people who'd sheltered Jews during the war, people who'd been honoured at Yad Vashem. There was a brief description of what each person on the list had done, and Sofia learned, for the first time, that for two months her grandfather had risked his life bringing food and clothing to fourteen Jews hiding in the woods close by his farm. Unlike so many others, they'd survived the war.

"But why did he never tell you this? Didn't anybody know?"

"Not even my father," Sofia replies.

She can't explain why. Perhaps it wasn't politic to tell such things; perhaps her grandfather didn't think of it as anything out of the ordinary, risking his life to save innocent, desperate people. He wasn't a complicated person, Sofia says, but he had dignity.

The conductor climbs back on board—a thin woman wearing black leggings and a wide shirt clasped by a belt so tight the cloth balloons like a tutu round her hips. By the time our stop comes up the tram has filled with passengers; we have to fight our way to the doors. And all the time I'm thinking of how we hide the most important things about ourselves, the best as well as the worst. Hide them from others, which can be like hiding from ourselves.

Later I ask Sofia to take us to St. George's Cathedral, the most beautiful church in the city, where, in spite of all the gilded mouldings and serpentine columns, your eyes can still find space to breathe. In an elaborately carved wooden frame hangs a portrait of Metropolitan Andrei Sheptytsky. His long white beard and hair make him look the standard patriarch: his face is thin, his eyes both deep and sharp.

It was this same Andrei Sheptytsky who helped save the lives of many Jewish children, some of them hidden in his private residence, teaching the monks Hebrew in the quiet of the library.

When we leave the cathedral I stand on the steps, across from a pale stone palace. What would it be like to live through a whole war inside that house, to work at a desk behind a small fortress of books, so intent that you forget to wonder who might be outside, looking up, calculating how much longer he will let you go on breathing?

I stare at a window where Sheptytsky might have stood in 1944, when the Soviets retook L'viv and placed him under house arrest. He died a few months afterwards; in peace, I hope, at last.

※◈※

Once we have seen the sights of L'viv—churches, parks, palaces: including the Palace of Happiness, where as many people go to divorce as to marry—I ask to visit two museums, the main ethnographic one downtown and the open-air museum on the outskirts of the city. I am looking for clues, I tell Sofia. The house where my mother was born was pulled down after the war—nothing remains of its furnishings, or of the life that went on inside its walls. Yet I want to find whatever traces I can of that life: leftovers, artifacts that were once as everyday as the mug I use to drink my tea, the brush I pull through my hair. Objects from which I can pull the dead, like scarves stashed up a magician's sleeve. I want to find my grandparents; I want to meet them on their own home ground.

The ethnographic museum, like so many of the stately buildings of L'viv, was once a bank. It's dark inside—individual galleries are lit when visitors come through—but the staircase looms, a mahogany Matterhorn under a gigantic chandelier. An incongruous setting for displays of homespun hemp, bast shoes, farm implements similar to the ones we saw on crossing the border from Poland. I find kilims like those my sister and brother and I, and all our cousins, rode our tricycles over in our parents' basements: a set of *skrynia*s, some roughly carved with what look like tally marks, others with perfect circles and checkerboards and blind arcades. How many of them held rags soaked in menstrual blood? There are photographs of village musicians dating from the early 1900s—did this one, this *ansambl troista muzyk*, with their shiny toy-soldiers' caps, their fiddles, clarinets, dulcimers, play at the dance where my grandparents met?

The display that most moves me is the one of children's toys: small clay whistles in the shape of roosters and goats and horses; wooden carts; birds whose heavy wings flap open at the tug of a string. My mother's childhood without toys—not even one clay whistle? And then I recall the potato masher. The only thing close to a doll in all these glass cases is a set of puppets made of wool and wood and animal hair, figures four inches high, mounted on sticks. Each one of them is a standard type: the sailor, the gypsy, the priest, two Jews with fur caps. At Christmas children would put on plays with these puppets, taking them from house to house. Living so far from the sea, never travelling farther than the nearest market town, what could those children have known of sailors? And what roles did they play, the Jews in their fur caps? Did Sofia's grandfather, when he was a small boy, put on such puppet plays? Did he think of those stick figures all those days he carried bread and milk, or a flask of clean water, to fugitives hiding in the forest? Nothing is innocent here, or rather, nothing is simple. Sometimes the resonances are so complex, you can't hear the words being spoken here and now.

We exchange the gloom of the ethnographic museum for a brilliant summer afternoon. The open-air museum is in a part of the city filled with private houses instead of apartment blocks; it would be heaven, Sofia says, to live here. We ride a jammed trolley bus to the nearest stop, then walk into a green world of birds calling out at staggered intervals, as if they are looking for someone they have no hope of finding. The whole city's out for the afternoon: parents with small children, elderly ladies, a stunning girl in a slip of peach satin; she carries herself as if in a dream, blind to the pudgy, balding man at her side.

This outdoor museum has the magic of that time-lapse photography I loved as a child, when the camera would reverse the decay of a flower so that dry, bleached petals would curve softly into bud. From miles around, centuries-old houses, schoolrooms, barns have been saved from demolition, repaired and then brought together, making a little world, immune to time and change. Everywhere, there's the smell of wood, green or seasoned. In the church it mixes with the warmth of beeswax; in the barns, with the scent of hay and remnants of the heavy smells of animals—their matted coats, their soft explosions of dung. Whole farmsteads have been brought here to the outskirts of L'viv; churches with gateways and palisades. I take picture after picture until the film runs out; I search my knapsack for the new roll and discover I've forgotten it at the hotel. I'm desolate, furious—and then I understand that memory is preparing me for something I would never be able to see with a camera at my eyes. For at the next turn on the leafy road, I find what I've been searching for ever since we crossed into Ukraine: a small house with whitewashed walls, its thatch crowned with a row of crossed sticks.

I step inside, and then I can't move; it's as though the air I'm breathing is the solid glass of paperweights. Out of time, out of place, I've found my grandmother's house, the very room where my mother was born. What I've always longed for, a desire like the small stones we pick up on a beach and carry in our pockets till their weight comes to feel part of our bones.

The guard understands without my speaking a word. She undoes the cordon meant to keep visitors out of the second room of the house, the *svitlytsia*, its solemn bed heaped with embroidered cushions. The windows in this room are larger, each with six small panes of glass: one of them is open, and I lean out into a small orchard, cherry and plum trees fenced off with interlacing willow boughs. A small girl falls through the leaves, her skirt caught on a broken bough. *You've still got your eyes, you've still got your legs. What are you wailing for?* I turn back to the room, but I can't tell anymore what is really here and what I am imagining. There's the *bambatel* on which my mother used to sleep, and beside it a cupboard with a tilting mirror. In it I can almost see their faces, side by side: the eighteen-year-old girl, the twenty-year-old man who will become my grandparents. Images formed on wavy glass, as tentative as breath. They dissolve into shadow first, then emptiness: the disappearing tricks of ghosts.

This pressure of lives lived through, and lost, makes me do something that feels both natural and strange: slipping off my shoes, I walk barefoot over the pressed clay floor. Powdery coolness, undulations almost too subtle to perceive. Ghostprints. Time stops, time winds back to be played out again, a long ribbon that fits my hand perfectly. I am in the Old Place, just as when I was a child, when words alone, the timbre of a loved voice, could make what I imagined real for me. This is no imagining: this is here and then, there and now, all at once; no borders anymore. I spend an hour in my mother's house, I spend no more than a moment, until the noise of other visitors slips my feet back into my shoes, walks me out into an ordinary summer afternoon. I pass a chicken coop, the exact size of a playhouse; its walls are the kind Vira would trick Haliu Puliu into painting, with a promise to play wedding.

By a garden filled with beans and cucumbers and dark feathers of dill, Michael and Sofia are waiting for me. Voices blare from a loudspeaker hidden somewhere at the other end of the park; they cut through the outdoor service that has started at the church across from us. We walk down the path past rowan and woolly-leaved hazel trees to an ice cream stand by the entrance. Chestnut is the best, Sofia says, but there's only vanilla left. We buy some anyway and leave the park for the road down to the trolley stop, eating chalky ice cream, breathing in black scarves of exhaust.

✖◈✖

After a drink at an outdoor café Sofia heads home, and we spend the evening walking through the city streets, like everyone else—except the beggars. According to Sofia lots of gypsies work the streets here, just as in Krakow, but we see only men with missing legs, elderly women with feet swollen to the size of small pumpkins. They cross themselves when you hand them the change from your pockets; they're not begging—you are giving alms. If you are a tourist, that is—most people who live here have no such thing as spare change.

And now, this pleasant summer evening in the city of L'viv, I come face to face with the question of belonging. I am a tourist: I give alms. But am I also, somehow, a native of this place, at however many removes? What in this country, its language and culture and history, has had a hand in making me who I am? What do I feel actually being here, strolling down Svoboda Prospekt, a boulevard stretching for a third of a mile across the centre of L'viv? The whole city seems to be on display here: roller skaters, cyclists, small children pushed in strollers trailing purple balloons. Teenagers posing for Polaroids by the Opera House, boys and men locked in chess games, bystanders passionately watching. Girlfriends strolling arm in arm, engaged couples, elderly neighbours, everyone dressed in their finery. And every one of them a stranger to me.

The boulevard ends at the monument to Ukraine's much-loved poet, Shevchenko. It was built only a few years ago as a response to the much older statue of Mickiewicz nearby. Fresh flowers find their way to Shevchenko's statue every day, but the monument's no shrine. An eight-year-old girl in red-and-white polka dots twirls on the granite base: a small boy shoots Dinky cars along the steps. But what to make of this throng of people—mostly men older than fifty—gathered by the monument and singing? A glimmer of gold teeth, untrained voices in a minor key. These are the songs we used to make fun of, my friends and I, shut up in a church basement on Bathurst Street on Saturday mornings while the "English" kids played hockey or baseball. But for these men on Svoboda Prospekt—Freedom Avenue—the blue sky and yellow wheat of Ukraine's flag is the whole world, and it is theirs at last.

Listening to their singing, I find my throat tighten, tears prickling my eyes. Several of the bystanders join in. My mouth opens but no sound comes out. I can't sing these patriotic songs, anymore than I can sing, "O Canada!" at home. This public display of loyalty to a nation, a homeland, a history, this simple act of belonging, is something I've never been able to perform. It has to do with how fraught and complex the worlds of nation and homeland are—how impossible to contain them in a few bars of music, a banner of words. It has to do with that most complicated world of all for me: language.

From the moment I became aware of words, I was never sure what my mother tongue should be. The Ukrainian of my infancy, of lullabies and nonsense rhymes, was my first experience of speech, but the language I used when I was old enough to speak for myself was English. With my grandparents I spoke baby Ukrainian, while they came to meet me halfway with their shaky English. After the McCarthy scare had passed, my parents tried to speak Ukrainian with my sister and brother and me at meal-times, but we never got much further than *proshu podai maslo*: please pass the butter. And though my brother has taught himself to hold his own in his parents' mother tongue, my tongue becomes a sieve whenever I try to speak Ukrainian. It's a lovely language, much softer than Russian; certain words resonate for me in ways that their English equivalents can never do, yet I can't shake off my shame at not being able to speak proper Ukrainian. And shame is a great silencer.

Here I am in L'viv, speaking German to my guide, English to my husband, and venturing into Ukrainian only when Sofia's not there to help. As when, tonight, I order dinner in the White Fountain Cafeteria. It's not the kind of elegant, expensive place where we take Sofia for lunch: here, the cutlery's aluminum; tired women dish out lukewarm potatoes, lapsed cutlets, peas the colour of asphalt. They are patient with my clumsy attempts to say the simplest words. For everything comes out wrong: phrases, inflections familiar to me since childhood hide in the corners of my head and pull faces.

We eat by the window, though there's nothing much to see. But just as we're getting up to leave, two deaf mutes walk inside, go up to the counter and, through a ballet of fingers, make known to the women what they want to eat and drink. The men carry their food outdoors, and though their hands are busy with their trays, something about their faces, the easy way they walk together, makes it seem as though they're deep in conversation still. As though the perfect pitch of speech can only be reached through silence.

※◈※

We see Sofia one last time before we leave L'viv. We are having lunch at the Café Kupol, in the spruce, elegant university district of L'viv. This café has a bohemian air: its walls are hung with photographs of people who lived in this city a hundred years ago; on our walk through the dense green of the Lychakiv cemetery this morning we must have passed by some of their angel- or lion-guarded graves. The photos seem to be portraits of friends, not families: in this one, two well-dressed men seem at first glance to be playing chess, but are really clasping hands.

We talk with Sofia in the fevered way people do when they realize they may never meet again. I try to explain my obsession with Staromischyna, the need I feel to visit a place where there's no family left to greet me. I can see from Sofia's face that she doesn't understand. "I want to see it for myself," I say, but my tongue slips, and what comes out instead is this: "I want to see myself."

Michael asks Sofia whether she would leave L'viv if she had the chance to live somewhere else: Berlin, London, Toronto. "Never," she replies. "Unless I fell in love with a foreigner, but even then—how could I leave my family, how could I abandon my friends?"

We know that Sofia's parents are divorced—she hasn't seen her father for years. Her mother works as a radio journalist, though it's been eight months since she last saw a paycheque. Somehow Sofia supports her mother, her grandmother and a younger brother who's still at university, all on one salary. But as she speaks, we begin to understand that this is only part of what keeps her in Ukraine. Sofia explains that she spends almost every evening with her friends, talking of everything under the sun and moon. As she speaks, I begin to understand the extraordinary depth of feeling, of loyalty and knowing, that friendship here demands.

Sofia gives us the name of the guide the foundation has arranged for us in Ternopil'; she tells us the quickest route by which to leave L'viv and wishes us a safe journey. We say goodbye, but as we start to walk away, Sofia calls after us. She says she hopes I'll find whatever it is I'm searching for.

17

Ternopil': field of thorns

Villas, leafy arcades, a stone lion, tamed by chemical rain. The road out of L'viv is so empty that the traffic cops can pull over every vehicle at the STOP-CONTROL they've set up at the city limits. Similar surveillance booths can be found at the entrance and exit of every city in Ukraine: this one is graced with a display of smashed cars—part object lesson, part found sculpture, part scavengers' joy. We show our papers and are sent on our way with the Ukrainian equivalent of *bon voyage*: *shchaslyvoho dorohu*.

It's a sweetly rolling countryside we're driving through, this hazy day in mid-July. Horses, goats and turkeys graze in ditches where daisies and poppies bloom. Mutts skulk in doorways; one is chained in the yard of a mobile home plastered with Marlboro signs. Still no storks, though I'm looking out for the huge, ungainly nests, a male perched on one long skinny leg, a female feeding their young. Storks, I recall, mate for life; they winter over in Egypt. Perhaps they've all decided to take up permanent residence there, an avian equivalent to Florida.

Every so often we pass wooden carts with metal rims on their wheels, pulling loads of fresh-cut hay and clover. Sometimes we see collective farm buildings in fields of white-flowering potatoes;

the rarest sight of all is a tractor. Women are out in the fields, stooped or bending straight from the hips. What has changed in their lives since the days when their great-grandmothers worked these fields for Polish noblemen? What is it like to live here— where do people live? The bus stops are deserted, the houses in the small towns seem sealed with decay, though they date from the sixties: skinny porch poles, sagging roofs. Sometimes we glimpse older houses in shades of lilac or cool, shadowy blues, and once, a wall painted with swans. But there are no signs of life spelled out in laundry lines, children's toys or bicycles.

At times we're the only traffic on the road—every other car has pulled over to the side, popular mechanics going on under smoking hoods. All the way from L'viv to Ternopil', only one western-style transport truck, and one man on a bicycle, outside a small town where volleyball is being played right at the highway's edge. Will it be like this in Pidvolochys'k? Will a similar highway run through Staromischyna, turning it into a mere drive-through? Where are the roads from my mother's stories, cart tracks that become brown rivers when the rains beat down?

A persistent smell of asphalt in the air; mistrust perching like a flock of crows on my ribs as we ride into Ternopil', the place where my grandmother and her daughters broke their journey on their way to Canada.

✕◈✕

Ternopil' was founded in 1540, when Zygmunt the First gave a massive grant of land to Hetman Jan Tarnowski, leader of the Polish army. Tarnowski named it "Field of Thorns," which seems sadly fitting now. By the end of the war, after the Red Army had seized the city back from the Germans street by street, there were only a handful of buildings left intact. A few of the ruined structures were rebuilt as they'd once been; most were replaced by

Soviet-style apartment blocks. We park by a barnlike cinema in which a porno film is playing; walk past a sepulchral *Univermag* store that seems to be a depot for all the defective merchandise the USSR ever produced: shoes, vases, pocketknives. Just as we reach the town's main square a thunderstorm breaks, but we keep on walking, looking for any building or simulation of a building old enough to have been glanced at by Olena and her children. It must have taken them some time to find a pharmacist who could treat my mother's trachoma: they must have stayed overnight at some boarding house by the station.

The station's up the hill. My guidebook tells me it's a reproduction finished the year I was born, yet as I walk inside I feel I'm on haunted ground: through this place those I love once passed. The building aspires to grandeur: art deco lamps like upside-down ice cream cones, a showy central staircase. Everywhere there's a buzz of buying and selling: fresh rolls, bottles of Fanta, translations of Danielle Steele as well as volumes on Ukrainian literary culture. There's even a row of Quick Jack gambling machines in one deserted, crepuscular hall. But the weary smell of sweat-soaked cloth, the constant shifting of bags, boxes, baskets—these wouldn't have changed since my grandmother's day.

I watch Olena and her daughters push their way through the crowded hall. They stumble out of the station, lugging their belongings—they can't afford a cart or cab—and walk into the same rainstorm that's drenching us, in spite of our umbrellas. The leather of their shoes squelches as they splash through puddles; the soaked wool of their dresses weighs them down as much as their bundles. They ignore the patriotic music gushing from the loudspeakers, they push past vendors and gypsies, vanishing down Chopin or Tatar street, looking for the kind of place where three people can find cheap lodgings for however long it takes to soothe Natalia's smarting eyes.

I want to call them back, just to show them a sidewalk stand displaying blackened sunflower seeds and a pale fan of bananas. That mysterious object of desire Vira and Natalia failed to puzzle out when they first saw it hanging in a plate glass window in this very city, more than sixty years ago. Now for sale on every corner, the world's least perishable, most easily transportable fruit. The one almost everyone here can now afford to buy.

❋❋❋

Our hotel has only recently been opened to foreigners. At the front desk, which is really a sentry post, stand the harpies. One has a dyed-black bouffant and a moustache with hairs like wayward feelers. Another sports gold fillings as big as medals, and the last looks as though she receives hourly transfusions of vinegar. They seize our passports as if to restore them to their rightful owners; they demand we fill out illegibly mimeographed forms on disintegrating pink paper; they speak no English and possess even less patience with my halting Ukrainian. Perhaps the harpies are in such fine form because an entire floor of the Hotel Ruta is filled with American missionaries, the ones who have postered the city with yellow signs advertising the "Victorious Living Mission," a title that seems to have eluded or defied translation.

Our room's on the top floor, reached by a wheezy elevator. The furniture, the wallpaper, the bedding have not been changed since 1963, but it's the most expensive room in the whole hotel: the presence of a massive refrigerator that we end up unplugging each night to silence what sounds like arctic blizzards pushes the room's price into the VIP range. Translated into American dollars this is supremely modest, but it's four times what a Ukrainian guest would pay. The Ruta brings out a slovenliness in us: within minutes our room is littered with receipts, passports, books and notebooks, plastic bags, sweat-stained moneyholders, worn socks, rinsed underwear, ashtray caches of glasses, earrings, watches.

Late the next morning I phone the Netherlands and hear from our son about the sailing he's done, the rowing camp he's signed up for, the old teak lifeboat he's helping to sand down and refinish with a friend he's just made. I'm relieved he isn't with us in Ternopil', and yet I'm sorry, too. Not just because of missing him, the very sight of his long, thin body, all knees and elbows still, but because of his way of looking at things, the newness of his eyes. He would see a different city from the one I do; he'd help me correct some of my shortsightedness. But the plastic card that has given me five minutes of his voice is running down; there's hardly time to say goodbye.

We walk out of the dark hotel into cool, glassy sunlight; we are supposed to meet the interpreter Sofia's arranged for us: German-speaking, I presume. To cheer me, Michael points out the pleasanter aspects of the city: genuine or replicated Habsburg-era buildings, a few with scaffolding outside and paint buckets in the windows; beds of marigolds in public squares, a young couple with a baby dressed up like a pasha. There's even a trailer advertising virtual reality sessions. But it's not till we reach the main square with its thickly planted chestnut trees, its dozen stone-dry fountains, that I stop imagining disaster. Here is our guide and translator, who will show us the sights of Ternopil' and accompany us to Staromischyna. She can't be more than twenty: her face is as glistening and open as an apple sliced in two. And so generous is her enthusiasm that the whole city is redeemed in the rush of her greeting:

"HelloIamsohappytomeetyouIhopesoverymuchthatIcan-helpyou."

Her name, like my grandmother's, is Olena, and though she's a biologist by training, her English is astounding. We go to a small basement restaurant across from the square, and over lunch, Olena tells us something of herself. She was born in Ternopil', into a family of doctors. Her parents are divorced, and she hasn't seen her father for many years, but her mother is lucky enough to own a house and garden near the hospital where she works. They would be honoured—she and her mother—if we would join them for supper at their home that evening, after we've visited the Regional Museum. It's one of the best in Ukraine, and tomorrow it will be closed; we really must spend some time there, look at the Zbruch idol, if nothing else. I'd hoped that we could head to Staromischyna today, but Olena's insistence, and the thought of seeing the Zbruch idol, persuade me to delay this homecoming until tomorrow.

The idol turns out to be a copy—the original, which dates from the eighth century, is in Krakow, in one of the many museums closed for renovations there. From what little I'd read in the *Encyclopedia of Ukraine*, I'd pictured a golden Buddha-like godlet; what I'm faced with is a column of dull grey stone, three metres high, carved with a figure in a round hat and skirt, holding a dove or a pipe in its hands. The guard, a middle-aged woman sitting on a folding chair, asks if we're from Canada, then tells us how lucky we are. *People here don't get paid anymore for the work they do—you have to scramble just to get by each day with enough food in your belly.* I try to tell her that I hope things will get better very soon. The woman sighs, leaning forward with her hands on her knees. I would like to say more, I would like to do something more than stand with my head slightly bowed in the electric light that's been switched on in our honour. But I move on, leaving the Zbruch idol behind, looking for objects from a far more recent past.

In one display I find a *mialka* or potato masher topped with a star-shaped piece of wood: was this what my mother dressed up in a square of black cloth snipped from a Sunday skirt? This photograph of Russian soldiers standing at the edge of a field, sometime during World War I—could these have been the men who rode into Staromischyna, ordering the villagers out to dig trenches? Beyond the edges of the picture, could you find my grandmother's sister, the nameless one who grazed her legs with the edge of a shovel, sat down in the dirt and chose to die? And this wall of documents dealing with the Polish-Ukrainian war of 1919–20: might they colour in some of the blankness that is Tomasz's early life? Dictionary in hand, Olena translates for me the oath of the Ukrainian Galician army, wrestling with the odd archaic words:

We swear this solemn oath to almighty God and promise to serve faithfully and obediently the West Ukrainian National Republic and its supreme power as vested in the government and army, the chiefs and their commanders. We swear to respect and defend them, also their commands and missions, to perform any service against any enemy who might be, and wherever the supreme power demands: on the water, on the land, in the air, in daytime and at night, in battle, in attacks and conflicts, and all different kinds of initiatives; in a word in every place, in every season, in every case to struggle boldly and courageously, not to desert our army's flags and weapons under any circumstances, never to come to the slightest mutual understanding with the enemy, always to behave in a way which military law demands and that becomes an honest military man, and in this manner to live and die in an honourable way. So help me God, Amen.

I try to imagine the effect of these words on a boy of eighteen, aching for action in some wider space than the confines of a house, a reading room, a village. The combination of generalities and specifics, the calls for unthinking obedience to a supreme command, but also for honesty and honour, make me dizzy. Did the young recruits say this oath instead of grace over the gluey mess of boiled, unroasted barley that was all they got to eat in training camp? Coming as so many of them surely did from mixed Ukrainian-Polish families, how did they respond to the charge never to come to the slightest mutual understanding with the enemy?

The guards are darkening the room, ready to shut the museum for the day. We walk past the panorama of the destruction of Ternopil' at the end of World War II, past the reconstruction of the village of Molotkiv, in which German soldiers shot every man, woman and child. I find myself thinking of my great-aunt Hannia's sons, wondering if I can learn more about what happened to them when I get to Staromischyna. I wonder, too, about Tomasz's half-brother Volodko, who seems to have vanished off the face of his native earth. The last display we pass is an enormous photograph of the gate of a concentration camp set up in Ternopil' by the Nazis: faces of children pressed against barbed wire. Whose children? It's closing time, the museum guards are tired, hungry and unpaid. And I am full of questions.

On the way to Olena's house we stop at several shops, trying to buy a map of the region. Maps are not to be had. Olena tells me not to worry—she knows how to get to Pidvolochys'k, which is only an hour's drive away; from there we can ask the way to Staromischyna. But now it's time for dinner; her mother is waiting for us; her grandmother would like to meet us, too. She was one of the physicians brought into Ternopil' after the Germans surrendered in 1944. She worked twelve hours a day in what could better be described as tidied debris than a clinic: she slept on a bed fashioned out of a desktop, sharing her mattress with a bucket placed to catch the rain falling through what remained of the roof.

Olena's grandmother is now a small, bent woman in a yellow head scarf; because of her wartime service she receives a pension just large enough to support Olena and her mother as well. Olena has a scholarship that has not been paid for the last eight months; her mother Olha's labour as a cardiologist working ten-hour days has been rewarded, these past four months, by payments in gas or electricity, or the occasional sack of flour. And yet the meal we are served is sumptuous: thin-skinned tomatoes tasting of sun, not plastic; cutlets done in a special local style; delicious bread and cakes. Wine, and fresh-pressed apple juice from the trees in the garden. Michael and I are not allowed to help; we sit idle on the sofa, leafing through books in Ukrainian and Russian, including a children's encyclopedia through which an oversized Lenin strides on almost every page. Olha's passion is fine art—once she visited the Hermitage, and the beauty of what she saw there enchants her still. She brings us her art books, one of them—*The Beauty of Man*—showing Michelangelo and Donatello, Bernini and Rodin as warm-ups to a monstrous work of steelman and peasant. They brandish a hammer and sickle, reminding us how deeply the past has bitten into the present here, of the persistence of mindsets as difficult to overthrow as any monumental sculpture.

We sit together talking of art and of families: my sister is an artist, and as I describe the marketplaces and the gardens she paints, the brightness of her colours, Olha's eyes widen. How she would love to see my sister's work, to meet my parents, my brother. I am moved by her generosity, her obvious pleasure in learning of other people's lives; I am humbled—the word, for once, seems right—by her quiet courage. She tells me they get by, the three of them, thanks to her mother's pension, but also to the garden with its fruit trees, its vegetable patch. I don't make the mistake of asking Olha's daughter if she would live elsewhere if she could: Olena has already told me how shocking she found it that a friend of hers who'd received a scholarship to study in the United States has decided to stay on there and not return. The grief this girl's family must feel—this is what weighs with Olena, not the dazzle of chances that have opened for her friend.

She hasn't travelled very far, Olena. Without the slightest stitch of irony, she has pointed out to us the Avenue of Eternal Glory, the everlasting flames lit for Fighters Against Fascism—some of them boys no older than herself when they were killed. What she sees is not rotting concrete and grandiose inscriptions, but the sacrifice of those who died so that this city could become her home. The parched fountains on Shevchenko Boulevard still flow for her, the fifty-year-old chestnut trees, their clustered leaves large as bear paws, are as miraculous yet customary to her as clouds must be to heavenbound saints.

What she, and others like her, will make of this place in the next twenty or thirty years may also be a miracle. I'm thinking of the brilliant faces of the gypsy children we saw on the street leading down from the railway station our first night in Ternopil'. Brilliant with happiness, inexplicable happiness, for their clothes were thinnest cotton, and heavy rain had chilled the evening air. Unlike the gypsy boys in Krakow, these children seemed free. Clutching the few kopecks we'd found for them, their faces ready to split with grins, they skipped and crowed, running back to their mother, emptying the coins into a cup she held out. Boys thin as stick figures, possessed by delight, this unexpected treasure of a few coins at the bottom of a paper cup.

I, too, am treasure-seeking, but with no such clarity of joy. The stories that make up what I know of the Old Place are a mixture of ashes and honey; dust and mould as well as the porcelain and lace tablecloths they cover. And there are secrets as well as stories. When Olena asks me, just before we say goodnight, what I'll want to do when we arrive in Staromischyna tomorrow, I don't mention finding out about the fate of Tomasz's nephews or his half-brother Volodko. I talk instead of tracking down the grave of my grand-mother's sister, finding at least the letters of her name. Of stand-ing for a moment on the site of my grandparents' fields, whether they're planted with wheat or under cement. Standing with the surveyor's plan in my hands, its buff envelope inscribed with the words *moyeh poleh*—my fields.

18

Staromischyna: blood for the ghosts

O n my way home at last, the place where my small portion of everything begins. My nerves are kites, half-fighting, half-climbing air dense with the familiarity of strangeness—a man marooned in tall grass, sharpening a scythe with a stone; a rough wooden cart with sloping sides pulled by two white workhorses, a foal skittering alongside. Olena sits in the back seat, delighted to be riding in a car, even so lowly a car as an elderly Opel Corsa. Michael's answering all the questions she asks about Canada. I can't say a word.

The car pushes on over a road that reeks of fresh tar. Small blue car; vast blue sky. I shut my eyes. We're only a few miles away from Staromischyna now, and I want to see it, one last time, through the map my mother's drawn for me, a map that might as well be etched on the backs of my eyelids.

First, the hill overlooking the village, and on top of that hill, the old church of St. Nikolai. Across from it a school, newly built, with huge and shining windows. The co-operative store, with its snowy shelves of sugar, salt and flour; the *chytalnia*, holding a few books and newspapers, several rows of rough wooden benches and a stage on which my thirteen-year-old mother saw her sweetheart off to war.

A road runs down the hill from the church, all the way to the river: along it grows *koliuchka*, the thorn hedge that can tear at your skin if you're not careful. If you follow this road to its very end, past weathered wooden fences keeping in goats and hens, you will come to my grandmother's house. You will know it's hers because of the sunflowers carved on the door and the pair of storks lording the roof. And because of the *lyokh*, whose entrance my mother has drawn to look like a roll of hay, like anything but what it really is: the entrance to a treasure hoard, hidden deep beneath the ground.

My grandmother's house, with its garden of hollyhocks and marigolds, its vegetable patch and flowering orchard, lies in a small valley: arrows point to the cemetery up the hill, and beyond it some thick, zigzaggy pencil lines sketch in the marshes bordering the Zbruch. Geese and ducks come here to teach their young to swim and eat the succulent weeds called *luska*. Horses like the white pair we passed on the road this morning are brought here to drink. Beyond the Zbruch is a blank space marked *Wheat. USSR.*

What's missing from my mother's map—or not missing, just assumed in the scribbling of names like Husak, Eschuk—are the people who lived here. Who loved and married, had children, worked what little land they owned, died and were buried, all in this nutshell world of Staromischyna. Their intimate knowledge of each other's affairs, the unstoppable interweaving of lives, so that when a woman of thirty, hearing a muffled shout on the road outside her house one April night, discovers a young man fresh from the tavern face down in the mud, she says to herself: "I'd better turn him over—who knows, he might be my son-in-law one day." Five years later, the young man marries her daughter, the girl she'd left sleeping the night she heard a cry on the road outside her door.

The very sounds of the Old Place leap up at me: cocks crowing, dogs yelping, men and women singing in the fields, sometimes for joy, sometimes just to keep themselves going after their bodies have all but given out. And the silence that roars in a child's ears when she looks up into a cloudless sky. Vira, six years old, clinging to the cousins who've come to do her mother's ploughing. When they finish, they let her tag along with them, two young, straight-backed men striding along a path through the wheat fields, back to their own village. When they get home, they will hoist her onto the back of a stout grey horse and lead her through the orchard so she can pick flowers straight from the trees, conjuring apples from the scent of petals. She wishes she were on that horse's back right now, shooing the flies that love to cluster in the corners of its eyes. It's hard to walk so far, so fast; all at once her feet refuse to go forward. Her cousins have vanished from her sight, just as her mother's house has vanished. She is stranded in a sea of freshly sown wheat; a bird she has no name for wheels above her in a sky as blue and endless as the eye of God painted on the ceiling of St. Nikolai.

"Pidvolochys'k," Olena calls out from the back seat. My eyes open onto a small town, the inevitable statue of Shevchenko at its edge. Trees, telephone wires, windows—everything's coated with dust stirred up from the road. Then nothing. The road goes on for another kilometre or so, a paved road that no one in my family would ever have known. And suddenly a name spelled on a clumsy sign, telling us that here is Staromischyna.

※◇※

Where does it begin? With black Cyrillic letters on a white background, hammered into an upright birch log on one end and a cement post on the other? Or with the old man pedalling a bicycle who stops so Olena can question him? He has lived here sixty years, he tells us: he knows of no family named Solowski. But he points out the way to St. Nikolai, up a steep, narrow lane. We drive as far as we can, park the car in front of a rusted gate and step out into the heat of noon.

When my grandmother was an eighteen-year-old girl conva-
lescing from typhus, when my grandfather came home from his
misery of a war, close to four hundred people lived in Staromischyna. Today the place seems deserted: full summer, yet no sounds
of children playing, no shouts from the fields, not even a radio
leaking music through a window. It's like looking at a photograph:
every detail's there, a whole world caught in a lens, yet nothing
moves but your eyes. For a while we stand gazing up at the white-
walled church, and then we see that we're not the only ones alive
here after all. Two old women lean against a fence across from us;
they watch us as if we're both significant and unnecessary appari-
tions. It's Olena who breaks the spell: she calls out to them, asking
the taller of the two if she knows anyone named Levkovych,
Solowski, Pokotylo—we are relations "from America" who've
come home after sixty years away.

I'm hanging back between the car and the daisies thrusting
through the fence; I'm studying the feet of these old women, the
thick socks, the stiff, battered shoes. It's as though I'm a child
again, the child I've seen through the unforgiving eyes of home
movies, a small girl curled into a ball on the floor, face down,
refusing to smile for the camera, to take part in whatever festivity
she's interrupting. I don't need any of this paraphernalia—local
experts, translator, relations ten times removed. What I want is
only this: to be invisible, to possess the mobility of a ghost, to be
in two places at once, then and now. But it's already too late—the
older woman calls out to me, asks me to come closer. Her name
is Varvara Hryhorivna Eschuk, her name appears on my mother's
map, she's the embodiment of that arrow signalling the neighbours up the road.

And as soon as she has acknowledged me as my mother's daughter, Olena Solowska's grandchild, the possibility of becoming
invisible, of walking forwards into the past, disappears forever. I
am in a Staromischyna where I must be shown round lest I lose

my way, miss the sights, like the perfect stranger I and my whole family have become here.

❊❊❊

When the Soviets marched into eastern Galicia three years after Olena and her children left for Canada, they began a program of land reform, confiscating the vast estates of the church and of the Polish gentry, redistributing some of this land and the livestock that went with it to the poorest of the peasants, earmarking most of it for future collective farms. Collectivization began in the spring of 1940, the year before the expiry of Olena's contract with the neighbour who'd rented her fields. The Ternopil' oblast in which Staromischyna is located had the second highest rate of households collectivized in western Ukraine. To make possible such a drastic change in the way land was owned and farmed, to eliminate oppo- sition to the new regime, the Soviets ordered mass deportations of villagers. How many of the families who farmed strips of land on the outskirts of Staromischyna would have been torn from their homes and shipped east, to Russia? Next to the human suffering that must have happened in this village, the material damage should seem insignificant. And yet it doesn't. The people who were forced from the village vanished long ago, but the ruined beauty of this place remains, and makes this loss continual.

The *chytalnia*, Varvara explains, was destroyed during the war; its site is marked only by a small pile of stones. That one graceful white-walled house with the portico? It's now a cultural centre— the priest used to live there once. "Was his name Swystun?" I ask, repeating the name I've read on so many death and birth and marriage certificates. Varvara nods. As for that grey concrete building it's the new school, for the older children; the young ones still go to classes in the old school, over there. It takes me a moment to realize that the small pink bungalow to which Varvara's pointing is that glorious modern building my mother so often described to me, the one whose huge windows were a source of stupefaction to her. The school's tin roof looks rusted through; great pieces of stucco have peeled from the walls, leaving turquoise scars: three fat geese waddle past the wooden door.

The door is shut; I make no move to open it. I know the school to be a mirage that would dissolve the moment I tried to enter it. At the open-air museum outside L'viv I'd seen the kind of school I knew my mother's to have been: long wooden desks, a display of stuffed birds, a crucifix over the chalkboard, all faithfully preserved. All I'd see inside the school at Staromischyna would be the past erased. I look away, over to the ugly metal roof of what used to be the priest's house. Olena questions me with her eyes: I confess that I was expecting at least one house with thatch. In England, I explain, only very wealthy people can afford thatched roofs—it's a sign of high social status to own an ancient cottage. Olena smiles politely: it's clear she can't believe anything so absurd.

Varvara Hryhorivna Eschuk is the village equivalent of a field marshall. Her uniform is a black kerchief, a dark skirt and sweater striped with thin white lines, and her husband's thick, gaping shoes—she tells us her feet are too swollen for anything else. When I ask about a large mound in the churchyard, a *mohyla* topped with a cross made of birch logs, Varvara calls out one word—*viyna*: the war. Beside the *mohyla* hangs a Ukrainian flag, its blue and yellow bleached by the sun. Olena apologizes for not being able to read the inscription on top of the cross; she has trouble with her eyes, she confesses: her mother is trying to arrange for her to see a specialist. Varvara's own eyes are too poor to read such small print, but she seizes on a young woman with a baby who has materialized out of nowhere. "Read what it says there," she commands, taking charge of the baby, as the woman dutifully spells out the verse. It asks the young men—the boys—of the village to sleep quietly here. They have fought for freedom and their homeland; they have met their fate. What dreams could be more beautiful?

Varvara leads us down the lane from the church onto the main road through the village. The words of the inscription are running in my head—I ask her if she knows what happened to a man named Volodymyr Pokotylo, my grandfather's half-brother. She never breaks her stride. "Killed," she says. "By the Fascists—or the Soviets—at the start of the war." I wait, but there's nothing more, just the facts, however inconclusive. I want to ask about Hannia and her sons but remember that they lived in another village; besides, I don't care to hear their lives chopped up by Varvara. Perhaps there'll be someone else I can ask, someone with a gift for storytelling. Varvara's style is that of an inquisitor: as we walk under the soft green slap of leaves, she stops at this gate, that fence, calling out to anyone old enough, "You there—do you remember Olena Solowska and her children?" Varvara explains that we're tourists—the word might as well be "aliens" or "idiots."

People come up to us to say they knew my family—a shy woman in a stained pinafore, Stefka Khory, remembers going to the village school with Vira. She stares at us for a moment, lifts her hands to her face; words fall like tears between her fingers. "She's saying she regrets her destiny," Olena explains. At first the phrase seems inflated, but it is, I come to understand, exactly right. Life is very hard now, Stefka tells us, folding her arms so that her breasts look like apples stashed in pockets on each side of her waist. In summer there's enough to eat, but once autumn's over things become impossible. People can barely afford to heat and light their houses; whatever pensions they receive are worth less than the pebbles on the road, and how can you live on stones? Perhaps, Stefka says, she will see the kind of life we have in Canada when she gets to heaven. Varvara shrugs, signalling her disbelief in the existence of either place or else the chance of Stefka's ever reaching them.

We continue along a road with no trace of any vicious hedge, or the earth that spring or autumn rain turned into thick brown soup. Light falls through the trees and the sleeves of dust on their branches; silence falls between us. I'm approaching the site of my grandmother's house the way my mother, as a child, approached the priest's egg-shaped glass through which she knew she'd see the whole of heaven. But as we stop before a metal fence and look— as Varvara bids us—at the squat modern house beyond, the glass becomes stone. It withholds what I'm searching for—not Olena's house, where my mother was born, but the ghost of that house, its tangible absence.

I take photograph after photograph of nothing. There's too much to see here: the chain-link fence that has replaced the wooden one; the ugly tin-roofed house with its large, badly fitted windows; the crowd of other houses, concrete telephone poles and thickly sprawling wires. My grandmother's house was sheltered by acres of orchard; when I ask where they are, Varvara tells me that everyone has chopped their fruit trees down—they need potatoes more than cherries to see them through the winters. The orchard in which a man embraced a woman, his lips travelling her stubbled head as if to address her every grief; the orchard where a small, skinny child was chased by an ancient schoolmaster roaring *bestia carnalia*—gone, as if they'd never been.

I stare through the mesh of the fence, searching the cluttered yard for some sign of a structure shaped like a bale of hay, a door leading down to the dark. It's the one thing my mother has asked me to try to find in Staromischyna. She knows, as I do, that the *lyokh* vanished long ago, its treasures stolen or rotted away. She hopes, as I do, that some trace of it remains, if only as a story still told in the village: how our family kept faith with those who trusted them with their most precious possessions. I ask Varvara what she knows about the root cellar that used to be here; she holds up her hands, then twists them round, palms up and empty.

As if to console me, she tells of how the *lyokhs* have changed with the times; nowadays their walls are made of concrete or cement blocks instead of clay. How can I tell her that the *lyokh* as it used to be is the heart of the Old Place for me—its heart because hidden, mysterious and thus alive?

The only thing that still exists from the world of my mother's stories is the pump at the end of the road. It's painted a bright blue instead of the bare metal my aunt remembers. I work the handle up and down, trying to draw water, and when a little trickles out I don't drink it but let it fall through my fingers onto the earth. I'd thought I would bring back a handful of that earth to my mother, but I can't force myself to stoop and gather it. For what good would it be without the things my people planted in it—an orchard, a house with clay walls, a heap of treasures waiting for their owners to return? I should have stolen a fistful of earth from the house at the open-air museum in L'viv; I should have realized that the Old Place could survive only as an exhibit in an open-air museum: clay and thatch plucked up by levers and pulleys, loaded onto a truck and driven hundreds of miles away. To become part of a zoo where, instead of animals, they keep the past.

As I follow Varvara down the road, I keep wondering why everything before me seems so emptied, so unreal. The Staromis-chyna that came to me through stories was like a length of cloth dense with embroidery; what I find here is the same cloth with the stitches picked out, a cloth of holes. I'm expected to respond to these holes; the camera stands in for me, clicks at a rooster on a dung heap, a long-abandoned stork nest on the tall stump of a tree. We turn back, take another turning of the road, past the house where I'm told Adela once lived. It looks more like a barn than a house, and I wonder whether Varvara, in spite of her brisk authority, is mistaken, or else inventing what she thinks I want to hear. She makes us stop before a large house with a steep drive, at the end of which a man of fifty seems to be sitting flush with the earth. Except that you can't sit if you have no legs. The man is lodged on his stumps, which rest on a round, wheeled, wooden board. By means of two large plugs with leather handles he pulls himself along the ground. There's no explanation as to how this man lost his legs; no indication on Varvara's part that explanations are called for.

"Yuri," Varvara bellows. "These Americans want to take your picture: stay still for a moment." I am ashamed to aim a camera in this man's direction, but he stops his painful push across the drive just as Varvara bids him: he rests on his stumps and looks straight up to the sky, as if doing so could make him taller.

"That," Varvara says, as we leave the man behind, "is where Adela's brother lived—Volodymyr. Not in that house, but the one that was there before the war."

However hard I try, I can't make a connection between the legless man and the man who once made skis for my aunt; between this modern house and the workshop it must have replaced. I ask Varvara about the war, what happened in the village. Some of her answers I can understand without Olena's help. The Germans weren't as cruel here as they were across the river on the Russian side. Only a few places were destroyed in Staromischyna. It was under the Soviets, after 1944, that the village changed into what's here now—modern houses, electricity. Everything from the old time was destroyed, pulled down. "Except for the church," I interrupt. I'd seen its date of completion carved into the lintel: 1888. Our house in Canada is twenty years older than St. Nikolai.

Varvara's tour stops in front of a metal gate. Beyond it dogs trot and a turkey gathers its chicks. Inside a screened, shallow box newly hatched ducklings are peeping. A small girl crouches over them, listening as if with her eyes alone, hazel eyes that become rounder and deeper as she looks up to see us. A man appears at the gate, a short man with a face that doesn't seem to belong to his old man's body. His face is round, almost unlined, with the kind of curved, hooded eyelids you find in medieval Flemish paintings. His eyes don't meet my face, even when Varvara explains that I am "family." For this young-old man Evhen turns out to be the son of Tomasz's stepbrother Mykola Pokotylo. He stands there contemplating Varvara's damaged shoes or the dust puddled round them. It's his wife, Stefania, a pleasant woman in her fifties, who finally asks us inside.

What protocol must returned prodigals follow? I don't want any of this—neither, it appears, does Evhen Pokotylo. He keeps his hands clasped behind his back, his eyes fastened to the ground. Yet his thoughts are as clear as if he'd spoken them: "These people who breeze into the village, showing off their good fortune like too many rings on their fingers—what do they want out of me?" Varvara claps her hands as if she's accomplished a good portion of her life's work, then takes her leave of us, her dark back with the thin white stripes melting into the mix of light and shadow on the road. I try to tell Stefania that we don't want to be any trouble, but she insists we have a bite to eat. Her husband still says nothing. The little girl, their granddaughter Olesia, follows us indoors, bunching her skirt in her hands, plucking at the little balloon of material she's made.

Is every homecoming in Staromischyna like this? The chore-ography, the stage set and props? We're taken to the parlour where we sit on a plastic sofa, while Stefania disappears and Evhen stares at our shoes. There's something so familiar to me in his wariness, something I've always known. And then it comes to me: this is the grandson of the man who Vira told me would refuse you the time of day and would never meet your gaze. The man who tossed Tomasz's children withered apples, saving the sweet ones for his grandchildren by blood, not marriage. Do genetics really work this way—not only the shape or shade of eyes but an oblique glance, a cast of mind passed down, for better or worse, along the generations?

Olena attempts conversation—she asks what's growing in the fields. The Colorado potato beetle, Evhen replies. It's destroying what had promised to be an exceptionally fine and plentiful crop. Everyone's in the potato fields, especially the children with their thin and agile fingers, pulling the bugs off one by one, crushing them in their hands. There are sprays, of course; they come all the way from France, but they're dangerous, you need masks to use them. After Chornobyl, people are suspicious of even the most helpful poisons.

In the silence that follows, the objects in the room jump out at me. An enlarged photograph on the wall of a uniformed young man, his dark-eyed, mustachioed face a study in blanks and shadows. This must be Evhen's father Mykola, who'd have been the same age as his stepbrother Tomasz. He'd have known everything I've been trying to discover of my grandfather's early life, and he's as silent as blanks and shadows can be. Across from this portrait sits a sofabed with a factory-made kilim tossed over it. A television set draped in lace, a telephone the colour of candied violets. Nothing in this modern parlour has the grace, the simple beauty, of the crudely fashioned chairs and tables, hanging cradles, carved chests we've seen in ethnographic museums. The only piece of furniture that seems to have been made by hand is a large plain wardrobe built of some light-coloured wood, with the barest ornamentation.

Evhen tells me that the wardrobe was made by his uncle Volodymyr. Sixty years ago, he adds, and it's still a fine piece of furniture. Not like what you buy today—pressboard, plywood—junk. Volodymyr was a *maister*, Evhen says: not a mere carpenter but a cabinetmaker. A clever man: people respected him for his head as well as his hands. Although—and here Evhen says something about his uncle that I don't understand. I have to ask Olena to translate it twice, and I still can't fathom what he means. The atmosphere in the room alters with my confusion; the air seems thicker, darker. Evhen is still talking, Olena translating. All that's left of Volodymyr, they tell me, is the furniture he made: tables, bedsteads, wardrobes scattered through the village. And as far away as Canada, I want to add: a miniature cupboard with a tilting mirror. Instead I repeat what Varvara has told me, that Volodymyr—my mother's uncle Volodko—was shot by Fascists at the start of the war. Evhen shakes his head; he addresses a piece of embroidery hung on the wall below his father's photograph:

"He died in Siberia—slave labour. The Red Army took him when they came back in '44."

I try to connect the man I know by his diminutive—Volodko—with his death in the harshest of exiles. I say one word to Evhen: "Why?"

He shrugs, not because he doesn't know the answer, but because of the stupidity of the question. When did the Russians ever need reasons for what they did? All he knows is this: Volodymyr was deported by the Russians; he died in a gulag, no one knows exactly when or where.

Stefania comes into the room with bowls of *borshch*, dark slices of honeycake. It's mid-afternoon, and we haven't eaten since breakfast: a roll each, bought off a bakery truck parked by our hotel. But I'm reluctant to eat, though the food smells delicious and Stefania's face lights with the pleasure of having guests. I like Stefania, I like the way her bright yellow sweater and purple skirt stick out their tongues at the drabness of her kerchief and lumpen sandals. But there's a stone in my stomach, put there by Evhen's talk about Volodko's death in Siberia; by what he said earlier, the words I couldn't understand. I look down into the *borshch*: its colour and thickness make me think of Odysseus spilling blood for the ghosts to drink and tell their stories. It makes me think of Persephone, too, prisoner of those six pomegranate seeds she ate in the garden of Hades.

But I know what's expected, I know enough not to give myself away. I pick up my spoon and drink the rich red *borshch*; I take a slice of honeycake as dark as earth. While I eat, I look at the photograph of my grandfather's stepbrother on the wall. I look at the face of his son, averted, deliberately emptied, like those wax-backed sketchpads, where you write with a leadless pencil over clear plastic—words or lines you can erase just by pulling up the sheet.

Stefania tries to fill the silence, talking of how most villagers get by thanks to their pigs and cow and the sauerkraut they put up each year—these days, no one can afford to get vitamin C from oranges. She tells us that her husband used to be a chauffeur until he had an accident and lost the use of one eye. He's been retired for seven years, now—

"I'll work until it's time for me to die," Evhen insists. And then he tells his wife to go and fetch the key to the church. Stefania, he explains, is in charge of changing the flowers, washing and iron-ing the altar cloths, caring for the priest's vestments at St. Niko-lai. He tells us this with the same detachment he showed on the subject of Colorado potato beetles. We would love to see the church, I say, speaking without Olena's help this once. I'm uneasy in this house where I've paid my dues, eaten *borshch* and honey-cake: I want to leave before I'm trapped here by that stone in my belly, the weight of everything I haven't asked or understood.

Michael asks to use the bathroom—we wait in the yard for him, then walk up the road together. Evhen and his wife with little Olesia between them, Olena holding a gigantic rubber plant that Stefania's decided to present her with. Michael joins me at the end of the procession. I look at him and he shakes his head.

"A bucket," he says. "Pulsing with maggots."

※◈※

When the Soviets took over Staromischyna, they decided to tear down St. Nikolai. Stefania tells us how the villagers refused to go off to work on the morning set for the demolition, how they formed a human chain round the church, saying, *You'll have to chop our arms off first.* They were banking on the newly collectivized fields needing the labour of those arms, and they won their gamble. The building stayed put, its doors locked, the interior stripped echoless.

The church has been open for several years now. In the porch stands a crude wooden statue of Christ on the cross, the wound in his side like a crumpled pink handkerchief, a dish of strawberry ice cream. Someone must have hidden the carving all those years when the church lay locked and dark; performed this small act of resurrection by placing the carving back where it had always been. Its presence tricks me into thinking that, as I step through the doors, I'll find the very skin of the past: oiled wood garlanded with periwinkle leaves, a scent of beeswax and roses.

Inside, where my mother remembers only the fatigue of standing or kneeling for hours on end, are the same oak pews you'd find in any Canadian church. The lamps, the gilded icon screen, the gilt statues of crowned saints: all were ordered new from the factory or collected from other churches in the neighbourhood, Stefania tells us—places that were falling into ruin. I look up at the ceiling to find the Virgin trampling a snake, her eyes upturned under lids like snapped blinds. Over the choir loft a greybeard Jehovah floats, wedged between a white disc that must be the sun, and a blue ring, like a Lifesaver sucked small.

They are fiercely proud of their church, the people of this village; its splendour and strangeness are far more powerful than anything that flashes on their television screens. Though maggots writhe in the buckets of their outhouses, God's house is a glory, a small space where everything gleams, new and thus perfect. The priest is a learned man, we're told—very "accurate," this is how Olena translates Stefania's description. No one could be stricter about how many flowers should be placed in the vases on the altar, how many inches apart those vases should be. This is a very good thing, it seems: God loves order, and in a world where everything's been dumped on its head and shaken to pieces, all that comes between shame and glory are those strictly specified inches.

Outside the church, near a small grove of ash trees, stands the belfry. It still shelters one bell, but the larger one that partnered it was stolen months ago, Evhen relates. He doesn't explain how or why anyone would steal something as loud, huge and heavy as a church bell. The belfry used to be made entirely of wood and thatch; now its cap and upper walls are sheet metal, yet it's the one object in all the photographs I take of Staromischyna that my mother will recognize. She will stare and stare at the image caught on a shiny rectangle of paper, her eyes travelling from the wooden planks at the bottom to the tower's slanting roof. She will tell me again the story of how the girls of the village would line up outside the church for confession and, feeling a sudden fall of rain on their hair, would look up to find the boys peeing on them from the belfry windows.

For a time I stand in the little cemetery behind the church, before the grave of my great-grandmother Rozalia—the mother of Tomasz and Hannia, of Adela and Volodko. All of her children are buried or will die in foreign places—Canada, Siberia, the west or north of Poland: could she ever have dreamed of lying so lonely in death? Between the graves Olesia kneels, plucking up dark, plumed weeds to feed to her ducklings. You can look out in different directions at the valley below and to a farther set of hills, studded with new brick houses, their roofs glittering in the sun. This is Volochys'k—Stefania points out the domes of an enormous church still under construction. When my mother was a child, those hills were Stalin's country; if your eyes were good enough, you could make out the shape of cows in the pastures or the glint of blades at harvest time, but you could no more imagine setting foot there than on the moon. As for the famine that went on far to the east in Stalin's country, that land of endless golden wheat—it could have happened on the moon as well, for all that Staromischyna knew of it. Now, should we wish, we could drive across the bridge spanning the Zbruch, with no fear of border guards pumping bullets in our backs. We could stand among the rash of new houses going up in Volochys'k and look back at Staromischyna, as any number of young, dead men had longed to do.

We say goodbye to Evhen, Stefania, Olesia, an awkward farewell, for we've tried to make them a gift of money, which they refuse to take until Michael persuades them to spend it on the church. Evhen asks me to give his greetings to his aunt Adela in Poland; then he shocks me by kissing my hand. We climb into the car, Olena balancing the heavy rubber plant on her lap, trying to keep the earth from spilling out as we jolt away.

XOX

Before heading back to Ternopil', we stop at Staromischyna's other cemetery, the one that lies in the valley and edges up a hillside on the very outskirts of the village. It's the one place where I feel safe here; the only place that speaks the past to me as if it were a living language. Years ago it was Vira and Natalia's chief refuge; now I've come to it to hide in waist-high grass under a lilac tree. All around me tiger lilies bloom and pale blue chicory; Olena points out a leaf called *Maty i Machukha*, Mother and Stepmother, one side of it smooth, the other rough. Bees drowse; dogs bark far away; wind shakes the trees and sets the grasses swaying. At last I'm alone and invisible, calmed by the blindness of the dead, the conversation of roots and earth and bone going on all round me.

When I look back at this journey to the Old Place, I'll remember how brief and vast it was, this time spent hiding between iron crosses and lilac leaves. Michael walks along whatever paths remain between the graves, searching for my family's names as if for children lost in a forest. Olena's identifying wildflowers: I know that she has to get home within the hour; I know we should have left this place by now. Yet I cannot move a finger, even an eyelid. Is it the pull of the dead that keeps me here, ancestors moving through my cells like those circus acrobats who swing from one pair of arms to another and another, making a human chain to bridge sheer air?

Any moment now Michael will come to me and hold out his hand. I will walk with him towards the gate, the car beyond the gate. But for the moments before that moment it's as if I am already walking. Towards a cliff edge from which I'll have to jump as surely as I'll have to go on breathing. And as I fall, I'll be thinking not of how far or fast I'm flying downwards, but of how I'll never be able to regain that clifftop, the lush, flower-shot grass through which I walked to the very edge of falling.

※◇※

Step by step by step
a child goes down to the dark.
What does she know, what does she fear?
A child who wakes in the night, pulled through
the throat of all she knows and cannot understand.
When can she speak? To whom? What can she ever tell?

Lightning shoves into our room like a searchlight. Seconds later, there's a crack of thunder overhead. The hotel has no fire escape or evacuation procedures: if worst comes to worst, all we'll be able to do is jump out the window, seven stories to the concrete below. I can't tell if it was the storm or my dreams that woke me: all I know is that I can't shut out the lightning. Even with my eyes closed tight, it scalds the dark. All I can do is stumble out of bed and plug in the refrigerator, hoping its moans will drown out the thunder breaking louder and closer.

Michael's sleeping through the storm as if it were nothing more than weather. He wakes only when I crawl into his narrow bed. There's scarcely room for him inside, yet somehow we manage to lie down together. I put my hand to his face, and he asks what time it is.

"Early."

"Don't worry about the storm—we'll be all right. Try to get some sleep."

"I can't," I say. "Bad dreams."

"About that man—Pokotylo?"

"No. Yes."

No more words for a while, just thunder, and gusts from the refrigerator, and lightning. Then my husband tells me one of the things he was thinking as we walked through Staromischyna. That no one could have hid anyone there without the whole village finding out. I don't reply. "Let's talk in the morning," Michael says. I lie crushed up beside him, listening to his steady breathing. It's as hard for me to fall asleep as it was when I was a child, terrified to go to bed if my closet door was open. I had convinced myself that a small, hunchbacked man materialized there each night. Once, when I was ill, I woke to find the door to my closet, which had been shut when I'd fallen asleep, sliding open again. I stared into the darkness, watching the hunchback creep towards me.

When he reached my bed, he leaned over, whispering something soft and thick, so close against my face I couldn't breathe. I screamed, waking my sister in the bed across from me and bringing my mother rushing down the hall. I was scolded for making a commotion, I was told to go back to sleep, and I did. I never saw the hunchbacked man again. But now, thinking of a locked wardrobe in a strange man's house, of a plate of blood-red soup set down before me, I feel that same soft thickness against my face, the thickness of words uttered in the dark. The words Evhen spoke about Volodko, words I had to ask Olena the meaning of again and again. Words I tried to put away from me after we left the Pokoty-los' house: *He had arguments with the Jews. Conflicts with Jews.*

Evhen would have been nine years old when the war started, a boy of fourteen at its end. What did he see, what does he really know of that time, of what happened to his uncle and why? The Russians pushed a gun at Volodko's back; they marched him to a train that carried him so far to the east, so far to the north that no one ever heard from him again. But when did this happen? At the start of the war, as Varvara suggested, when the Bolsheviks arrested hundreds of thousands of Ukrainian nationalists, so-called enemies of the people, executing some, deporting others? Or at the end of the war, as Evhen remembers it—when the Russians reoccupied eastern Galicia, and after almost all the Jews there had been murdered? Which version is accurate, whom do I trust? Magisterial Varvara, airily assigning Volodko's death to Fascists or Bolsheviks, as if they were one and the same? Or blank-faced Evhen, who never once looked me in the eyes?

Arguments, conflicts—what do the words mean? I know that for centuries the Jews of Galicia allied themselves with the Poles, not the Ukrainians, who were, after all, only another minority, as oppressed as they. Would the Jews have welcomed the Russians in 1939, grateful for their lifting of restrictions placed on them by the Poles? Both Volodko's parents were Ukrainian; he may have grown up a patriot. The grave mound by St. Nikolai, next to the blue and yellow flag—is that where Volodko should rest? Was he a partisan, an anti-Bolshevik? Why did the Russians arrest him— what had he done? *When did the Russians ever need reasons for what they did?* They could have shot him straight out; instead they hauled him to the gulag, worked him to death, threw his body away. *What dreams could be more beautiful?*

Everything I know, everything I don't know shakes on a blade of lightning. I thought I was prepared, I was expecting ghosts— but not this one. Conflicts with Jews, arguments: when, why?

Volodko would have started his training as a cabinetmaker in the mid-1930s, a period when, from what I've read, many Poles were entering trades that had traditionally been Jewish domains. What kind of turf wars would have occurred even in sleepy towns like Pidvolochys'k? And what would a man who'd had this kind of conflict do when the Jews of Pidvolochys'k were being murdered? Olena can't help me unravel this; she's given me the words, nothing more. It could mean anything, she said, driving back to Ternopil', hugging her rubber plant. "Anything and nothing." I want to believe that "nothing." I want my fears about Volodko to be as groundless as my mother's fears about a chest of blood-stained rags. But what of the difference made by history, the context in which all these words are stuck? Exterminations. Deportations. Adela will know; I will have to ask Adela about her brother's death, his life before the war. About Hannia's sons, too, the ones who were tortured and killed. All the questions I need to ask; the stories I have yet to hear. The heart's two chambers—everything I most desire, everything I most fear.

I'd planned to spend days in the village, looking, listening. I'd wanted to find my grandparents' fields, I'd wanted to steal the past right out of the arms of the present. Now all I can think of is rushing back to Poland, to a small town by the Baltic, to an old woman who may or may not remember what happened in a small village on the Russian border, more than half a century ago. "Let's talk in the morning," Michael said. He sleeps soundly, the way you can sleep if you're a total stranger in this place. I lie breathing in the salt of his skin, longing to be like him: no ties, here; no secrets, no uncertainty.

But we can't leave, not yet. We'll have to go back to the Old Place. Not Staromischyna this time, but Pidvolochys'k. There's something I didn't think to ask Varvara, that I couldn't ask Evhen: if Volodko perished in a gulag, what happened to Helka and Blumen? *What happened, exactly?* Adela will tell me about her brother, but for Helka I must find someone else. Someone to tell this story as an act of witness and grim homage, a form of service for the dead.

19

---

a ditch and two rivers

The electrical storm spares the Hotel Ruta. Waking to the screech of roosters, we breakfast off rolls saved from last night's dinner, drive to Olena's house and then head out for Pidvolochys'k under a sky that holds no memory of last night's rains. The road's almost empty, except for a procession of men with scythes and sacks of new-mown hay strapped to the backs of their bicycles. They put into sad relief the pylons we pass by, the telephone poles and crumbling bus shelters decorated with mosaic tiles. Trees are the real beauty of this landscape: clumps of silvery maples; acacias, their brown exploded pods hanging udderlike; birches with trunks slender as cigarettes. And always puddles of ducks and geese, the one sign of super-abundance. They fetch a good price at market, Olena explains: you can stuff their feathers into quilts and pillows; render their fat for frying.

When we pull into the town, Olena asks what I'll be looking for. The *gimnazium* Vira attended, I say. The morgue where she left flowers for the blue-caped bodies of Polish university students. The studio where my grandmother was photographed with her two daughters and an empty space to be filled in with her husband's image. The railway station where Tomasz boarded a train for Danzig. I've seen a photo of that station, taken just before World War I; in front of its two-storey neoclassical facade two young men with walking sticks lean like twin Charlie Chaplins. I tell all this to Olena, keeping secret what I really want out of this town with its gently rotting villas, azure patches showing through the whitewash, plaster garlands sad as sighs.

We find a place to park the car down a side street, by a house hemmed in with flowers. A woman in her early sixties is standing on the porch. Olena calls out to her. We're looking for buildings that would have been here in 1936, she says. The woman shakes her head; she moved here after the war. But she knows someone, a former schoolteacher, who has lived here all her life—she's the very person to help us. The woman disappears indoors for a moment; reappears with her son, a young man of twenty-five. He's wearing jeans and a designer T-shirt scribbled over in French, which he doesn't speak. He's studying at the university in Lublin to become a priest, he tells us: while he's home for the summer, he's being coached in Polish by the woman he'll take us to meet.

The way to the schoolteacher's house lies down a maze of alleyways and across backyards, along the baked dust of side streets and the desert of the main road. No one, it seems, has painted or patched a facade here since before the war; everything slopes towards ruin. We come upon a child with a puppy who has run away; she lavishes kisses on the prodigal, then holds him at arm's length, turning into a small copy of her mother: "Now I'm going to have to punish you!" A boy coasts by on a skateboard: everyone else in the town seems to be dead or sleeping. We have to knock many times at the schoolteacher's house: when she comes to the door, it's as if she's been woken from a spell. Before she lets us in, she looks at us a long while, her blue eyes magnified by thick spectacles.

This is no peasant woman with a kerchief and unlaced boots: she has the air of an exasperated duchess and is dressed with an elegance not incompatible with poverty. Stanislawa Jadwiga

Brodanchuk—she writes her name down for us, the typically Polish first names, the unmistakably Ukrainian surname. If it's her husband's, he is long gone—there's no sign of him here, not even a photograph. The house is airless and smells of rotting wood: the sitting room's taken up by a huge table on which books and ironing are piled. A few things from the old time remain—a crazily tilting stove, made out of primrose yellow tiles; an antique vase holding shrivelled black-eyed Susans. The whole house is giving way to gravity, to intricate, unstoppable decay.

When Olena asks whether the *gimnazium* my aunt attended in 1936 is still standing, she is met with a reproof. Pidvolochys'k, the teacher remarks, drawing out her vowels, giving certain words a peculiar emphasis, is a *small* town—only in *Ternopil'* was there a *gimnazium*. The disdain in her voice is as strong as the lenses that turn her eyes to ponds. Yes, there was an institute for older children, the ones too clever or rich to be finished off by the village school. My aunt might have gone there—it's at the edge of town, not far from the cemetery, if we really wish to see it. As for the railway station, it was levelled in the war. She shrugs, falls silent. Olena whispers that the teacher's Ukrainian is thick with Polish words, her manner of speaking old-fashioned. The arrogance and reserve come through without translation: if you can divide all people into sleeves or pockets, she's a pocket. What she knows and won't tell could fill a whole town. But I've come here to find things out, and this elderly woman is the only one who can help me. Were there many Jewish people in Pidvolochys'k before the war? I ask. What happened to them?

Immediately the teacher's expression alters. This is not a foolish or ignorant question, she seems to say; this is something worth speaking of. *Sumna istoria*, she sighs. A sad story. When the Germans occupied the town they rounded up the Jews, who were a considerable presence, some of them wealthy enough to own fine houses or apartments. The Jews were marched to a place on the road to Staromischyna. The Germans made them dig a great ditch and then throw logs across it. They made the Jews cross these logs, and while they were crossing, they shot them. Children, men and women, people with their lives just beginning; old people, like herself. The ditch heaving with bodies, the dead upon the living. It was horrible, beyond description.

After the war, when the Russians came back, they found the camp, dug up the bodies from that ditch and brought them to be buried in the town cemetery, side by side with the Poles. But first they took whatever gold they could find still stuck to the bodies, to teeth and to finger bones. And then the Russians filled in the ditch and built an outdoor restaurant on top of it. One Jewish man who survived the war had wanted to put up a memorial, but he didn't succeed. He's dead now, buried with the others. And nobody knows any of this, or wants to remember.

"You—what do you know?" the teacher asks the young man studying to be a priest. Her voice carries clear across the room; there's no refusing it. He says he knew that Poles and Jews lie side by side in the cemetery, but nothing of how or why this came to be.

"And the houses the Jews were forced to abandon. Such ignorant people moved in—they knew nothing, they broke windows, burned anything they could find for fuel: doors, wardrobes, carvings. Everything ruined. The Russians demolished what was left—so there's nothing to help us remember. Memory," she says, looking up through her heavy glasses, "memory should be dark, like blood. But it's only water after all."

The teacher shows us out through the same damp corridor we entered by. I lag behind, turning over these extraordinary stories she has told us: the reburial of the murdered Jews, the transformation of a site for mass murder into a picnic spot. It takes me some time to reach the doorway where Stanislawa Jadwiga is waiting. She steps outside with us, and I ask if I may take her photograph. She makes an impatient gesture with her hands.

"I'm too old," she says, "too ugly. Take a picture of the girl instead." She's pointing to Olena, whom she has scolded and corrected throughout the conversation. I've already taken her picture, I say—I would like to take yours. And I lift the camera towards the fine bones of this woman's face, the gigantic, liquid eyes, the still-beautiful hair, swept up and pinned at the back of her head. I wonder what she's doing here, why she didn't leave after the war, like all the other Poles who chose or were forced to flee what had become Ukraine. The shutter clicks, catching an expression more fluent than contempt or resignation. She knows an enormous amount: she refuses to forget. And she, like her house, is dying.

Back in the dust and heat we follow our guide in the direction the teacher has sketched out for us, through a part of town we haven't seen before: streets of small, carefully tended houses surrounded by fruit trees, riots of hollyhock and clematis. At last we come to a square red-brick building; its stepped gable echoes the facades of churches in the oldest parts of Krakow. This is the school that twelve-year-old Vira attended, sitting next to the Jewish children on the outcasts' bench. I think I'm seeing everything so clearly in this doubled light of past and present, but Michael points out what I haven't noticed: bullet holes in the brick around the school's main door. Trees throw shadows like water on the walls: all I can think of is how thirsty I am, and how tired Olena must be. But when the young man asks if we'd like to see the cemetery the schoolteacher spoke of, I say yes, following him down the road and through an iron gate.

Here is a different kind of root cellar, holding bodies instead of carrots and china. In between nettles and thick-roped brambles, small, toppled statues lie. There are many graves without any other marker than rusted metal rods spelling out the customary space a life takes up of earth. In Kazimiersz, on the outskirts of Krakow, we saw a wall made of fragments of Jewish gravestones, a wall that made me think of a mouth of smashed teeth carefully cemented together. Here there is only a green luxuriance under which the bodies of Jews and Poles lie intermixed. Perhaps Helka and Blumen are buried here; or perhaps, by some extraordinary chance, they managed to escape, to die in their beds, somewhere far enough away. Whatever their fate, I mourn them in each one of their neighbours who perished so unspeakably.

Our guide leads us back to the side street where we've left our car, and when we try to offer him something for the time and trouble he's taken, he shakes his head. "For books," we say. "All students need to buy books." Again, he refuses. His mother joins us; she wears a housedress stained from gardening, but her dignity is a match for that of the schoolteacher. "You are strangers here, you need our help—why should we want your money?" We take the young man's photograph and wish him well with his studies in Lublin. He nods, smiles. *En Afrique*, his T-shirt says, *il fait très chaud*.

※◇※

"And now?" Olena asks, as we drive out of Pidvolochys'k. I'm jumpy after all I've learned, but I speak as calmly as I can. "Now," I say, "we're going to look for one last thing. A river, wide and deep enough that a man and horse can drown in it without a hope of being saved."

We pass the turnoff to Staromischyna and park just before the bridge, where a sign spells out ZBRUCH. I stand looking out at the water, then walk away. From St. Nikolai's churchyard the Zbruch had been a blue fold in a green plain: here it seems like a mere canal. Is it the wishfulness of fiction, the fallacy of memory I've been staring at? Varvara had told me that the *staw* had disappeared, the marshes where ducks and geese once fed on peppery weeds. But if the Zbruch itself is only this thin seam of water, then what of the stories I've been told of soldiers stationed on its banks, of terrible drownings? If they're all exaggerations, even fables, then how reliable are any of the others given me to map the past?

Those stories told throughout my childhood—I never stopped to ask myself, are they true? By being stories, they were the truest things I knew. They were like the books in which I lost myself, books about flying carpets and magic amulets that could take you across continents and eons in a single moment. To listen to my family's stories round a dinner table, or in a chance moment on a streetcar ride, was to enter an endless enchantment of words; my life was braided into the lives of my ancestors with no mark of beginning or end. But now, standing at the edge of this blank and shrunken river, where reality seems to confound or abolish memory, enchantment stops.

A few old women have brought their cows to graze here: the grass is thick and rough, without flowers. Small willows grow on one section of the riverbank, and there are poplars, too, but mostly the valley is empty. I'm about to return to the car where I've left Michael and Olena, when I find myself walking down the bright and slippery grass. I have come here to find a river, even if this puddle's all there is to be found. Close by the bridge there's a broad, flat stone; I sit down on it, out of the wind that has begun to rattle the willows. Kicking off my shoes, I put my feet in the water. It seems to me that I could walk across the Zbruch as if it were still and shallow as paper. And that all I'd find when I crossed the water would be the same shore where I'm sitting now.

Where is the current my mother spoke of, the one that tugged at her as she lay all slimed with the body's mud, each beat of her heart a fist-sized explosion? If I were to lie down in these waters, would I, too, be washed clean? My skin feels written over with stories. Family stories, and the ones I've heard from Sofia, and Evhen Pokotylo, and Stanislawa Jadwiga. Right now I long to be empty of stories, to be quit of their identifying marks, the way I once had a mole burned from the back of my neck. If only it were simple, this business of belonging. If what you were born to were something you could sit down to or refuse at table; something you could put on or take off—a wreath or woven belt. If history had nothing to do with it, if history were only a book and not a burden you carry in your bones.

When I return to the car, I find Olena and Michael standing on the bridge, talking to an old woman dressed like so many others here in the costume of poverty: a skirt and jacket made out of cloth so worn it looks beaten; pilled woollen socks, sagging, laceless shoes. "I've found out the whole history of the river," Olena calls out. "This person," she explains, "is from Volochys'k." The woman smiles up at me, her gums showing a few splayed teeth.

"Our poor river." She sighs. "You see that place on the hill?" She points to the new, shining houses in the distance. "We call it Tsarskoe Selo: it's where the manager of the factory lives, and all his friends and family. A factory that makes sugar. To build that factory, they changed the shape of the Zbruch. Engineers, machinery, everything."

For a moment I can't believe what she is telling me. And then—I can't help myself—story floods in. I'm thinking of Myhailo Petrylo's sons, who grew up to be engineers. I wonder if they had anything to do with the narrowing of the Zbruch, along whose banks their father rode with Natalia and Vira, staring the future in the face.

"It used to be deep and wide, and very beautiful," the old woman says. "If you could have seen the flowers that grew along the banks, the orchards coming down right to the water."

There's still such grief in her for the lost beauty of the river. Her face must once have been handsome—you can see that from her cheekbones and her eyes. She talks unstoppably, as though she has no one else to give her stories to. She was a child during the war—eleven years old by the time the Russians came back and the fighting ended. "Listen," she says. "It's better to have nothing but a loaf of bread, and peace, than to have everything you want, and war.

Can you understand? I have pictures in my eyes; I still wake up in the night and see things I can never forget. We would run, all the children, run from one village to the next, trying to get away from the killing. But wherever we ran, there would be more and more blood pouring into the earth. When I was a child, things were terrible because of the war. Now I'm old, and life is still so terrible. Our land is rich, why are its people so poor?"

How can we answer her? We stand together in silence, and then, as a courtesy, as a kind of tribute, Michael asks if he can take a picture of us all. The woman's face fills with the pain of what she knows. "I don't want people to see me like this, I don't want strangers to say this is what we're like here, this is all we are." But she stands with us on the bridge, and the camera catches a bent old woman leaning on a stick, her eyes looking away. Behind her, between willow boughs and grass, are blue handfuls of river. We say our farewells as we have said them to Varvara Hryhorivna and Stanislawa Jadwiga: we take our leave of this woman whose name we've never asked, perhaps because she seems so much a part of the landscape as to have or need no name at all.

When we get back to Ternopil', we leave the car, as before, in a parking lot guarded by two boys who look no older than our sons. They offer us all kinds of extra services—bottled mineral water, a carwash that will strip the fur of dust we've so carefully accumulated on the local roads. Olena has told us that the sum these boys or their bosses charge to keep our car from being stripped of parts is scandalous. Still, the lot is crammed: not only foreign cars but the local ambulance as well. We pay what we're asked; we want to be sure we'll have a way of leaving Ternopil' first thing in the morning. For we are returning to Poland tomorrow, days earlier than we'd planned. As we walk towards the steel gate at the end of the lot, I notice a small table shoved up against a wall: on it, a deck of cards and something that looks like one of the toys my brother and I used to play cowboys with when we were small. A gun.

⁜

Long before sunrise, women in shock orange vests are sweeping the roads with birch brooms. At the very outskirts of Ternopil', screened by huge stalks of angelica, sit three metal huts painted a bright red and offering different grades of benzine. We stop to fill up the tank or, rather, to purchase what the attendant declares he'll sell us, the extra half-litre sloshing from the nozzle of the hose, soaking the earth below. Still, he wishes us *shchaslyvoho dorohu* as we drive off in the direction of L'viv.

We decide to stop there for an hour or so to say goodbye to Sofia. She's at her office on Teatralna Street, where she works at the foundation that has helped us enter Ukraine. We meet her boss, Sashko, a man my age, in jeans and T-shirt and a beard that looks a little like a rumpled bed. He's just come back from Uzhorod, where he's been trying to set up credit unions as a way to encourage small businesses. He tells us he has the best people in western Ukraine working on any number of projects. But he's returned to a crisis. Without any warning the government in Kyiv has changed the law concerning gifts of computer equipment to organizations like Sashko's: a form of luxury tax has been imposed, and somehow he has to pluck thousands of dollars out of the morning air.

Sashko in blue jeans, Sofia in a sundress, a Xerox machine humming in the background, faxes coming through and computer screens lit up. The distance we've travelled between the lane winding through Staromischyna and this office on Teatralna Street seems immense. Between the fresh, undamaged faces of Sofia and Olena, and "the archive of memory" preserved by old women with cavernous eyes, plundered teeth, ruined feet. Witnesses, not just to what happened in the Old Place so many years ago, but to the persistence of memory itself.

Sashko and Sofia wave us off from the courtyard. They've said nothing about our early departure from Ukraine, and I've made no excuses, though I'm seized by guilt as soon as we join the highway to the border. I could have spent at least another day in my mother's village, looking for my grandparents' fields, their children's graves. I could have asked more questions—about the root cellar and its treasures, about that grave mound in the churchyard with its small birch cross. But I'm afflicted—there's no other word—by panic; I carry it like a money belt tied round my waist, its edges pressing into my gut. Panic sown by a man's blank face and the words that turned a landscape into a minefield. By a schoolteacher's magnified eyes. By everything I know and don't know: by all there is to understand. And the only help I can find for this panic is my great-aunt Adela, the stories only she can give me.

Crossing back over the border, I keep hearing Stefka Khory lamenting her destiny, or the old woman from Volochys'k—a woman ten years younger than my mother and looking more than ten years older. I can't help wondering what life would have been like for them, what it would be offering now to Olena and her mother, if eastern Galicia had remained part of Poland. Fewer hardships; greater hope? But no singing such as we heard in L'viv at the Shevchenko monument; no such monument in a city that once banned the teaching of Ukrainian in its university.

Poland, Ukraine: I don't want to have to choose between them or to parcel out my loyalties. Nor do I want to forget a woman with bright red hair, a flag of hair waving at the bottom of a pit. What I really want, I tell Michael, is to go home. He doesn't answer: the silence in the car fills with longing like a body of water. You can't bundle it into your arms; the harder you try to hold it, the faster it pours away. And I am left with two rivers: one blue and open to the sky, and one gone underground, its water dense as ashes.

20

Skarszewy: skeleton speech

Poland is deluged. Days and nights of continuous rain have blackened the sky. The Odra River, which forms a portion of the western border, has burst its banks. In the heart of Wroclaw, on whose outskirts we spent our first night in this country, skiffs and rowboats ply the central square. We learn all this at the restaurant where we stop for lunch; we also learn that these are the worst floods Poland has seen in two hundred years: 15 per cent of the country is under water. Conditions are terrible in the Czech Republic, where the trouble started; now parts of Germany, Belgium and France are threatened.

We weave in and out of thunderstorms, slowing for downpours that send water thick as icing down the windshield. Passing flooded meadows, I see a stork at last. White breast; a black sheen like an opera cloak slipping down its back. And a beak like a pair of long red scissors jabbing forward with each step, reminding me that storks are not just rooftop angels, but predators as well. Everything I look at in this drowning landscape acquires the abrupt, inevitable shape of images in dreams, vanishing as quickly. Ribboned shrines with statues of the Virgin made of a plaster like calcified egg whites. English graffiti on a signpost at the entrance to a small village: *Welcome to Hell*. People peering anxiously along the edge of the Vistula River, as water the colour of milky coffee rushes past, thick with branches and blots of foam.

We're heading for the coast, past Warsaw and northwest into Pomerania, which seems to have been spared the rains drenching the rest of Poland. We're heading for a small town that features in none of our guidebooks: Skarszewy, where Adela lives with her daughter, and where her sons and their wives and children are coming to meet us, all but Adela's granddaughter Katarzyna. She is the only one of the family who speaks English; she is the only one who isn't a stranger to me. Months ago, by purest serendipity, I met her in Umeå, a town in the north of Sweden. I was attending a conference held at the university there, the same place where Katarzyna happened to be studying for her doctorate in ethnology.

As we race towards this reunion with family I've never seen and of whom I have so much to ask, it helps, a little, to think of that meeting with Katarzyna. The landscape of Umeå could belong to northern Ontario: in May the birch trees were just starting to bud and the grass was ice-burned, still. Umeå could also be the north of Poland. I'd wondered, driving in from the airport, if Katarzyna had grown up, as I did, singing folk songs about birch trees in the meadow. Of course she hadn't—at the age when I was singing those pastoral songs, she was growing up in the ferment of *Solidarnosz*, and then the grimness of martial law.

It took me some time after I'd unpacked my suitcase to pick up the phone and call the woman who's my cousin only by a split and slender thread. All through my adolescence I had talked of "my family in Eastern Europe"—it seemed such a romantic connection to possess. Yet as I dialled Katarzyna's number, it occurred to me that despite being family, we had almost nothing in common; we might not even like each other. But it was too late for second thoughts: a clear, courteous voice at the other end of the line was inviting me to dinner the following night. It was an older voice than I'd expected, and this puzzled me until I recalled that prewar photograph of Hannia and her family, from which I'd conjured up my Katarzyna: a pale, ghost-blonde girl at her First Communion.

The evening was a pleasure: Katarzyna's fiancé had cooked a fine dinner; the table was set with crystal and candles, all in my honour. We talked for hours about books, politics, ethnology and economics, the Samaria Gorge, Algonquin Park. And all the time I was stealing glances at my cousin, trying to find resemblances—our eyes and hair seemed to be the same colour; we both had long and narrow feet. Suddenly I realized I was exhausted; though the sky out the picture window seemed no darker than when I'd arrived just before seven, it was now nearly twelve. Midnight sun or not, it was time for me to take my leave, yet I hadn't begun to ask what I needed to know. When I told Katarzyna that I was interested in her father's family, whatever stories she could tell me, she apologized, saying she knew almost nothing. Adela, she explained, had never been much of a storyteller; in fact, Adela always sighed when pressed to speak—I shouldn't take offence at this.

And yet I did get the bare bones—the wishbone—of a story that night. When Adela had been in her early twenties, she'd fallen in love with a Ukrainian who'd died before the war. And though she'd married the man who became Katarzyna's grandfather—a good man, a kind man—it was the young Ukrainian she had loved. His photograph was still in Adela's possession; I must ask her to show it to me when I went to Skarszewy, Katarzyna said.

Going back to my hotel, I found the night was bright as day; it was graduation time at the university, and all the students were blowing horns and whistles, drunk on light alone. I had to be up early, as a friend was taking me north to the Arctic Circle, and we had many hours of travelling ahead of us. We would drive on long, straight highways past endless lines of fir trees and occasional white threads of birch. My friend would point out to me the places where lingonberries and blueberries were gathered every summer by busloads of Poles. They could often make more money selling three weeks' berry-picking to Swedish companies than they could from a whole year of "real work" at home.

My friend would go on to tell me about an exhibition by a Sami artist, one of the most powerful she'd ever seen. The artist, while working in Paris, had chanced upon a cache of glass slides on which some early-twentieth-century photographer, caught up in the vogue of examining so-called racial types, had recorded the faces of Sami people he'd lived with in the north of Sweden. Lifting slide after slide to the light, the Sami artist had come face to face with an image of his own grandparents. He'd made copies of the portraits and brought them back to Sweden. The places that the *Parisien* had photographed are deserted now, the home of industries of one kind or another; the Sami artist took his own pictures of the empty forest and, against a blown-up version of this landscape, hung the photos he'd made from the Parisian slides. In the branches of trees, on the slopes of hills, he gathered the faces of the dead. They spoke so strongly, my friend says, of who they were and of what was being taken from their children and grandchildren.

"You should do something like that when you go to Ukraine," she would urge me. "Even if the house where your mother was born has been torn down, even if nothing's left but the land itself, you could put their photographs there, the faces of your grand-parents, the children your mother and your aunt used to be." Glass ghosts brought back, if not to life, then to the next best thing: to memory.

It was something I never thought of doing in Staromischyna; I only remember it now, driving to see Adela. I tell myself that Staromischyna was too crowded a place—you'd need the bareness, the openness of the north for the kind of effect my friend had described. But perhaps in Skarszewy I'll be able to do something similar. Looking at photographs from sixty years ago, looking so intently that they'll achieve the brightness and transparency of glass.

❋❋❋

Skarszewy's a small, sombre place, built of brick and stone. Its patron saint is John the Baptist, and his severed head, eyes sealed shut, appears on plaques and signs throughout the town. Six thousand people live here, many of them workers in the shipyards of Gdynia. "This clean full of verdure town has the sewer system," the local guidebook tells us: in 1189, when Skarszewy was presented to the Knights of St. John of Jerusalem by Duke Grymislaw, it was surely not so blessed, although a hundred years later the Germans would name it Schöneck, "which means a beauty spot."

When they first arrived here with their two surviving children, Adela and her husband found a house to live in on the edge of town, close to the fields they would farm. But now Adela lives with her daughter in one of the apartment blocks by the allotment gardens, and it's here we find her at last, on a street named, like so many Polish streets, after Copernicus. We ring the buzzer bearing Adela's surname, Wolanik, and announce ourselves; the door unlocks as solemnly as if it were made of bronze, not plywood. Before I climb halfway up the stairs, I'm locked in a bearhug by Adela's son Bazyli. He is Katarzyna's father, my elder by twelve years. And though I've never seen even a photograph of him, I feel we've known each other always. We speak German together, he fluently, I with the adroitness of someone waltzing blindfold. But the warmth with which he welcomes us, the intelligent humour in his words and face accomplish something I'd thought impossible: he makes us feel at home.

Irena, Bazyli's sister, embraces us as her mother walks towards us. Adela's tall and thin, with a grave face and olive skin. Her thick, grey hair waves back from her brow; she has the same brown eyes as her half-brother Tomasz. Adela's eyes glisten as she takes a long look at me, and she sighs, as Katarzyna warned she would.

Were I to walk out the door, descend the stairs and vanish from Skarszewy, this would be enough for her—that she's seen both Olena and Tomasz in my face.

We sit down to a meal Bazyli calls *Abendessen*—a snack, he explains, since their main meal is eaten at midday. But the table is loaded with chicken and ham, and a salad topped by a mushroom design made from eggs and tomatoes, with corn kernels as the spots on the mushroom caps. I'm moved by this way of marking off the day, the simple meal, from the ordinary; I express my thanks in German, which Bazyli has to correct for himself before translating it all into Polish. Sometimes my mouth fills with gaps—I forget the simplest words, like *laufen* and *verstecken*: to run, to hide. At other times I pour out a mishmash, saying *glühend*—German for red hot—when I mean *klebrig*, sticky. The table's littered with what gets left out in translation: nuances, resonances scattered like breadcrusts.

What's oddest of all is that I end by telling stories about the Old Place to Bazyli and Irena, who were born in Staromischyna. Tales of a world more remote to them, I realize, than it has ever been to me. What does Adela make of these stories? Do they force her to remember a time and place she's worked so hard, these past fifty years, to forget? Or is everything in them as new and strange to her as it is to her children? It's here at the table with us, the chasm I'm trying to bridge with words split into two voices, Bazyli's and mine, and then bound up again in the laughter or sighs of our listeners. Everything's come full circle, round this table where we eat and drink together, telling and listening to stories.

The kitchen is barely big enough for two, and Lilli, Bazyli's wife, a lovely, quiet woman, insists on helping Irena with the dishes while we sit in the living room and rest after our journey. When Irena joins us, she brings a plate of cakes and gigantic cups of coffee. She must be ten years older than I am; she works as a bookkeeper in the next, much larger town, Starograd Gdansk.

That and Skarszewy make up the orbit of her life; she hasn't travelled much, even in Poland. Years ago Irena had written to Natalia
and Vira, asking whether they could help her come to Canada; she
thought she might even find a Canadian husband. Looking at
Irena's pleasant face, the fine darkness of her hair and eyes, I wonder
what she must be thinking now. For the visit to Canada never came
off. Irena would have had to stay for at least six months to make it
worthwhile; Vira still had a full practice then; my mother had been
scheduled for surgery on her back. Still, I can't help thinking what
might have happened had Irena paid that visit. Would I have made
friends with her, the way girls often do with women who fall somewhere between the roles of aunt and older sister?

When it's time for us to go to the hotel Irena has picked out for
us, Bazyli and Lilli drive ahead to show the way. Irena comes along
for the ride, and when we finally arrive, she faces the man at the
check-in desk with half-suspicious, half-exultant eyes. *Wollen Sie
ein französisches Bett?* Do we want a French bed? the man asks.
Michael and I stare at one another until we realize that we're
being offered a double rather than two single beds. We all troop
upstairs to look at the room; Irena gapes at the French bed and
German television set, the gleaming bathroom, the futurist décor.
It's far more expensive than anything we'd have chosen for
ourselves, but we can't let Irena down by asking for something less
opulent. I want to suggest that she take the room as our guest, and
that we sleep in her room in Skarszewy, but I can't—shyness and
something like shame get in my way.

Driving back to Skarszewy the next morning we stop by a
meadow drenched with cornflowers. When Adela opens her door
to us, I hold out a fistful of blue, the way a child would, and she is
as delighted as a child. For the first and only time in our visit her
face lightens; joy lifts the stones from the pockets of her eyes. For
a long moment she stands on the threshold, burying her face in
flowers.

※◇※

> The commune of Skarszewy was a mainly agricultural region so it is ecologically clean and belongs to the cleanest regions of the Gdansk province. The lakes have the first class of water cleanness. Smokes emitted from the settlements and industrial works remain within the bounds of norms. The town has a purification plant and a litter stockyard.

I'm not amused by the English of the tourist brochure, wouldn't presume to be amused given the poorness of my scraps of Polish. I'm worried that the mayor, or whoever commissioned this pamphlet, protests too much about the safety of this region where my family was resettled. Invisibility, of course, is no guarantee of dangers overcome. Bazyli tells us how, at some of the army bases newly vacated by the Russians, you can find benzine seeping from the soil.

Walking through Skarszewy with Bazyli and Lilli, we pass crumbling buildings, their windows rotting out, grime lodged in the stucco like dirt under skin. Along the central square named after that same General Haller whose superbly equipped troops defeated the Ukrainian Galician army, a few people are doing their weekend shopping: the drunkest man I've ever seen moves down a side street with elaborate care, as if performing a monstrously tricky dance step on a ballroom floor. We pass an abandoned skating rink, weeds jutting up through cracks in the cement. Only a few years ago, Bazyli tells us, it was kept in perfect condition by a teacher and the students who shared his passion for hockey—now the teacher has to hold down three jobs just to make ends meet.

Bazyli moved away from here more than thirty years ago to attend university; he now lives in Slupsk, a town that, unlike Skarszewy, merits a mention in our guidebook. But there's neither apology nor nostalgia in his voice as he shows us round, even when we visit the "castle" hill where he used to play with his friends when he was a boy. His only memory of Staromischyna has to do with the end of the war, when the Russians were on their way to retake the village and towns they'd abandoned in 1941. Three-year-old Bazyli was hiding with his parents in a cellar while a German sniper waited for the Russians in the attic of a house across the way. Between the two buildings was a cleared space, a courtyard perfect for running. And Bazyli, restless and unable to interpret his parents' terror, somehow slipped up to the courtyard where he began to run about, his arms flailing, his feet kicking an imaginary ball. It was only when his mother grabbed him in her arms that he looked up and saw the sniper who'd been training his rifle on that invisible ball.

In the former castle of the Knights of St. John a small museum has been established. The work of a local farmer who's also a woodcarver and poet is on display; one of the carvings shows a family being forced from their home at gunpoint by German soldiers. From the outbreak of the war Poles were arrested, imprisoned in the cellars below the museum, tortured, interrogated and shot in the forest nearby. The town's small Jewish population was annihilated; local priests and teachers—anyone capable of offering resistance—were deported to concentration camps where most of them perished. Almost half of Skarszewy was destroyed. Thus the new home where the Wolanik family found itself at the end of the war was a bereaved and damaged place, and the mournfulness I can't help feeling here, under this pewter sky, has deeper roots and more complex causes than I first imagined.

In the adjoining room of the museum we find a small display dedicated to the memory of Jozef Wybicki, the author of what, since 1926, has been Poland's national anthem, "Dabrowski's Legions." A manuscript copy of this anthem lies under glass, and I ask Bazyli to sing a few bars for me. For a moment he looks startled, and then, in the small whitewashed room, empty except for ourselves, he sings not just the opening but the whole first verse: *Jeszcze Polska nie zginela*, Poland has not perished yet.

I am listening to my half-cousin twice-removed sing the anthem of a country that is his only because of a shuffling of diplomatic cards at a place with the comical name, to English ears, of Potsdam. The first line of this Polish anthem is almost identical to Ukraine's: *Shche ne vmerla, Ukraina*, Ukraine is not dead yet. Bazyli sings with flair as well as conviction: in German I compliment his voice; in German he laughs off my praise. The irony of this being the one language we share, bearing as it does the echoes of SS troops and of the peaceful burgers who named this place Schöneck.

On the way home we go to a shop where Bazyli buys candles in small glass lamps. For he's ending this tour by way of the small cemetery where his father's buried. I've asked him what his father was like—knowing, from Katarzyna, the story of Adela's first love, the Ukrainian who'd died so young. Bazyli says his father was a good man, a quiet man, who spent a lifetime doing work he had no liking for. He'd wanted to be a teacher; because of the war and the harsh conditions of the peace that followed, he ended up farming poor land in a strange place and died after an illness in which he lost the use of his body, from his legs all the way to his tongue. It's Bazyli who has had the life his father wanted. I wonder if he's thinking this as he lights candles under the stiffly carved letters of his father's name.

※◊※

I'm sitting with Adela and Bazyli at a table cleared of yet another enormous meal. My tape recorder stays at the bottom of my briefcase; even my pen and notebook cause uneasiness. "Don't write this down," Bazyli says, when Adela mentions a name, a date. "This may not be accurate, it's been a long time since we left

Staromischyna." I close my notebook, hoping my own memory will prove reliable, listening to Bazyli translate my questions and Adela's answers.

Katarzyna has warned me that Adela is no storyteller: Bazyli confides that, just over the past few weeks, his mother has started forgetting things. But isn't it true that as people age, their oldest memories take on such clarity that they can see straight down to where their lives began?

The questions go badly.

I start to ask about Staromischyna, what it was like before the war. I mean to add details, hooks to pull in Adela's thoughts like a school of fish, but immediately she frowns.

It's too far away. What can I tell you?

Everything, I want to say. Everything I'm frightened of asking. But I start with something certain, something my mother's often told me: how Adela helped Olena with the twins, after Tomasz had left for Canada. Could she tell me about those children?

No.

Is this denial or withdrawal? Has my mother confused Adela with someone else? Or is Adela refusing to remember what she knows, to speak about the past and thus restore the power it once held when it was all too present?

I ask about Tomasz, what she knew of him, the time he spent in the war between Poles and Ukrainians.

He was so much older than me. And then he went away. Tomek. I hardly knew him.

Tomek. Would you call a stranger by a pet name? I try again—was his father, Jan Solowski, Polish?

Yes.

Instead of asking about Tomasz's sister Hannia, I pull out the photograph my mother gave me—a girl dressed for her First Communion, two boys, looking like brothers, and two women, one old, the other young.

Adela looks at the photo from a distance.

The older woman is Hannia. The younger one is her son's wife, Olga, with her children.

Is Hannia still alive?

She died fourteen years ago, in Wroclaw.

And during the war?

On Adela's face, an expression of locked pain. Everything I'm asking her now is what she turned her back on forever, when she was given a few hours to gather her belongings and board a train crammed with deportees. Abandoning her language, her home and landscape, her family, the graves of the Ukrainian man she loved and of a small son. Abandoning them or sealing them inside her.

Natalia and Vira—they want to know what happened to Hannia during the war.

Her sons were killed. Franek and Voytek.

How were they killed?

Franek was a soldier—he died early in the war. But Voytek was killed.

How?

Her voice becomes impatient. *He was beaten to death. First tortured, then beaten.*

Why?

Adela shrugs. *He was a Pole. The men who killed him didn't want Poles in our village.*

Bazyli speaks for the first time, instead of merely translating. He knows very little of this history, he says. But he tells me that he remembers his aunt Hannia, her terrible grief the few times she spoke of Voytek's death.

People in the village tried to warn him. They told him to hide. But he said, "I've done nothing wrong, I'm not going to run away." And they came for him that night.

My mother once told me that as far as she knew from letters sent to Olena after the war, it was partisans who killed Hannia's son. *Banderivtsi*, followers of Stepan Bandera, after whom so many streets in Ukraine are now named. There's a theory among certain historians that many of the atrocities attributed to the *Banderivtsi* were really carried out by KGB agents trying to destroy any show of Ukrainianness. These historians base their claims, they say, on archival material that has only now come to light. I'm suspicious of all readings of history that come too close to what we most want to be true. But whatever the merits of these claims, to Adela they'd be only so much water against the rock of her belief: her nephew was killed for being a Pole.

I ask Adela about what she remembers of *pasifikatsia*.

Nothing.

Again, I can't tell whether she remembers nothing or whether she means that no violence of that kind ever happened to her. I can't tell, and I can't press her on the question. It's not what I expected, this conversation. It's like forcing someone to dig up a grave.

Adela's exhausted. I apologize and ask if we might talk together later, when she's rested. For I still have to question her about her brother Volodko.

She sighs and puts her hands together on the table. Something far sadder than a smile appears on her lips, and for the first time she speaks without any prompting:

When Tomek came back to Poland, he would sit at the dinner table with Natalia on one side of him, Vira on the other. They'd link arms and sway from side to side, singing a rhyme he'd made up, a song ending with the words, "to Canada, to Canada." And Olena would be standing on the other side of the table, standing as if frozen, watching her daughters singing with their father.

One thing more.

When it came time for Tomek's children to leave the village, to walk along the lane with their bundles in their arms, they cried so hard the blood streamed from their noses.

❊❈❊

While Adela sleeps, Bazyli and Lilli, Michael and I walk out again, this time along a path that takes us to a cluster of small allotment gardens, belonging to whoever can afford to buy them. They remind me of my grandmother's garden at the house on Dover-court Road. Long, narrow strips thick with raspberry canes and strawberries, plum and cherry trees, strictly staked beans and luxu-riating squashes. And flowers, too—red climbing roses, gargan-tuan daisies.

Bazyli unlocks the door of a hut lost in a tangle of vines. The allotment gardens are full of small structures made of wood, concrete, corrugated iron: each one a single room with a bed, a chair, a table. People often spend summer nights here, he tells us. I think of the crowding in the apartment block where Adela and Irena live, how what Bazyli calls *Katzenjammer*—teenage pop-rock—pounds through the walls. I think of the sweetness of a night spent among leaves and flowers, the quietness of moths.

Under a leaden sky, we stoop to pick the last of the strawber-ries: the earth under them is coarse grey powder. Before we leave, I ask Bazyli and Lilli if they'll pose for a photo on the porch. They put their arms round each other as if they were still the lovers who met as students thirty years ago. It will be a wonderful photo-graph, and it will be ruined by being exposed, accidentally, before the roll of film is finished. But none of us know this as Bazyli and Lilli stand framed by roses, while birds sing through the rain that has finally begun to fall.

※◇※

From the glass-fronted cupboard in the dining room Adela brings down a thick square book.

It's like any family album—a few clear shots in a sea of blurs. Birthdays, anniversaries, parties, always a table round which people are gathered, a table laden with food and flowers. And suddenly the shock of seeing my four-year-old self and six-year-old sister, white-gloved, in pale organdy dresses, leaving the Dovercourt house for Vira's wedding.

The photos shift from colour to black and white, from Skarszewy to Staromischyna. There are only half a dozen photos from the Old Place in the album, photos Adela was able to pack up in the panic of leaving. Young and handsome men in Polish army uniforms; a group of men and women outside what could be the priest's house or a villa in Pidvolochys'k. Here is the same photograph I've stared at so many times in my mother's album, a studio portrait of Natalia and Vira with Adela and the elegant young woman who taught my mother embroidery. Adela's finger rests on the image of herself taken sixty-one years ago: stately, dark-eyed, her whole life waiting to happen. Of the photograph Katarzyna spoke of, the portrait of Adela's Ukrainian lover, there isn't a sign, not even an empty place. But turning the page, I find at last what I've been looking for. A studio portrait of Volodymyr Pokotylo, the only image of him I will ever see. A scarred image, with a crease running diagonally from top to bottom.

When was he born? My mother had thought Volodko was born five years after Tomasz, in 1905, but the birthdate Adela tells me is 1914. This would make him only twenty-two the year Olena and her children left for Canada. Yet in this portrait he looks older than thirty, the age he was when his life effectively ended. This may have to do with the suit he wears, a good dark suit that's a little too short, a little too tight, and the tense pose the suit obliges him to strike. Only the hat resting on a small table gives an air of easy elegance. A beige hat with a wide dark ribbon and a little dip in the crown. A homburg—the kind of hat you'd expect an aspiring artisan, a master cabinetmaker to wear.

I signal to Bazyli, who has seen these photographs too many times before and has pulled away from the table. I hesitate for a moment, knowing that what I'm going to ask Adela now will be far more painful than the questions I put earlier. I ask her what happened to Volodymyr during the war.

Adela's face is as pale as always. Her eyes are still. Bazyli immediately translates the few words she says: *Things were terrible then.*

I tell her that I know her brother was deported to Siberia, that he died in a gulag. When was he arrested?

Towards the end. 1944.

Why? I ask, remembering Evhen's reply to the same question. What had he done?

For the first time Adela gives me a sharp look, the kind you'd give a thief or fool.

If they didn't like your face, your way of walking down the street, they'd arrest you—the Russians.

And now I summon all my courage. I start by conveying her nephew's greetings. At the name, Evhen Pokotylo, Adela makes the slightest nod. I tell her what Evhen had spoken of: conflicts, arguments with Jews. What can she tell me of this? Did it have anything to do with her brother's arrest?

There's no change in Adela's face or in the sadness of her sigh. *This happened when he was very young, setting up in his work. He had a hard time. There were already many cabinetmakers in Pidvolochys'k— Jewish men, competition. They made things difficult for him.*

She waits for a moment, her lips moving slightly, but no sound comes out. Then she speaks again.

I saw him only once after he was taken to prison, in Czortkow. I brought him bread to eat. We weren't allowed to speak to one another. Perhaps he was helping the partisans—perhaps he was just a cabinet-maker, a capitalist. I never found out why they arrested him.

What should I make of this—what can I make? Is it a question of making, or of accepting the one certainty in this mess of shadows? That I will never know about Volodko, one way or the other. That I will have to live with not knowing.

"Adela," I say, as gently as I can, "if you're not too tired—there's something else I'd like to ask."

Adela's eyes are closed, her skin grey. The something else will have to wait.

※◇※

Are we, in the end, only what we can remember? Or are we also all that lies deep inside us, stored in the niches of a long, dark corridor whose door we shut behind us long ago? The painfulness of remembering—the physical process of recall. How we speak of triggering memory, as if it were a loaded gun.

At the hotel that night I can't sleep. The bedroom is windowless, but it feels as if the neon from the sign outside is cutting under my eyelids. I leave Michael to the embrace of our French bed and steal into the sitting room of our suite, to the briefcase of Xeroxes and photographs I've brought like ballast for this journey. But holding the close-typed papers in my hands, all I can see is the photo Adela showed me of Volodko. What can you tell of a person—his character, his life, the end he'll meet—from such a photograph? The dark, wavy hair, parted at the side and cresting up from his forehead: the same huge eyes as Adela, the brown eyes he had in common with his half-brother Tomasz. Nothing in that face to show either hate or compassion; only the frozen stare into a lens, the apparatus of remembering. If only I had something to compare this image with, if I had a photograph of that Carpathian farmer who took milk and bread each day to people hiding in a forest—because he was a decent man, and he could not stop being who he was. But all I have is Volodko's image or, rather, my memory of a face taken from a photograph. He is handsome, that is all I know. A grave, handsome man, whose clothes are too small for his body.

In 1936 Volodko would have been twenty-two—let me keep him there for now, in that almost innocent time before the war, before he dressed in a tight-fitting suit and homburg hat. Let him stay the younger brother who made a mirrored cupboard for the *svitlytsia* in Tomasz's house and a miniature of that cupboard for Olena to take away into a foreign place. When he was that bereft young man who sent a letter all the way to Canada, a letter Tomasz intercepted and threw away unread, a letter of whose existence only Volodko, Tomasz and Natalia ever knew.

For there's something else that I must tell, something without photographs or stamps with Polish eagles to authenticate it. A story I've been carrying with me like a jewel sewn up in the hem of a coat; a story told to me in a car driving through the dark of a winter's night. Out of that dark a woman's voice speaking with the urgency of a child.

There were things you never spoke about and never understood. Knowing and understanding aren't the same thing. I only know what I heard; I saw nothing. Because it was dark, because it was the middle of the night, and no lights were ever left burning.

It was late and it was dark and I woke up from my bed, the bambatel *I had to sleep on. It was hard and narrow, I was always afraid of falling off. I would lie very still and sometimes I would think, "This is what it will be like to lie in my coffin." So when I woke that night, I didn't move. I was listening to what woke me, a sound I'd never heard before, though I knew it was my mother's voice. She wasn't shouting, she wasn't even speaking, it was something like singing, but it wasn't singing. I got out of my bed so quietly; I walked across to where my mother was sleeping.*

She wasn't there, only my sister was in the bed, my sister dreaming quietly for once. She didn't hear what I couldn't stop hearing, my mother's voice, coming from a different place, not where she'd sing when she spent the night sewing. I left the room, I crossed the hall, I opened the door of the svitlytsia. *Everything was dark, everything was quiet except for my mother's voice. It was coming from the bed piled with cushions, where no one ever slept. Beside my mother, his arms around her, his whole body listening to the voice pouring out of her, was a stranger who was no stranger. I thought at first it was my father, I thought he'd come home to us again. But it wasn't my father, I knew that as I stood there in the dark, not seeing them and they not seeing me.*

When I first heard this story, long after Olena had died, it was as though my mother were telling me a dream. She told me it once again, before I set out on this journey, as if she were giving me permission to remember. Adela is only five years older than my mother; she would have been nineteen in 1936. Did she know of this passion on Olena's part? Can she tell me what Volodko said when he watched Olena walk out of the village forever, a woman eleven years older than he, a strong, proud, lonely woman?

I want to speak to Adela, who loved one man and married another; I want to tell her what I think I know. That a woman who'd lived alone for so many years had listened to the whispering of lovers as they walked down the lane outside her home; had listened to the neighbours' talk of how her husband had found himself a wife in Canada and would never return to her. That her husband chose not to know what he'd learned from the handwriting on a letter. And that my mother, that fourteen-year-old girl whose aunts were already talking to her of marriage, but who had never in her life seen an adult's naked body, had had the courage to protect her father and her mother. Had spoken her love for both her parents by keeping perfect silence, so that even her sister never learned from Natalia what she knew.

Telling this secret now, turning it from secret to story, has been as difficult for me as keeping silence was for my mother. For I was brought up in the force field of my grandmother's pride; the very air we breathed flashed warnings: *People are always watching, waiting to drag you into the mud.* Olena and her daughters were born into a world where shame had the power to annihilate. Yet I see nothing shameful in what my mother has confessed to me. It's a branch of light in an otherwise invisible sky; it makes my grandparents' marriage—a marriage made for love, a marriage that endured so many years of separation and struggle—not a fairy tale, but a story, made as all true stories are, out of the fallible flesh and blood of perfectly ordinary, perfectly remarkable people.

A free, unfocused light, this story. A light in which I see, as if I'd never lost them, Tomasz and Olena. See them with my adult's eyes, as they finally see me: a woman, no longer a child. Seeing them like this, I can keep them with me as long as I live. This is what remembering and imagining can give us: this moment of recognition, this clarity that is a form of blessing between the living and the dead.

There is so little to remind us of anyone—an anecdote, a conversation at table. But every memory is turned over and over again, every word, however chance, written in the heart in the hope that memory will fulfill itself, and become flesh, and that the wanderers will find a way home, and the perished, those whose lack we always feel, will step through the door finally and stroke our hair with dreaming, habitual fondness, not having meant to keep us waiting long.

❊❋❊

At our hotel the next morning we watch the news, shot after shot of Poland sinking under floodwaters neither sandbags nor prayers can stop. We learn that all border-crossings into Germany have been shut, except for the one at Szczecin. We phone the Netherlands, speak to our son, tell him we'll be coming back early, will see him the day after tomorrow. It's harder to think of what I'll say to Adela—her youngest son Eugeniusz is driving up with his family to meet us this very afternoon. On our way to Skarszewy I thumb through the dictionary looking for words of apology; correct, useless words: *Sorge, Schade, es tut mir Leid.*

In the end we've spent only a handful of hours with my Polish family. Intense and often exhausting, this time spent talking in a language that is no one's mother tongue; talk between strangers who are also blood relations, from cultures at various removes—some extreme—from one another. Yet always this extraordinary gift: the grace of their generous welcome.

We gather one last time round the dining table: tomatoes and cucumbers, jellied chicken, tea in narrow glasses, gigantic cups of coffee. Irena and Lilli disappear into the kitchen to pack food for us to take along, in case we have to wait for six to twelve hours at the border, as the news reports have warned us. We hand over the gifts we've been saving for Eugeniusz and his wife and children; we say our goodbyes, promising we'll be back soon. Bazyli insists on seeing us off; Adela honours us by walking down the six flights of stairs and out into the rain to wave goodbye. And it is an honour, her refusal to concede the painfulness of the descent, the effort it will be, once the embraces are over and the car pulls away, to walk back up again.

As we drive off, I wave as long as I can, long after the apartment building and the two figures standing in the rain have vanished. All that I didn't ask, all that I couldn't say. It's not that I may never see Adela again, it's that I saw her and could only look at her silence, the way I saw people standing on the sandbagged banks of the Vistula, helplessly watching water pool round fragile islands of treetops. I had come to her for stories and been met with skeleton speech: I had stood outside the locked house of memory and stared up at a presence in the upper windows, a presence gliding by so quickly you might think it never showed itself at all. Memory invisible until it becomes story, though story itself can be as different from what truly happened as the flood's milk-and-coffee colour is from the clearness of water.

On the road to Szczecin we pass men holding out eels that drip like lengths of rubber hose. Great grey folds of rain blur everything around us; the ditches have become ponds, the roads, streams. And it seems as if more than the rivers are flooding, it seems as if time itself has risen from its channel and is overflowing the banks meant to keep it contained. Past and present awash, nothing to stand between them and the future.

epilogue

_____

homecoming

no, I do not long, long, slowly for the past.
I am happy it is gone. If I long for it,
it is for the hope of it curled like burnt
paper.

Dionne Brand, *Land to Light On*

Did I find what I was looking for? Has this journey changed me? I did so little of what I thought I would—I never found my grandparents' fields, the graves of my infant uncle and aunt, or of Olena's nameless sister. I bring back no handful of originary soil, only a few dozen photographs, making copies of them for my mother, who recognizes almost nothing that they show. After we've looked at all the photographs, we go downstairs to fetch the jars of *borshch* that she has made for me. We go to the basement, the storage room with its shelves of tinned fruit, of pickles and preserves, and the ancient fridge that still sends electric shocks like little barbs through my skin. But before we head back upstairs, I stop by the door to the furnace room. Is it still there, I ask—the little cupboard with the tilting mirror? Is it still on the shelf above my father's workbench?

Moments later I am holding the cupboard in my arms, bidding my mother goodbye. She has made me a present of the one memento she has of her father's half-brother Volodko. I have told her, as best I could, what I'd learned about her uncle's fate, but as I leave she says, "I wish I knew what happened to him." As if I'd never spoken; as if my story failed to feed something hungrier than curiosity. When I get home, I carry the cupboard from room to room, looking for some place to put it, to show it off, but it doesn't seem to fit anywhere—the wood's too red, the shape too strange. Finally I set it down on a table top and take my first full look at it. I open the little doors with their flimsy latches, test the emptiness inside. For the first time I notice the flowers carved on the top of the cupboard, run my fingertips along the marks left by the chisel. And last of all I tilt the mirror, in its scalloped frame, so that I see my face marked by the flaws in the glass: not the spots of tarnish I'd remembered, but a series of vertical lines. When I step back from the mirror, they seem to divide my reflection, making it shift and blur, as if it were crossing border after border.

Does the mirror fill with other faces when I'm not there to see? Faces of ghosts, some radiant, others sombre, locked in uncertainty? And what of the Old Place, that imagined world that was mine from childhood? Is it still there for me, a hotel my dreams check into when my mind runs away from home? Has it become like the glass paintings I bought at the Halitsky market in L'viv: small, fragile, contracted to the point of darkness in their heavy frames? I have a sudden picture of Sofia in that flea market, trying on a turquoise ring; I remember her words in the Café Kupol. To know where you belong, what claims not just affection but allegiance make: I envy her this. To know, infallibly, where home is, to feel instinctively at home.

All my life my head has been painted with the sky of the Old Place. So that the standard get-acquainted question, "Where are you from?" was something I could never answer the way so many of my "English" friends might do, with one name, one place. When I was a child, I invented alternative origins for myself: I was an Italian war orphan, the child of Swedish circus artists or one of a clan of Smiths and Joneses. Later, I wanted to dis-invent myself, pretend I came from nowhere, nothing but clear and empty water. I know now there's no water clear or empty enough. I know that what I really want is only this: to be at home. Home, as the dictionary defines it, "a fixed dwelling-place, one's habitual or proper abode. The place of one's dwelling and nurturing, also with reference to the grave or future state. A place, region or state to which one properly belongs, in which one's affections centre, or where one finds rest, refuge or satisfaction. One's own country, one's native land, the place where one's ancestors dwelt."

Yet even as I read this litany of definitions, the conflicts and contradictions leap up at me. Rest, refuge, satisfaction—none of these fit what I feel about Staromischyna, or about the Ontario to which I have returned. Perhaps home is only this: inhabiting uncertainty, the arguments desire picks with fear. Not belonging, but longing—that we may live in the present, without craving the past or forcing the future. *Sweet home, sweet home*, my grand-mother would say as we drove her back to the house on Dover-court Road after some outing to the cottage or suburbs. Both sadness and pleasure in her voice: home lost, home found.

I write this in my study, in a stone house by a river. As I write, I look up at the windowsill, where, cradled in a wineglass, lies an image of a thatched and whitewashed house against a brown-black sky. In China they bury eggs, often for many, many years. The eggs are rich, marbled with the dark in which they've lain, and their savour is apparently exquisite. If I were to bury that egg painted with the house in which my mother was born, I would never want to dig it up again. I would want something new to grow from it, something marked by the past, but shaped by the pressures, the possibilities of the present. For without these borders of the only home I know—a home that is open, conflicted, uncertain—no departures can occur at all.

acknowledgements

This book could not have been written without the help of Natalie Solowska Kulyk and Vera Solowska Duane, whose stories fill its pages, though the turns given to these stories, and the inevitable errors that have crept into the telling, are mine alone. I can never thank them enough for sharing with me their stories of their own lives and those of their parents, and for giving me the freedom and encouragement to write those lives as I felt I must. I thank my mother, especially, for this extraordinary gift.

I want also to acknowledge here the invaluable help of my father Joseph Kulyk, my sister Karen Kulyk and my brother Robert Joseph Kulyk. This book is written for them and for Vera's children, and for all of our children who, though they may never have met their great-grandparents, have heard at least some of their stories.

I owe a debt of lasting love and thankfulness to my family and to two people who are family by adoption: my godmother Anna Yawyliak Ksenych and her husband Jack Ksenych, who have shared with me so many stories of their own Old Place and of this country. I also wish to thank Katrusia Stefaniuk, who shared some of her family's most moving stories with me. I am particularly grateful to John Matushak, who helped illuminate for me my grandfather's early years in Canada, and to Olya Kaluck for her kindness from a long way back. My great-aunt Adela Wolanik and her family, especially Irena and Bazyli and Lilli Wolanik, were hospitality itself when I visited them in Poland; I also wish to thank Katarzyna Wolanik Boström and her husband Gert-Olof Boström for the tremendous kindness they showed me.

I could not have travelled to Ukraine without the generous assistance of Dr. Bohdan Hawrylyshyn and Ms. Olena Mazirko of the Renaissance Foundation in Geneva; I am deeply grateful to Sofia Onufriw and Olena Melnyk, my guides and translators in L'viv and Ternopil', and to Sashko Sofiy of the Renaissance Foundation in L'viv for the time and effort they took on my behalf. Morris T. Cherneskey obligingly shared family documents and information with me, as did my cousin Dr. Walter Teteruck. And Professors Nancy Burke of the University of Warsaw and Irena Przemecka of the Jagiellonian University in Krakow gave us excellent advice and assistance during our time in Poland.

Catherine Byron, Michael Keefer, Myrna Kostash, Anna Simon and Rhea Tregebov have read this manuscript with great care and insight; they have my deepest thanks. Natalka Husar has, with her customary verve and grace, shared both stories and images with me: John Walsh valiantly laboured over microfilms of newspaper reports from 1930s Toronto, looking for traces of my grandfather's political history. I also wish to thank Janet Turnbull Irving for her expert advice and welcome support. Becky Vogan, once again, has been a peerless copy editor, and Nicole Langlois' cheerful and adept editorial assistance has been invaluable. I am especially grateful to my editor at HarperCollins, Iris Tupholme, for having so generously assisted me, not only with the revision of this manuscript but with its very genesis.

A host of friends helped in the actual production of this book, offering hospitality, much-needed books and articles and other material assistance for our travels: Geneviève and Bernard Bauer, Catherine Byron, Beverly and Stephanie Cohen, Maria Carmen Garcia Salguero and Juan Serrano Jiménez, Ian and Jean Grieve, Vivian Hart, Avril Harvey, Geoff Hemstedt, Isabel and Bob Huggan, Leon Kozicki, Elisabeth Mårald, Olivier and Alicia Martin, Gerry and Glenn Minard, Danielle Schaub, Joop Steenman and Conny Steenman-Marcusse, Wanda and Piotr Syrowinski, Virginia Poza and Michael Tregebov, Pat and Brian Wills. And I am sincerely grateful to the University of Guelph for granting me a sabbatical leave to research and write and undertake the travel for this book.

Finally, I thank my sons for their company and curiosity on many journeys. And as always, Michael, whose loving support and steadfastness have been a lifeline, both in the Old Place and at home.

sources of quotations

page vii. "Memory is the sense of loss . . . waiting long." Marilynne Robinson, *Housekeeping*. New York: Bantam, 1987, pp. 194–5.

page 4. "is a wish, or a truth . . . satisfy their wishes." Randall Jarrell, Introduction, *The Anchor Book of Stories*. New York: Doubleday Anchor, 1958, p. ix.

pages 7–8. "All water . . . 'flooding.'" Toni Morrison, "The Site of Memory," in *Inventing the Truth: The Art and Craft of Memoir*, ed. William Zinsser. Boston: Houghton Mifflin, 1987, p. 119.

page 15. "is all we know of infinity, the insolence of fate." Clark Blaise, *I Had a Father: A Post-Modern Autobiography*. Toronto: HarperCollins, 1993, p. 16.

page 16. "to want, and not to have—to want and want." Virginia Woolf, *To the Lighthouse*, included in *Three Great Novels*. London: Penguin, 1992, p. 417.

page 16. "to walk with the dead . . . vantage point." Margaret Forster, *Hidden Lives: A Family Memoir*. London: Penguin, 1996, p. 309.

pages 18–9. "The smell . . . pits." Isaac Babel, "Crossing the Zubrich," in *Lyubka the Cossack, and Other Stories*, tr. Andrew R. MacAndrew. New York: Signet, 1963, pp. 108–9.

page 70. "unjust city." The 1930s witnessed many protest and hunger marches in Toronto; if Tim Buck did attend the demonstration Mr. Matushak described, it would have had to take place after 1934, when Buck, "the victim of political persecution by a Canadian state which had launched an 'Anti-Red' campaign in the 1920s," was released from prison. It is certainly true that those providing social assistance in Depression-era Toronto both penalized and demonized single men: police were instructed to remove transients from public parks and places and to force them to register themselves with civic officials as "poor," so that they might be kept under surveillance as members of a new (and humiliating) social category. By 1935 men attempting to qualify for social assistance in Toronto had not only to fulfill a one-year residency requirement, but also to be British subjects, a development that must have been devastating for those named Solowski or Matushak. Non-British immigrant men were thus relegated to "a 'double ghetto' of their own as class and ethnicity reinforced their otherness from Toronto's civic 'community.'"

The quotations in this footnote are taken from a report prepared for me by John Walsh, a doctoral student at the University of Guelph. He concludes his report with a remark that reinforces the complex interdependence of private story and public history in giving us an accurate, or representative, account of the past: "The social history of this period suggests that a large (but not 30,000 persons) protest of the nature described by Mr. Matushak could have happened, even if various historical texts cannot confirm that it really did happen."

page 92. "She . . . cross with her." Anton Chekhov, "Peasants," in *The Portable Chekhov*, ed. Avrahm Yarmolinsky. London: Penguin, 1977, pp. 326–7.

page 109. "'Travel' . . . 'journey.'" Bruce Chatwin, *The Songlines*. London: Penguin, 1988, p. 194.

page 136. "getting dressed for Easter . . . rise above them." Margaret Forster, *Hidden Lives: A Family Memoir*. London: Penguin, 1996, p. 163.

page 165. "How does the old country . . . got to do with me?" Myrna Kostash, *Bloodlines: A Journey into Eastern Europe*. Vancouver: Douglas & McIntyre, 1993, p. 2.

page 168. ". . . fortified towns . . . Varangian arms . . ." "Galicia," *Encyclopedia of Ukraine*, Vol. II, ed. Volodymyr Kubijovyc. Toronto: University of Toronto Press, 1988, p. 4.

page 169. "the Galician misery." Stanislaw Szczepanowski, quoted by Orest Subtelny (as "The Misery of Galicia") in *Ukraine, a History*. Toronto: University of Toronto Press, 1990, p. 310.

page 170. "personal subjection," "whereby . . . property rights." "Galicia." *Encyclopedia of Ukraine*, Vol. II, p. 6.

page 170. "only one elementary school . . . 220 Galicians." Orest Subtelny in *Ukrainians in North America: An Illustrated History*. Toronto: University of Toronto Press, 1991, p. 8.

page 171. "that they could only supply . . . of the year." Norman Davies, *The Heart of Europe: A Short History of Poland*. Oxford: Oxford University Press, 1986, p. 256.

pages 175–6. "To the Ukrainian People . . . L'viv, first of November, 1918." Broadsheet on display in the Regional Museum, Ternopil', Ukraine.

page 176. "On 16 July 1919 . . . Eastern Ukraine." Orest Subtelny, *Ukraine, a History*, p. 370.

page 177. "choice of nightmares." Joseph Conrad, *Heart of Darkness*, ed. Robert Hampson. London: Penguin, 1995, p. 101.

page 179. "The 'pacification' of Ukraine . . . wrecked . . . ." *The Manchester Guardian Weekly*, Friday, October 17, 1930, quoted by Samuel A. Wallace and Yaroslaw Chyz, *Western Ukraine Under Polish Yoke: Polonization, Colonization, "Pacification."* New York: The Ukrainian Review, 1931, p. 46.

page 181. "who personally . . . Eastern Galicia." *Ibid.*, p. 24.

pages 181–2. "In each case . . . has resulted." *Ibid.*, pp. 24–6.

page 184. "Social Distress . . . anxiety." Norman Davies, *The Heart of Europe*, p. 126.

page 185. "a murderous struggle . . . generations." Orest Subtelny, *Ukraine, a History*, p. 475.

page 199. "the most tragic nation in Europe." Adam Michnik, *Letters from Prison and Other Essays*, tr. Maya Latynski. Berkeley: University of California Press, 1985, p. 92.

page 200. "well-named Bohdan, given by God." Wojciech Miaskowski, quoted by Frank E. Sysyn, "The Jewish Factor in the Khmelnytsky Uprising," in *Ukrainian-Jewish Relations in Historical Perspective*, ed. Howard Aster and Peter J. Potichnyj, second edition. Edmonton: Canadian Institute of Ukrainian Studies, University of Alberta, 1990, p. 43. Sysyn contrasts Miaskowski's panegyric to Khmelnytsky with the denunciation by Miaskowski's Jewish contemporary, the chronicler Nathan Hanover, who writes of Chmielnicki, as Khmelnytsky is known to Polish speakers, as "the archenemy Chmiel, may his name be blotted out, may God send a curse upon him" (Sysyn, p. 43). Stressing the absence of impartial and adequate historical sources apropos the Cossack Revolt of 1648 and the "social warfare" that broke out alongside it, Sysyn remarks, "We shall never know certainly how many Jews were massacred." Urging that "it is time to put to rest tendencies by Ukrainian scholars to minimize the number and of Jewish scholars to use inflated statistics," he ends by conceding that "1648 will continue to have very different connotations for Jewish, Ukrainian and Polish collective memories and traditions . . ." (Sysyn, pp. 50–2).

pages 200–1. "The Ukrainians were like wild animals," "the long Polish struggle against the Ukrainian invaders." Louis Begley, *Wartime Lies*. London: Picador, 1992, pp. 138, 107.

page 201. "markedly warped." John-Paul Himka, "Ukrainian-Jewish Antagonism in the Galician Countryside During the Late Nineteenth Century," in *Ukrainian-Jewish Relations in Historical Perspective*, ed. Howard Aster and Peter J. Potichnyj, second edition. Edmonton: Canadian Institute of Ukrainian Studies, University of Alberta, 1990, p. 114. Himka also quotes the Ukrainian "poet and publicist Ivan Franko," who stated that "the overwhelming majority [of Jews] in Galicia are even poorer and more unfortunate than our peasants." *Ibid.*, p. 120.

page 202. "the Jews of Galicia . . . as the peasants," "vulnerable, dispersed . . . nation in Galicia." *Ibid.*, pp. 119, 142.

page 202. "No steel . . . place." Isaac Babel, *Lyubka the Cossack, and Other Stories*, tr. Andrew R. MacAndrew. New York: Signet, 1963, p. 90.

page 203. "Her skinny legs . . . in the world." *Ibid.*, p. 109.

page 205. "The ghettos of Eastern Europe . . . building," "'a portable kingdom' . . . men's hearts." Bruce Chatwin, *The Songlines*. London: Penguin, 1988, p. 195.

page 206. "Jewish stores . . . *Judenrein*," "a poor and fairly backward . . . matzo on Passover." Abraham Brumberg, "The Last Jews in Warsaw." *Granta*, no. 55 (Autumn 1996), pp. 243–54.

page 209. "outcasts . . . sanctity of man," "I want you to be a good Jew . . . my faith." Quoted by Taras Hunczak, "Ukrainian-Jewish Relations During the Soviet and Nazi Occupations," in *Ukraine During World War II: History and Its Aftermath, A Symposium*, ed. Yury Boshyk. Edmonton: Canadian Institute of Ukrainian Studies, 1986, pp. 49, 50. Sheptytsky's response to the extraordinary pressures of his times and the position he occupied is one of considerable complexity. As Harold Troper and Morton Weinfeld point out, "Sheptytsky's humanity when it came to the Jews did not prevent his endorsing a Nazi scheme to organize a Waffen SS unit from Ukrainian volunteers in late 1943." *Old Wounds: Jews, Ukrainians and the Hunt for Nazi War Criminals in Canada*. Chapel Hill: University of North Carolina Press, 1989, p. 19. "Although it violated Nazi standards of racial purity," Troper and Weinfeld observe, "Heinrich Himmler approved recruitment of non-Aryan units for the Waffen SS. What role these post-Stalingrad organized units were to have in the ongoing Holocaust, whether they were envisioned as cannon fodder for the faltering German military machine or as back-up for the hard-pressed and racially pure SS units and *Wehrmacht* are points of historical discussion." p. 19. Ukrainian leaders, they point out, hoped that the 13,000 man Galicia Division would "become the focal point for Ukrainian resistance to the Soviet advance on western Ukraine," p. 22. A significant number of veterans of the Galicia Division settled in Canada after the war, and became involved in the controversy surrounding the formation and proceedings of the Deschênes Commission (1985–87). As Troper and Weinfeld observe, it was Judge Jules Deschênes's ruling, in the *Report of the Commission of Inquiry on War Criminals*, "that membership in the Division, like membership of the Waffen SS generally, was not in itself a war crime." p.300.

page 209. "the best possibilities . . . genuine and mutual," "the ruts of prejudice and hatred." Eva Hoffman, *Shtetl: The Life and Death of a Small Town, and the World of Polish Jews*. Boston: Houghton Mifflin, 1997, pp. 5, 18. Eva Hoffman's introduction to *Shtetl* makes clear her refusal of the thesis that "one can speak of Polish anti-Semitism, as if that attitude were an essential and unchangeable feature of Polish character." She describes her book, which I discovered at the end of writing *Honey and Ashes*, as "an effort to counter . . . the notion that ordinary Poles were naturally inclined, by virtue of their congenital anti-Semitism, to participate in the genocide, and that Poles even today must be viewed with extreme suspicion or condemned as guilty for the fate of the Jews in their country." Her aim, she states, "is not to absolve any more than it is to condemn, but it is, at the very least, to complicate and historicize this picture" (*Shtetl*, p. 5). This perspective, I would like to suggest, is one that might be applied, *mutatis mutandis*, to relations between Jews and Ukrainians. Works such as Howard Aster and Peter J. Potichnyj's *Jewish-Ukrainian Relations: Two Solitudes* represent a start in this crucial task of recognizing what Hoffman calls "the terrible complexity of everyone's circumstances and behavior" (*Shtetl*, p. 6). "If cross-cultural discussions of difficult histories are to be at all fruitful," she insists, "they need to start with acknowledgement of complexity rather than insistence on reductiveness" (*Shtetl*, p. 15).

page 210. "New Jerusalem." I am grateful to Dr. John C. Lehr of the University of Winnipeg for acquainting me with this particular aspect of immigration to the Canadian prairies.

page 213. "What else . . . not yet become. . . ." David Malouf, *An Imaginary Life.* Toronto: Vintage Canada, 1996, p. 135.

page 216. "Vodka Line." Geoffrey York, "'Vodka Line' symbolizes East-West gulf: border-crossing a journey through time." *The Globe and Mail*, Saturday, July 5, 1997, A1.

page 217. "in which Jews have said they feel safest." I am grateful to Dr. Bohdan Hawrylyshyn for providing me with this information and with the overview about the present state of affairs in Ukraine contained in this paragraph.

page 219. "the wars, famine . . . population of Ukraine." George Wesely, in John Noble et al., *Russia, Ukraine and Belarus: Lonely Planet Travel Survival Kit.* Hawthorn, Australia: Lonely Planet Publications, 1991, p. 880.

page 221. "the imagination of disaster." Henry James, quoted by Morton Zabel in *The Portable Henry James*, ed. Morton Zabel. London: Penguin, 1977, p. 14. The entire quotation reads: "I have the imagination of disaster—and see life indeed as ferocious and sinister."

page 224. "the incomparable trauma of rejection." Mavis Gallant, "Varieties of Exile," in *Home Truths.* Toronto: Macmillan, 1982, p. 268.

page 226. "Despite stories . . . discomfort." George Wesely, *Lonely Planet*, p. 16.

pages 228–9. "those zillions of care parcels . . . families in Ukraine," "laced with a sort of guilty superiority," "romantic . . . blue-washed walls," "folkloric rash," "ghost of limited possibilities." Natalka Husar, *Pandora's Parcel to Ukraine*, in *Black Sea Blue.* Regina: Rosemount Art Gallery, n.d., pp. 55, 56.

page 267. "We swear . . . Amen." Text displayed in the Regional Museum, Ternopil', Ukraine.

page 302. "the archive of memory." Aby Warburg, quoted by Simon Schama in *Landscape and Memory.* London: Fontana Press, 1996, p. 212.

pages 308, 311. *Skarszewy.* Booklet published by the Commune of Skarszewy, Poland, n.d.

page 326. "no, I do not long . . . burnt paper." Dionne Brand, *Land to Light On.* Toronto: McClelland & Stewart, 1997, p. 68.

page 328. "a fixed dwelling-place . . . ancestors dwelt." *Shorter Oxford English Dictionary.* Oxford: Oxford University Press, 1933.

selective bibliography

Aster, Howard, and Peter J. Potichnyj. *Jewish-Ukrainian Relations: Two Solitudes*. Revised edition. Oakville: Mosaic Press, 1987.

—————, eds. *Ukrainian-Jewish Relations in Historical Perspective*. Second edition. Edmonton: Canadian Institute of Ukrainian Studies, 1990.

Babel, Isaac. "Crossing the Zubrich." In *Lyubka the Cossack, and Other Stories*. Tr. Andrew R. MacAndrew. New York: Signet, 1963.

Begley, Louis. *Wartime Lies*. London: Picador, 1992.

Boshyk, Yury, ed. *Ukraine During World War II: History and Its Aftermath, A Symposium*. Edmonton: Canadian Institute of Ukrainian Studies, 1986.

Brumberg, Abraham. "The Last Jews in Warsaw." *Granta*, no. 55 (Autumn 1996): 243–54.

Chekhov, Anton. *The Portable Chekhov*. Ed. Avrahm Yarmolinsky. London: Penguin, 1977.

Davies, Norman. *The Heart of Europe: A Short History of Poland*. Oxford: Oxford University Press, 1986.

Encyclopedia Britannica. Eleventh edition. Cambridge: Cambridge University Press, 1910.

Encyclopedia of Ukraine. Ed. Volodymyr Kubijovyc. Toronto: University of Toronto Press, 1988.

Himka, John-Paul. *Galician Villagers and the Ukrainian National Movement in the Nineteenth Century*. Edmonton: Canadian Institute of Ukrainian Studies, 1988.

—————. "Ukrainian-Jewish Antagonism in the Galician Countryside During the Late Nineteenth Century." In *Ukrainian-Jewish Relations in Historical Perspective*. Second edition. Edmonton: Canadian Institute of Ukrainian Studies, 1990. 111–58.

Hoffman, Eva. *Shtetl: The Life and Death of a Small Town and the World of Polish Jews*. Boston: Houghton Mifflin, 1997.

Husar, Natalka, et al. *Black Sea Blue*. Regina: Rosemount Art Gallery, n.d.

Katz, Yossi, and John C. Lehr. "Jewish Settlements in Western Canada." *Journal of Cultural Geography* 14 (Fall/Winter 1993): 49–57.

Kostash, Myrna. *Bloodlines: A Journey into Eastern Europe*. Vancouver: Douglas & McIntyre, 1993.

Lysenko, Vera. *Yellow Boots*. Edmonton: NeWest Press and Canadian Institute of Ukrainian Studies, 1992.

Marples, David R. "The Ukrainians in Eastern Poland Under Soviet Occupation 1939–41:

A Study in Soviet Rural Policy." In *The Soviet Takeover of the Polish Eastern Provinces*. Ed. Keith Sword. London: Macmillan, 1991.

Michnik, Adam. *Letters from Prison and Other Essays*. Tr. Maya Latynski. Berkeley: University of California Press, 1985.

Noble, John, et al. *Lonely Planet Travel Survival Kit: Russia, Ukraine and Belarus*. Hawthorn, Australia: Lonely Planet Publications, 1991.

Pinkus, Oscar. *The House of Ashes*. London: I. B. Tauris, 1991.

Potichnyj, Peter J., ed. *Poland and Ukraine Past and Present*. Edmonton: Canadian Institute of Ukrainian Studies, 1980.

Richmond, Theo. *Konin, a Quest*. London: Vintage, 1996.

Schama, Simon. *Landscape and Memory*. London: Fontana, 1996.

Subtelny, Orest. *Ukraine, a History*. Toronto: University of Toronto Press, 1990.

—————. *Ukrainians in North America: An Illustrated History*. Toronto: University of Toronto Press, 1991.

Sysyn, Frank E. "The Jewish Factor in the Khmelnytsky Uprising." In *Ukrainian-Jewish Relations in Historical Perspective*. Second edition. Edmonton: Canadian Institute of Ukrainian Studies, 1990. 43–54.

Tregebov, Rhea. *Mapping the Chaos*. Montreal: Véhicule Press, 1995.

Troper, Harold, and Morton Weinfeld. *Old Wounds: Jews, Ukrainians and the Hunt for Nazi War Criminals in Canada*. Chapel Hill: University of North Carolina Press, 1989.

Wallace, Samuel A., and Yaroslaw Chyz. *Western Ukraine Under Polish Yoke: Polonization, Colonization, "Pacification."* New York: *The Ukrainian Review*, 1931.

Wiesel, Marion, ed. *To Give Them Light: The Legacy of Roman Vishniac*. London: Viking, 1993.

York, Geoffrey. "'Vodka Line' symbolizes East-West gulf: border-crossing a journey through time." *The Globe and Mail*, Saturday, July 5, 1997. A1.

Zinsser, William, ed. *Inventing the Truth: The Art and Craft of Memoir*. Boston: Houghton Mifflin, 1987.